A Historical and Cultural Analysis of Women Land Rights in Kisii County, Kenya, 1895 - 1970

Mallion K. Onyambu, Nicolas E. Makana &
Prisca T. Tanui

Nsemia

First Edition: May 2023

Published by: Nsemia Inc. Publishers (www.nsemia.com)
Oakville, Ontario, Canada

Cover Concept by: Authors
Cover illustration by: Robert Maina Kambo
Cover Design by: Linda Kiboma
Layout Design: Bethsheba Nyabuto

Note for Librarians:

A cataloguing record for this book is available from Kenya
National Library Services.

ISBN: 978-9966-082-92-3

Dedication

This work is dedicated to the Almighty God, the Creator and Giver of all things, and to the women out there who work very hard to make ends meet and inspire change in their families and the society at large.

Acknowledgment

I would like to take this opportunity to convey my sincere gratitude to my mentors and co-authors, Prof. Nicholas Makana and Dr. Priscah Tanui, who assisted in conceptualizing the historical and cultural issues of gender and land in Gusii that are covered in this book. Furthermore, with their assistance, we were able to go through several copies of the initial drafts of this document. Also, their observations and criticisms played a critical role in developing and refining the book, and; they also assisted in the sourcing of research materials, which was pivotal in the development of this study.

Also, our special thanks go to the Librarian and Staff of the Margaret Thatcher Library of Moi University, who assisted in sourcing various materials in the form of books, journals, and manuscripts that assisted in the development of this book.

In addition, our sincere gratitudes go to the staff of the Kenya National Archives, who assisted in the sourcing of archival information, which was also pivotal in providing evidence on various historical issues and events captured in this document.

Our special gratitude also goes to the many informants and interviewees in Kisii County, a majority of whom were elderly men and women who managed to spare their time and energy to give crucial primary information and insightful narratives as they relate to gender and land use issues in Gusii.

In the same breath, we thank the academic staff and postgraduate students in the Department of History, at Moi University, who were able to spare their precious time to provide critiques of this work and enriching comments that helped refine this book.

Last but not least, special thanks go to our families for the immense support given when researching, and developing this book. Without their patience, and material and non-material support, this research would not have been brought to fruition.

About the Authors

Mallion Onyambu is currently a History Lecturer at Kisii University, Kenya where she has been working since 2014. Over the years, Onyambu has taught undergraduate and postgraduate courses and has also supervised students at postgraduate level. Concerning her academic background, Onyambu pursued her undergraduate studies in the early 1990s at Kenyatta University, Kenya where she graduated with a Bachelor of Education, Arts Degree. After many years of teaching in Kenyan high schools, she enrolled and completed her master's Degree in History from Moi University, Kenya in 2013. Later on, she enrolled for PhD training at the same University which she completed in 2022. Her research interests are in areas of gender studies, land use policy and planning, and Economic and African History.

Nicholas E. Makana (PhD), is an Associate Professor of History at Moi University, Eldoret, Kenya. He is the author of " Changing Patterns of Indigenous Economic Systems: A Study in Agrarian Change and Rural Transformation in Western Kenya, 1930-1960". His other publications have appeared in the Journal of African Economic History, Africa in History (A Journal of Method), Journal of Third World Studies, International Journal of Sustainable Development, Journal of Social Policy and Society and Ufahamu (A Journal of African Studies)

Prisca Tanui Too holds a Ph.D. in History from Kenyatta University, Nairobi, MPhil in History from Moi University, Eldoret, and BA in History and religious studies from Egerton University, Nakuru. She is currently a Senior Lecturer in the Department of History, Political Science and Public Administration at Moi University where she has taught for more than 20 years. Her areas of research interest include African History, Gender Studies and Economic History, and she has published widely in those areas.

What Others Say About This Book

I am impressed with the historical reconstruction of gender with an emphasis on women's land ownership and usefructoral issues in Kenya as represented by the Kisii community. The authors put their hearts and souls into this work which has resulted in very useful insights. What comes out, most explicitly, is how practical and applicable women's ownership and usefruct are.

The work is good reading and the ideas presented herein stand to benefit those who lay their hands on the work. On my part, I now have a fresh understanding of things in a manner that I did not appreciate before. I saw my mother's conduct in some of the descriptions of land usefructoral attitudes and behaviours, and how they came to be. I found that to be a real eye-opener.

Another great attribute of this book is how very thorough it is on women's agentive navigation, negotiation and alternative approaches. The authors do a great job in their friendly, upbeat style of depicting them. This book covers the range of emotions and behaviours of women concerning land use from a historical standpoint and how they best dealt with the glaring policy and masculinity challenges of the day.

Beyond that, *A Historical and Cultural Analysis of Women's Land Rights in Kisii County, Kenya 1895 to 1970* is a great reference tool that includes an insightful blueprint that helps to identify impediments to women's land rights, the means with which they were dealt with and the impact thereof on women and society. My favourite part, though, is the knitting and weaving of archival materials punctuated with oral accounts from the research which speak to the heart of what history is and gives a reader the synergy between primary and secondary sources of historical accounts. Thank you to the author for writing such an outstanding book!

Duncan M. Mukhwana, PhD
Lecturer of History, Department of History, Political Science
& Public Administration
Moi University

The aspect of gender and land ownership control in Kenya is an emotive issue that requires scholars, policy makers and interventionists to infer through an inner lens in understanding the differential power relations that exist between men and women that are continually negotiated, renegotiated, contested and resisted in different ways. One thing I like about this book is that it brings, to the fore evidence of how women's and men's power relations are reflected in differentiated access to land resources in a culturally grounded community of Gusii. The book enlightens us on the struggles that exist in the Gusii community over land ownership, access and utilization that is often symbolic and constituted within the broader realm of sociocultural norms in a patriarchal society which in turn shape gendered identity and inequity. The book gives the readers an opportunity to reimagine how property relations and gendered struggles over resource ownership, access and use can be addressed from a gender perspective in the world of limited opportunities.

Peter Gutwa Oino, PhD
Dean School of Arts and Social Sciences,
Kisii University.

The land question in Kenya is an emotive issue and is often the cause of conflict among communities, clans and households. As this book clearly shows, land policies, many of them shaped by events of the time, have impacted the perceptions with which land is handled. In precolonial times, the land belonged to the community and each person used it based on their needs. With colonialism, traditional institutions and their authority faded away and land, in addition to being a tool for food production, became an instrument of capitalism with the issuance of title deeds.

The book underlines the impact all these changes have had on women's access to and use of land in Gusii. Largely, these changes have tightened men's control of land, given that titles were usually in men's names as only men could inherit family land. The Constitution of Kenya, promulgated in 2010, attempts to cure this by giving equal rights of inheritance to children regardless of gender. However, it is too early to assess whether this has created any meaningful impact on women's land rights and use in Gusii.

The historical perspectives offered in this book are useful not only in understanding the past but could also be the basis for extrapolation into the future. In this respect, one could interrogate the culture of land subdivision and how that impacts the productivity of the land and its capacity to feed the community. At what point does the community put a break on the unit of subdivision as a means of assuring that land, despite being of commercial value, remains a source of livelihood? And how would all those changes impact gender access to and use of to the land?

Matunda Nyanchama, PhD
Publisher, Nsemia Inc. Publishers

Table of Contents

Dedication i

Acknowledgment... iii

About the Authors v

What Others Say About This Book vii

List of Tables xv

List of Figures..xv

Foreword 1

Preface.. 5

Chapter One: Introduction..................................... 7

Study Location...11

Research Methodology 16

Research Design 16

Conclusion..18

**Chapter Two: A Broad Perspective on Land Use and Gender
Issues 19**

Introduction 19

Pre-colonial Land Tenure Systems and Gender Relations........19

The Impact of Colonial Land Policies on Gender Relations 31

Land Tenure in Relation to Gender in the Post-Colonial Period
....45

Contextual Framework of the Study 55

The Property Rights Theory 55

Agency Theory 56

Conceptual Framework 58

Conclusion..58

**Chapter Three: Gusii Indigenous Land Practices, Initial Colonial
Land Policies and Their Impact Upon Gender Relations in the
Pre-Colonial Period, 1850-1920........................... 59**

Introduction..59

The Gusii Concept of Land 60

Modes of Land Acquisition 66

Customary Land Tenure System and its Implication on Gender Relations in Pre-colonial Gusii 75

Initial Colonial Land Policies 84

Conclusion...95

Chapter Four: Colonial Land Policies and Gender Relations In Gusii-Land, 1920-193 97

Introduction...97

The Post-WWI and its aftermath in Kisii, 1920-1922 97

The Dual Policy and its attempted implementation in Kisii ..104

The Great Depression and its Aftermath in Gusii, 1929-1939 109

Gusii Response to the Colonial Expansion of Economic Space in the 1930s and its Implications on Gender Relations 117

Conclusion...126

Chapter Five: Gendered Land Use and Women Response During The Second World War, 1939-1945 129

Introduction...129

Human Resource, Military Conscriptions and Land Use in Kisii in the War-time..130

Impact of Conscription on Gender 133

Increased Demand for Agricultural Production and the War Efforts in Kisii 137

Institutional and Statutory Production Control Measure and Policy Pronouncement During the War in Kisii 143

Market and Price Incentives in Gusii War Production 145

War Time Technical and Technological Support to Gusii Production 149

Gusii Women's Response to the War Complexities of Land Access, Use and Control..152

Conclusion 156

Chapter Six: Post WWII Agrarian Reform Agenda and its Impact Upon Gender Relations In Kisii 1945-1960 159

Introduction...159

Post WW II Colonial Agrarian Reform and its Implications for Kisii, 1945-1960 160

The Intervention of the Swynnerton Plan, 1954 173

The Practicality of the Swynnerton Recommendations on Gusii
Agriculture..174

Land Kleptocracy and Gendered Relations among the Gusii 177

Conclusion 187

**Chapter Seven: Post-Colonial Land Ownership and Gender
Rights, 1960-1970** **189**

Introduction 189

The Colonial Legacy and the Evolution of Land Policy...........190

Implications for the Specific Case of Kisii............................194

Further Initiatives to Promote Cash Crops in Kisii 196

Further Expansion of Economic Space & the Need to Maximise
on Market Opportunities...199

Continuity & Change in Land Regime and Legal Framework at
Independence...201

The Impact of Kenya's Post-Colonial Land Policies on Gender
Relations in Kisii...206

Gusii Women's Agentive Response to Constricted Economic
Space...210

Conclusion...218

Chapter Eight: Conclusion **221**

Bibliography **229**

A. Archival Materials...229

B. Oral Respondents 232

C. Articles 235

D. Books 240

E. International Organizations..249

F. Theses 250

G. Internet Sources...251

Glossary of Gusii Terms Used in The Book..........................253

Appendices **255**

Appendix I: Informed Consent Letter 255

Appendix II: Interview Schedule...255

Appendix III: Interview Schedule For Chiefs/Assistant Chiefs258

Appendix IV: Focus Group Discussion Guide.......................259

List of Tables

Table 3.1: Units of African Labour In Employment 1919-1924 .93

Table 3.2: Maize & Wimbi produced by the Gusii between 1936-1938 105

Table 4.1: Planned conscription of labour in Nyanza Province 1944 126

Table 5.1: Land acreage committed to coffee growing in the Gusii Highlands, 1946-1950 163

Table 5.2: Average annual homicide rates per 100,000 people (1955-1956) 165

Table 5.3: Produce in bags marketed in South Nyanza 1948/49 and 1949/50 166

Table 6.1: Gusii population Density per square mile 199

List of Figures

Figure 1.1: Map of Kenya Showing Location of Kisii County 8

Figure 1.2: Map of Kisii County showing the nine constituencies...9

Figure 1.1 Conceptual Framework 52

Foreword

Mainstreaming gender discourse has gained theoretical and interpretative acceptance in academic spheres. The gender perspective has unravelled new information and provided a fresh look at content that was otherwise considered established. Onyambu, M. K., *et al* would have customarily examined the historical and cultural land rights in Kisii County, a topic that has been the focus of many scholars. However, the gender perspective, as interrogated in this work, especially with respect to women's rights to land, presents fresh insights into the subject.

This book explores the evolving nature of gender inequalities in access to productive resources, specifically agricultural land, addressing not only the impacts of changes brought by European capitalism to African pre-colonial economies but also voices women's responses to the same. The seven-chapter book focuses on the interplay between gender relations and land rights, ownership, access and control during the colonial and post-independence periods to create an understanding of gender inequality in land rights as they existed in the precolonial period. Beginning in 1895 when Kenya became a British protectorate, the book delves into the consequences of gender discrimination and disparity in land access and control, which the authors note, is dominated by a patriarchal culture in Kenya, whereby socio-cultural factors limit women's access to and rights over many resources, land included.

In essence, the authors examine the issues related to gender relations, colonial and post-colonial land policies on property rights, and ownership. Its general objective is to establish the impact of colonial and post-colonial land policies on gendered relations, property rights and ownership in Kisii. All seven chapters contribute to the realization of that objective in a consistent, harmonious and coherent manner. The authors ably show the relationship between pre-colonial land tenure systems and gender relations in Kisii, the effects of colonial and post-colonial land policies on gender relations, and Gusii women's response to gendered land rights and ownership.

The authors are articulate and focused, and use rich data all of which make the book to be is a well-documented account of the subject. Their arguments are plausible and well-situated in relevant and extensive literature. The style and language of writing are friendly which broadens the reader's appeal and reach.

Chapter one ably conceptualizes the study in its theoretical and methodological aegis. Chapter two, using the precolonial setup, affirms that the property rights of individuals include the use of resources supported by the force of etiquette, social custom, ostracism, and formal legally enacted laws, thus situating the study within the property rights theory together with the Agency theory used in much of the study. The chapter also discusses indigenous land tenure and gendered relations in Gusii. Chapter Three analyzes the effects of nascent colonial policies and the question of land access, control and ownership and the authors affirm that colonial policies between 1920 and 1939 had the net effect of constricting women's access, control, ownership and utilization of land as ownership became more competitive and contested.

Chapter four interrogates the importance of land in agricultural production in Kisii and the resultant gender-related issues which, the authors affirm, became more manifest as the colonial state navigated the challenges of increased agricultural production and the cash crop economy during and after the Second World War thereby exacerbating competition and contestation over this scarce resource by further constricting control and access of women to land as a key factor of production. This presented a scenario characterized by hunger for land both for men and women leading to strained gender relationships over questions of access, use and ownership of this constricting resource.

Chapter Five focuses on Post World War II agrarian reconstruction reforms (ALDEV and Swynnerton Plan and land kleptocracy) and the impact of the same on gendered relations in Kisii. The chapter demonstrates how land reforms in access, use and ownership among the Gusii as Kenya attained independence resulted in the issuance of individual land title deeds which legalized and legitimized individual ownership of land by Gusii men to the disenfranchisement of Gusii women. The last chapter explores how the early independence dynamics (including the colonial legacy, the Sessional Paper Number 10 of 1965, and gendered kleptocracy) played out in Kisii with the futile attempts by the state to settle the gender land question among the Gusii. Onyambu and her co-authors finally note that the transfer of land rights, during independence, to Africans (Gusii) failed to fundamentally alter long-standing impediments to land access use and ownership by women in Kisii.

Having read through the book, and having done much research in the area, I am satisfied that Onyambu and her co-authors have done a thorough work in examining issues related to Kisii land as a resource and its accessibility, ownership and utility between the gender. The work demonstrates rich background information on the area's history, theory and methodology. The rigour with which content is compiled, analyzed and synthesized, gives credence to the quality of the work as a resourceful textbook of history and a reference book for tertiary and post-tertiary students and experts in the field of gender, agricultural studies and researchers in the history of the Gusii. I am certain that the book will attract a wide readership based on its high academic discourse.

Professor Samson Moenga M Omwoyo
Professor of History, Kabarak University

Preface

The study set out to investigate the effects of gendered land ownership, access, control and use with a specific focus on the Gusii of Kenya. The research was thus problematized in terms of the imperative to seek an answer to the fundamental question: what accounts for the marginal position of women among the Gusii concerning access, control and use of land? The objectives guiding the study were: to analyze the relationship between pre-colonial land tenure systems and gender relations, establish the effects of colonial land policies on gender relations and examine gender rights in relation to land ownership.

The study site was in Gusii, specifically, the current Kisii County, one of the 47 counties in Kenya. Counties came into being in line with the constitution of Kenya 2010 which created the devolved system of governance. The study targeted one hundred oral respondents aged sixty years and above. This target population was selected for the interview due to the fact that they were old enough and were most likely to have acquired historical and cultural information, especially as regards the pre-colonial and colonial land use system. The study was conducted within the context of agency and property rights theories that permitted the historicization (i.e. the chronological and critical analysis) of the land question through the pre-colonial, colonial and post-colonial epochs.

The historical research design was employed in the study. Consequently, the data informing the study is derived from both primary and secondary sources. Primary sources entailed the conduct of oral interviews with target participants identified through the snowball sampling technique. Individual views and perspectives were subject to an authentication process through group oral interviews and discussions. In addition, a wide range of documents derived from the Kenya National Archives constituted a key component of primary sources. These included district and provincial annual and quarterly reports and official commentary from the Department of Agriculture.

The data derived from primary sources were used either to corroborate or critique information attributed to secondary sources such as books, dissertations and government publications. Such analysis of primary and secondary data yielded both quantitative and qualitative data thematically organized in a historical narrative.

The study found that the dynamics of Gusii societal organization during the pre-colonial period guaranteed greater security to women as pertains to land access, control and use than was the case in the colonial and post-colonial periods. Conversely, it also emerged from the study that the onset of colonialism destabilized and distorted the workings of the Gusii traditional structure, thereby occasioning the vulnerability of women in relation to land. The study further established that the consolidation of capitalist ethos wrought by the entrenchment of the market economy continuously exacerbated the marginalization and vulnerability of Gusii women in matters of land access and use. The study concluded that, far from being reduced to mere passive victims of the resultant constricted economic space, Gusii women have always been positively responsive through the design of multiple coping strategies cumulatively empowering them to remain shapers of their economic destiny.

Chapter One

Introduction

Gender inequalities in access to productive resources, including agricultural land, continue to be a major concern, particularly in low-income countries. Many studies on gender relations and land rights tend to address the changes brought by European capitalism to African pre-colonial economies. This book focuses on the interplay between gender relations and land rights, ownership, access and control from 1920 to 1970 to create an understanding of women's responses to gender inequality in land rights.

The Sustainable Development Goals (SDGs) adopted in 2015 recognize that to end poverty (Goal 1), it was necessary to ensure equal rights in ownership and control over land, as well as equal rights to inheritance of productive resources[1]. The SDGs contend that to achieve gender equality and empower all women and girls (Goal 5), policies and legal reforms are needed to give them equal rights and access to ownership and control over land and other economic resources. In this study, gender issues on land rights are explored from the women's perspective.

Anseeuw, Wily, Cotula and Taylor[2] report that globally, over the past three decades, gender issues on land ownership and control have gained prominence in development policy. Allendorf[3] asserts that women's land ownership is associated with increased bargaining power in the household, better child nutrition, lower exposure to HIV/AIDS[4] and higher protection from domestic violence. Food and Agricultural Organisation (FAO)[5] reports that, despite these efforts, women who comprise over half of the world's population,

---

1 United Nations, (2015). Transforming Our World: The 2030 Agenda for Sustainable Development. New York. Pg. 20.
2 Anseeuw, W., L. Alden Wily, L. Cotula, and M. Taylor. 2012. "Land Rights and the Rush for Land: Findings of the Global Commercial Pressures on Land Research Project". ILC, Rome. Pg. 14
3 Allendorf, K. (2007). "Do women's land rights promote empowerment and child health in Nepal?" World Development 35(11): 1975–1988.
4 Strickland, R. (2004). 'To Have and To Hold: Women's Property and Inheritance Rights in the Context of HIV/AIDS in Sub-Saharan Africa'. Washington, DC: International Center for Research on Women. Available at: www.icrw.org/docs/2004_paper_haveandhold.pdf
5 FAO. (2011). "Gender differences in assets". ESA Working Paper No. 11-12.

rarely own any reasonable forms of property; do not have adequate access to the same, and do not even make major decisions on the allocation and use of such property. However, FAO notes that the consequence of gender discrimination in land access and control is evident particularly in the developing world since the pre-colonial, colonial and post-colonial periods.

Ochieng[6] finds that before the advent of colonialism, the inward migration of communities defined land acquisition, ownership, and use. Communities settled in areas distinct to them. The solution for a need for land was to expand into unoccupied areas. In other situations, some communities conquered others to occupy their land (inter-tribal wars). Even so, the conquered community could still relocate to another place and find new land.

Caline[7] adds that the first European settlers arrived in 1902 and 1915, and the Crown Land Ordinance recognized "native rights" in lands reserved for the Kenyans. Anderson[8] avers that in 1926, this was further defined by the creation of "African Reserves" for each of Kenya's "tribes," leaving the "White Highlands" for the Europeans, which consisted of large parts of Kiambu and Murang'a as well as areas farther north around Nyeri and Nanyuki, and great tracts of land in the Rift Valley, and far to the west on the plateaus beyond.

Lonsdale and Berman[9] reveal that the establishment of capitalist estate production depended upon the appropriation of African land. But this partial separation of Africans from their means of production did not have an immediate adverse effect on their well-being, save in the case of the pastoralists who suffered immeasurably larger losses than the cultivators. On the contrary, African farmers enjoyed enormous access to exploitable land, as both the British pax enabled them to use areas previously left empty for reasons of defence, and as white land ownership made available to their tenants' hoes the acres that settlers could not yet afford to plough.

However, in the long run, the British colonialists even made worse land injustices in Kenya at the time. They came up with several laws and concessions, which included the Land Acquisition Act (1894), Crown Lands Ordinance (1902), Crown Lands Ordinance

6 Ochien W, R. (1985). A History of Kenya. Macmillan Press Ltd.
7 Caroline E. (2005: 16). Imperial Reckoning: The Untold Story of Britain's Gulag in Kenya, Owl Books.
8 Anderson, M, D. (2000) "Master and Servant in Colonial Kenya. The Journal of African History, Vol. 41, No. 3, pp. 459-485.
9 Lonsdale, J. and Berman, B. (1979). 'Coping with the contradictions: The Development of the Colonial State in Kenya, 1894-1914,' Journal of African History 20.

(1915), and the Kenya Native Areas Ordinance (1926) to alienate the coastal and mainland communities further from their land.

Ochieng[10] observes that in 1918, the Resident Native Ordinance was passed to demand that squatter payments were made in labour and not in kind or cash. This was done to keep the squatter farms from competing with or even eclipsing settler farms. "Conditions for squatters began deteriorating from the mid-1920s, at first imperceptibly, then dramatically from the 1930s."

Ndege[11] notes that at any rate, British colonial economic policy in Kenya included Land alienation for European settlers, African taxation, and African migrant/forced labour development of settler-dominated agricultural production and peasant commodity production, export production, rail and road transport and communication, education and health.

Ochieng further notes that by the mid-1930s, about one-fifth of all usable land in Kenya was under the exclusive control of the settlers. In addition, the state provided the settlers and corporate capital with the necessary infrastructural, agricultural and marketing services and credit facilities. Land alienation and the establishment of native reserves restructured the land tenure system, which was later perpetuated by African patriarchy. Ndeda[12] shows how colonialism was discriminatory to African women and how women were overburdened in the reserves in the absence of their labour migrant male folk. Women became the sole agricultural producers in the reserves. They planted, weeded, harvested, stored and managed their food harvests all these in the absence of men. Since then, World Bank[13] has noted that access, ownership and control over land, resources and benefits are determined by socio-cultural norms which have significant impacts on gender relations.

Anseeuw, Wily, Cotula and Taylor[14] note that generally in Africa, women's insecure land tenure and property rights can be linked to a mix of economic and social pressures that have profoundly

10 Ochien W, R. (1985). *A History of Kenya*. Macmillan Press Ltd.
11 Ndege O.P. (2006). Colonialism and its Legacies in Kenya. Lecture delivered during Fulbright – Hays Group project abroad program: July 5th to August 6th 2009 at the Moi University Main Campus.
12 Ndeda, J.M., (1993) The Impact of Male Migration on Rural Women: A case Study of Siaya District c. 1894-1963. Ph.D. Thesis, Kenyatta University.
13 World Bank. (2004). *"Gender Country Profiles"* Retrieved March 30, 2018 from www.worldbank.org/afr/gender/countryprofile.
14 Anseeuw, W., L. Alden W, L. Cotula, and M. Taylor. (2012). Land Rights and the Rush for Land: Findings of the Global Commercial Pressures on Land Research Project. ILC, Rome.

transformed social structures and land tenure systems. These include colonial and post-colonial private property legislation, an influx of investments, commodification of land, growth of land markets and rise in competition over land.

Qvist[15] finds that in Egypt, laws and cultural practices are highly predisposed by Islamic law. In theory, women and men have equal rights to land tenure in Egypt. Nevertheless, traditional structures continue to abet discrimination against women. In Ghana, women's access to land and usage is determined by men as a matter of patriarchal cultural tradition, where higher tenure security for women reduces productivity losses on women's plots.[16] However, in Rwanda, regularization of women's land rights through titling programmes increased investment in land soil conservation in women's plots.[17]

In Kenya, which is dominated by patriarchal cultures in many cases, socio-cultural factors limit women's access to and rights over resources. Men as *de facto* heads of households have the largest role in decision-making about resources at both the household and community levels, implying that women have disproportionately fewer rights to land and property.[18] Despite Kenya's efforts to promote gender equality, not much has been achieved and there are no equal rights in ownership, or control over land and other productive resources.[19]

In Gusii, for instance, access to and control over means and benefits of production show constraints in relation to gender. These inequalities make women more vulnerable to poverty than men in Gusii, therefore, the need for policy movement towards the provision of gender-equitable land reforms.[20] The significance of land reform policies depends on ensuring gender equality both in practice and in principle.

---

15 Qvist, E. (1995). Women's access, control and tenure of land, property and settlement. Retrieved   March 30, 2018 from www.sli.unimelb.edu.au.
16 Goldstein, M. and Udry, C. (2008). "The Profits of Power: Land Rights and Agricultural Investment   in Ghana." Journal of Political Economy 116 (6):981–1022.
17 Croppenstedt, A.; Goldstein, M.; and Rosas, N. (2013). "Gender and Agriculture: Inefficiencies, Segregation, and Low Productivity Traps." The World Bank Research Observer 28(1):79-109.
18 Doss, C. (2005). "The Effects of Intrahousehold Property Ownership on Expenditure Patterns in Ghana." Journal of African Economies 15(1):149–80.
19 Davison J. (1988). Land and Women's Agricultural Production: The Context in Agriculture, Women and Land the African Experience. J Davison (ed), West view Press, Boulder and London.
20 Lastarria-Cornhiel, S. (1995). Impact of privatization on gender and property rights in Africa. World   Development, 25(8), 1317-1333.

Land gives social and economic power and the impact can be almost immediate. Therefore, giving women land means giving them power. It is not surprising that women have such a hard time obtaining control of this valuable asset. However, the research in Kenya conducted by Nzioki Kameri-Mboti[21] confirms that land decides the economic well-being, social status and political power of individuals in society. As Sarpong[22] points on the status of gender, land access and control, this book specifically examines gender, land access and control in the Gusii context, which as Moore[23] opines reflects gender disparity in land access, ownership and control happens in many African settings.

In Gusii, gender relations on land ownership, access and control are culture-specific and are characterized by differential relations of power between men and women. Power relations are continually being negotiated, contested and resisted in various ways. The focus of this research is on women's and men's differentiated access to land, and the gender relations that both influenced and are affected by land ownership and control in Gusii. The study presents the findings based on Gusii people's gender relations in land tenure from the perspective of their history and culture between 1920-1970.

Study Location

The research site was Gusii and specifically Kisii County, one of the 47 counties in Kenya courtesy of the Constitution of Kenya, 2010, which created the county system of governance. It shares common borders with Nyamira County to the North East, Narok County to the South and Homabay and Migori Counties to the West. Kisii County lies between latitude 0 30' and 1 0' South and longitude 34 38' and 35 0' East. The county covers a total area of 1,332.7 km square and is divided into nine constituencies namely: Kitutu Chache North, Kitutu Chache South, Nyaribari Masaba, Nyaribari Chache, Bomachoge Borabu, Bomachoge Chache, Bobasi, South Mugirango and Bonchari. It has 9 sub-counties and 45 Wards. Population densities are high in areas with large proportions of

---

21 Nzioki, A. (2009). The Effect of land tenure on women's access and control of land in Kenya. Retrieved May 20, 2018 from www.jstore.org/stable/151481
22 Sarpong, P. (1974). Ghana in Retrospect: Some aspects of Ghanaian culture. Accra: Ghana Publishing Company.
23 Moore, D. (1996). Marxism, Culture and Political Ecology: Environmental Struggles in Zimbabwe's Eastern Highlands. In Peet, R. and Watts, M. (editors), *Liberation Ecologies: Environment, Development, Social Movements*. London: Routledge.

arable land such as Kitutu Chache South (1348 people km square), Nyaribari Chache (1128 people km square), Bomachoge Borabu (992 people km square), Bomachoge Chache (992 people km square) respectively.

The county is characterized by a hilly topography with several ridges and valleys. It is endowed with several permanent rivers that flow from East to West into Lake Victoria. Soils in the county are generally good and fertile allowing for agricultural activities.

The county has a highland equatorial climate resulting in a bimodal rainfall pattern with two rainy seasons, the long rains occurring between February and June and the short rains occurring between September and early December. The adequate rainfall, coupled with moderate temperature is suitable for growing crops like tea, coffee, maize, beans, finger millet, potatoes, bananas and groundnuts. This also makes it possible to practice dairy farming in the county.[24]

The area also consists of several escarpments, hills and mountains, like the Vinyo Escarpment to the South West of the region which is bisected by a large gorge through which River Gucha flows into Lake Victoria. As well, there is the Manga Escarpment to the North West which is broken by deep valleys that form the source of several streams and rivers.[25] The most prominent rivers draining Guisii land are the Gucha and Sondu. Gucha River has its source in North Mugirango and traverses Kitutu, Nyaribari, Bobasi, Machoge and South Mugirango before entering Homa Bay County where it drains into Lake Victoria.

The Sondu River starts in the Sotik/Borabu area and flows in the Northern parts of Guise along the boundary with Kericho County. The river enters Nyakach and then drains into Lake Victoria. The region also possesses many swamps in valley bottoms like Sironga, Riamoni, Nyanturago and Chirichiro.[26] Blessed with fertile soils of volcanic origin, Gusii, as a whole, is an area of high agricultural potential. Relief, drainage and existing rock formations have influenced the soil formation in the area. For this reason, the land is ideal for growing the variety of crops mentioned previously such as coffee, tea, pyrethrum, maize and bananas.[27]

---

24 http://www.kisii.go.ke/index.php/county-profile/vision-and-mission
25 Ibid
26 Ibid.
27 Government of Kenya (1984). *Kisii Development Plan*. Nairobi: Government Printer.

Gusii can be divided into two ecological zones based on the differences in altitude, rainfall, temperatures and soil distribution. These zones have, over the years, been recognized by the Gusii who refer to the lower ecological zone in the West as Chache (West) and the higher ecological zone in the East as Masaba. These ecological differences have also influenced land use patterns and population distribution differences.[28]

Apart from agriculture, the Gusii community practices various economic activities such as traditional crafts production, various forms of trade (e.g., in agricultural produce and soap stone curvings) and embroidery. The region is particularly well endowed in diverse natural resources and minerals such as traces of iron ore, salt, copper, and soapstone as well as plant resources such as wood and papyrus. These resources enable the Gusii to undertake various industrial production activities to produce various goods that they needed for their sustenance.[29]

---

28   Ibid.
29   Ibid.

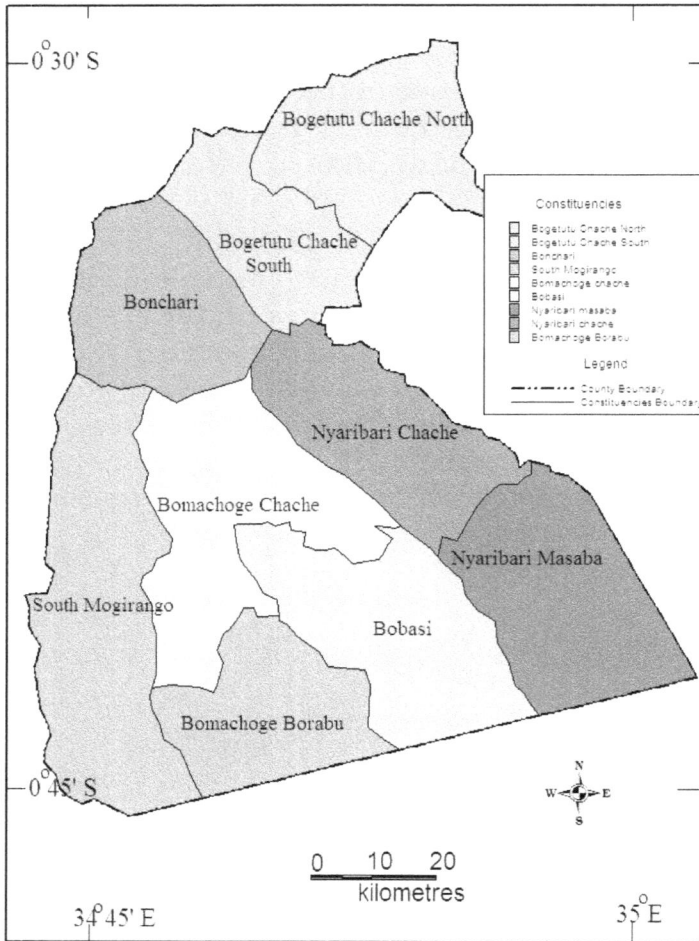

Figure 1.1: Map of Kenya Showing Location of Kisii County
Source; Geography Department; Moi University, 2019

Figure 1.2: Map of Kisii County showing the nine constituencies

Source; Geography Department; Moi University

Nasimiyu R. contends that, in Africa and by extension Kenya, the assumption was that land was majorly a patriarchal issue and women were on the periphery and passive recipients of acquisition, access, control and usage[30]. The book is mainly concerned with three inter-related issues namely: gender relations, colonial and post-colonial land policies on property rights, and ownership. Not much study has been done on the relationship between these three issues. It is on this basis the book sought to examine women's responses over time on issues of land access, ownership, control and usage with a particular focus on Gusii. Consequently, the fundamental

30 Nasimiyu R. (1995) Women in the colonial economy of Bungoma; The Role of Women in Agriculture 1902-1960. Journal of Eastern African Research and Development No. 15

15

issue concerns the extent to which differentiated access, control and ownership of land has impacted women in Gusii. The specific objectives of this book are to establish the relationship between indigenous land tenure systems and gender relations; identify the effects of colonial land policies on gender relations, and examine gender rights in relation to land rights and ownership in the post-colonial period in Gusii.

The study covers the period between 1895 and 1970 in Gusii. The year 1895, for purposes of this study, marks the start of the colonial era. However, Chapter Two tackles a section of the precolonial period specifically from 1850 to 1895, a period that beacons the precolonial land tenure as a basis for comparison with the colonial land tenure. The year 1970 marks the endpoint of the study. This is conceptualized on the first development plan of independent Kenya to enable assessing the continuity and change in independent Kenya.

Research Methodology

This section contains the methodology and procedures used in conducting the research. This included research design, area of study, target population, data gathering methods and tools; sampling and sampling procedures as well as data analysis.

Research Design

This study was based on the historical descriptive design method and its related multi-method qualitative approach in order to facilitate cross-checking of data and to, increase reliability. This was done to solicit views, opinions and comments on the gender relations in ownership and control of land in Gusii. This ensured the studied community was the subject of the research but not to be used merely as passive objects of the study because most study communities seem to be tired of being passive objects of discussion.

The study analyzed both primary and secondary data. Primary sources included archival and oral interviews. The Kenya National Archives in Nairobi was the main source of archival materials consulted. Various documents including district annual reports, land reports, ownership and control, and handing over reports for both colonial and post-colonial periods were analyzed. These documents provided historical data on land tenure and land policies and gender relations. The pre and post-independence development plans, sessional papers and statistical abstracts were other sources of primary data. These highlighted the official position regarding gender relations in general and gave valuable data on ownership and control of land in Gusii. Data from the archives was complemented and corroborated with data derived from oral interviews and secondary sources.

To extract oral data, interviews were conducted with the help of a questionnaire guide that was divided into various sub-themes on gender relations in ownership and control of land in Gusii during the period of study. Besides the oral interviews, case studies were conducted for selected informants. This was to capture the voices of the informants on the changing gender relations in ownership and control of land between 1920 and 1970. The collection of oral data involved the use of various sampling procedures. In the study area, purposive sampling was used. The COUNTY had nine electoral CONSTITUENCIES: Bobasi, Bonchari, Bomachoge Borabu, Bomachoge Chache, Kitutu Chache North, Kitutu Chache South, Nyaribari Chach, The age bracket of oral informants was taken into account. Informants were both women and men from the age of 60 years and above. The researcher identified the respondents through the snowball sampling technique. The use of contact persons was crucial to the researcher because some respondents were not free to talk about issues of land to strangers. To conduct the oral and semi-structured interviews, open-ended guiding questions were applied to some of the respondents. Oral interviews were used on specific women with land ownership-related problems identified through snowballing and focus group discussions. The researcher recorded the information using a tape recorder and notes.

In the interviews, the researcher used probing questions for clarification or even seeking more explanation. At the end of each day, the researcher organized the data collected according to themes and periods. The tape recorder was used with the informants' consent with the interviews specifically focused on land ownership and gender relations. Where informants were reluctant to indicate the acreage of their land during the oral interviews direct observation was adopted to determine gender relations in ownership and control of land. This was to ascertain some of the issues raised particularly concerning the deteriorating gender relations in ownership and control of land.

Secondary data also form part of the evidence used in this study. These include published accounts by early foreign travellers, missionaries and colonial administrators. Other sources of secondary data include journal articles, books, theses, seminar and conference papers, magazines and newspapers. These secondary data were gathered from various libraries including the Moi Library (Kenyatta University), the Institute of Development Studies, the Institute of African Studies, and the British Institute in Eastern Africa (IBEA) in Nairobi.

The secondary data gave various interpretations of scholars on gender relations in ownership and control of land not only in Kenya but also across Africa. The secondary data was used to corroborate the primary data. This helped to fill the gap in relations in ownership and control of land that the study intended to fill. Collected data were analyzed qualitatively. In addition, some basic simple descriptive tables were used to show the numerical data in the distribution of the respondents. Thematic and characterization of the finding validated the accuracy of this piece of historical work. The data were classified according to their content, and the specific historical timeframes within which events and developments took place. This was important because historical inquiry requires the establishment of the historical specificity of social phenomena in terms of their constituent elements and the relations between these elements over time. Since gender studies are contemporary, corroborating information with the past was essential to retain the historical significance, therefore, historicizing gender. The reliability of the collected data was through triangulation of data from both primary and secondary sources while the researcher validated the data through corroborating archival material with oral data and secondary data.

Conclusion

Chapter one provides preparation process for the research as it lays the foundation of the study by setting the objectives, the research design and methodology. It also contends that gender inequalities, as relates to access and ownership of land continue to be a major concern in Africa in general, and Kenya in particular. The Chapter also consists of the study location which is the Gusii region , and specifically the current Kisii County.

Chapter Two

A Broad Perspective on Land Use and Gender Issues

Introduction

Concerns about women in relation to ownership and control of land have been raised over the years at different but interrelated levels. Land resources are central to the lives of people in countries whose economic development and subsistence depend on the resources. This section provides a contextual analysis of land use and ownership as relates to gender. In particular, the section examines gender relations in ownership and control of land in developed and developing countries and analyses traditional land tenure and gender relations.

The section further describes the impact of colonial land policies on Gusii and gender land relations. In addition, it investigates issues of land tenure in relation to gender in the post-colonial period. It also shows what has been done in previous studies and clarifies the meaning of concepts used in this book in order to build theoretical departure points. It also identifies research gaps that are filled by this study.

Pre-colonial Land Tenure Systems and Gender Relations

This section focuses on the interplay between indigenous land tenure systems and gender relations from 1920 to 1970 with the aim of creating an understanding of women's responses to gender inequality in land rights. According to Gyekye[1], globally, indigenous land tenure systems were governed by cultural customary laws of the people, deeply rooted in communal land tenure systems, which assured community members' access to land. Land tenure systems consist of the social relations that are established around natural resources, particularly land, water, and trees; they determine who can use what resources and how the resources are to be used. However, Lundika[2]

---

1 Gyekye, K. (1998). African Cultural Values: An Introduction, Accra, Sankofa Publishing Company, Ghana.
2 Lundika, R, W. (2010). Land Rental Markets, Investment and Productivity Under Customary Land Tenure Systems In Malawi; PhD Thesis, Norwegian University of Life Sciences

in his title, "Land Rental Markets in Malawi," opines that existing socio-cultural institutions do not all the time provide secure tenure rights equally to women and men in communities.

Giovarelli, Wamalwa, and Hannay[3] argue that access to and control of property, whether customary, statutory, or religious, provide economic entry for women to key markets and social access to non-market institutions at household and community levels of governance, where they contribute to decision-making. On the other hand, the FAO[4] notes that, in societies where there is a high degree of gender inequality, women's secondary status, lower socialization, undervalued productive work, and illiteracy often makes women's opportunities difficult to attain.

Furthermore, in some places, as observed in Macedonia and Uzbekistan, daughters do not inherit any land, despite Muslim norms that entitle them to inherit some family land. Daughters concede their rights to brothers to avoid conflict and maintain support from the extended family. In such instances, wives and daughters may not insist on having their names included on the title to household land because of potential conflicts with husbands or their families. In Brazil, few women are aware of whose name is on the land title and do not request that joint titles be issued. In Bolivia, Giovarelli and Renee[5] reveal that some men were titling land in their sons' names, stripping their daughters and wives of legal land rights.

In many Asian societies, due to sociocultural constructs in the patriarchal mindset prevalent, women's right to land is still an issue on the margin of the mainstream development agenda. Consequently, in those places, policies and laws are not gender-sensitive and fail to consider differentiated impacts on women and men. In rural China, women are equal under formal law. However, because rural land is owned by collective communes which gave 30-year use rights to individuals, women (who usually relocate to their husbands' native villages upon marriage) often effectively do not have rights to land[6].

3 Giovarelli, R., Wamalwa, B and Hannay, L. (2013). Land Tenure, Property Rights, and Gender: Challenges and Approaches for Strengthening Women's Land Tenure and Property Rights. Property Rights and Resource Governance Briefing Paper #7. DC. Washington: U.S. Agency for International Development.
4 FAO, (2010). Gender and Land Rights Database. Rome: FAO.
5 Giovarelli, R. (2006). "Overcoming Gender Biases in Established and Transitional Property Rights Systems." In Land Law Reform: Achieving Development Policy Objectives, ed. J. W. Bruce, 67–106. Washington, DC: World Bank.
6 https://www.landesa.org/what-we-do/china/, 2020

In the Indian context, marriage plays a crucial role in the socio-economic status of women. A woman's life is almost always divided into pre-marriage and post-marriage status. However, the problem arises when a woman becomes a widow. There is no question of re-marriage or owning the husband's property. Back at her home, she is treated merely as a burden and not a co-owner of the family property. Hence, in these countries, due to structural and cultural violence, women with no or insecure land rights are more likely to suffer from acts such as gender-based violence, social stigma and isolation, rape and killings. In some countries, widows are forcefully evicted by in-laws.[7]

In Africa, indigenous/customary land tenure remains the predominant model of landholding in rural contexts and land remains the cornerstone of rural livelihood security. Improving land tenure security is often equated with the integration of customary land law into the modern statutory law of the state. As Payne[8] rightly puts it, land rights were, derived from membership of the community and, traditionally, no cash payment was made for such rights. Instead, a token payment was often made. This token payment is referred to as 'drink money' in Ghana and 'cattle or beer money' in some other countries in the sub-region.

Raymond[9], however, notes that as pressure on traditional property rights in land increased with increasing population and urbanization, this token payment has tended to increase to the extent that it approximates open market values. Though Raymond's study is significant, it does not indicate the place of women in land rights, ownership and control, hence the need for the current study.

Kameri and Mbote[10] find that in most Kenyan communities' land ownership rights are often vested in a community or other corporate structures such as lineage or clan. A significant proportion of land is not controlled by individuals but rather by groups and managed

---

7 Fryer, R. G. (2010). The importance of segregation, discrimination, peer dynamics and identity in   explaining trends in Racial Achievement gap. In: Benhabib J, Mathew AB and Jackson O (eds)   Handbook of Social Economics. Amsterdam: North-Holland, pp. 165–1192.

8 Payne, G. (1997) Urban Land Tenure and Property Rights in Developing Countries: A Review, Intermediate Technology Publications, London.

9 Raymond, N. (1987). "Land rights systems and agricultural development in sub-Saharan Africa". The World Bank research observer. Vol 2, no. 2 (July 1987), pp. 143-169.

10 Kameri-Mbote, P. (2005). "Inheritance, Laws and Practices affecting Kenyan Women." In Makumi Mwagiru (ed.), African Regional Security in the Age of Globalisation. Nairobi: Heinrich Boll Foundation.

according to community rules. As noted by Raymond[11], under most systems of customary law, women do not own or inherit land, partly because of the perception that women are part of the wealth of the community and therefore cannot be the locus of land rights' grants.

The foregoing studies are significant as they point out the need for women's empowerment in land rights, ownership, usage and control. However, they fall short in including women's responses to land rights, ownership, control and usage.

Corroborating Kameri-Mbote's findings, Ingunn Ikdahl[12] and colleagues aver that, for most women, access to land is via a system of vicarious ownership through men: as husbands, fathers, uncles, brothers, and sons. Customary rules, therefore, have the effect of excluding females from the clan or communal entity.

A study by Makura-Paradza[13] in Zimbabwe on women's land rights vulnerability concluded that the role of patriarchy was sometimes overemphasized in studies of women's land rights vulnerability in the developing world. Another study by Chigbu[14] in Nigeria showed that the land challenges women face sometimes come about as a result of the "actions and inactions" of women.

These studies are important to the current study as they illustrate why patriarchy is only one of several institutions governing land access along with governance structures and institutions. In this study, the research investigates whether patriarchy was still an impediment to women's inclusion in land ownership, usage and control.

Feder & Noronha[15] categorize African indigenous land tenure systems into three categories: countries that allow the acquisition of individual titles, although some rights of title-holders may be restricted; countries that recognize different types of tenure including individual property rights, customary tenure and public lands; and countries that vest land ownership in the state and grant individuals only use rights. Given these variations, the data

---

11 Ibid
12 Ingunn Ikdahl et al. (2005). Human rights, Formalisation and Women's Land Rights in Southern and Eastern Africa. Studies in Women's Law No. 57. Institute of Women's Law, University of Oslo.
13 Makura-Paradza, G. (2010). Single Women, Land and Livelihood Vulnerability; Wageningen Publishers: Wageningen. The Netherlands.
14 Chigbu, U.E. (2019). Masculinity, men and patriarchal issues aside: How do women's actions impede women's access to land? Matters arising from a peri-rural community in Nigeria. Land Use Policy, 81, 39–48.
15 Raymond, N. (1987). Land rights systems and agricultural development in sub-Saharan Africa". The World Bank research observer–2(2): 143-169.

from household and farm surveys on ownership may represent very different rights in different countries, depending on the existing customary and statutory legal frameworks. Though this study focuses on the African land tenure system, however, its broad focus does not provide particular attention to women's specific responses to land rights, ownership, control and access. Therefore, understanding ownership rights and gender relations in the context of the Gusii community where much of the land ownership took place under customary tenure systems is paramount.

In Ethiopia for example, Kebede[16] avers that the Ethiopian law puts it clear that land is officially owned by the state and Ethiopians only have land use rights. These use rights, which can be certified, allow alienation through inheritance, renting out or division between spouses in the case of divorce. However, regional land laws further influence who can use the land. In some regions, inheritance rules require that household members who inherit land live in rural areas and participate in agricultural work. Some regional laws also restrict how much of the holding can be rented out and whether land use rights can be used as collateral. This is significant to this study as it will elucidate how such land laws influence land ownership, access and control in the case of women in Gusii.

In the case of Tanzania, Namubiru-Mwaura[17] revealed that four land tenure systems coexist. Village land rights are held collectively by the villages and can be communal or individualized; they can also be registered and certified. Customary rights of occupancy are given for village land that is governed by customary laws. The rights are perpetual and may be transferred through bequest and sale, including to those outside of the community, with the consent of the village council. Statutory laws allow equal land ownership rights for men and women but they do not protect women against discriminatory customary practices. From the above case, it is not clear whether the same happens in Gusii. Therefore, the study investigates how customary land rights affected women's access to land, ownership, use and control.

In Uganda, two main types of tenure are recognized: customary and leasehold. Most rural land is under customary tenure (75-80%)

16 Kebede, B.; Land Tenure and Common Pool Resources in Rural Ethiopia: A Study Based on Fifteen Sites; African Development Review; 14(1):113–149; 2002.

17 Namubiru-Mwaura, E. L., Knox, A., and Hughes, A. (2012) Customary Land Tenure in Liberia: Findings and Implications Drawn from 11 Case Studies. Liberia Land Policy & Institutional Support (LPIS) Project (USAID).

and only about 15-20% of rural people have land that is formally registered. Owners of customary land can obtain certificates for the land they occupy and convert these certificates to a freehold title. The constitution of Uganda protects women from discrimination based on gender, protects their rights to own property, and protects the rights of women during and after the disillusion of marriage. However, it can be argued that to a certain extent, customary laws are discriminatory against women, although the extent of the discrimination varies by region. This study is significant in that it will supplement findings from Gusii, which also manifest customary laws that are discriminatory against women concerning land rights.

In Malawi, USAID[18] found that, under the constitution, women and men have equal rights to own land but there are no laws governing matrimonial property. Moreover, when it comes to land ownership, it is traditional norms and customs that dominate. Under patrilineal traditions prevalent in the north, women cannot own or inherit land; they obtain access to land through male family members. Matrilineal customs, which are found in the central and southern regions, are more egalitarian and often give women more land rights.

As we shall show, this study contradicts other studies which have found that women neither have rights to own land nor control it.

In Nigeria, Peterman, Quisumbing, Behrman, and Nkonya[19] note that the 1978 Land Use Act nationalized all land to remove the customary tenure system, and Nigerian women and men could apply for two types of land use certificates - customary and statutory - both of which were for a fixed term. In general, these certificates cannot be transferred, even within the lineage, without government approval. While statutory laws state that men and women have similar inheritance rights, the law only applies to women married under statutory law. In Northern Nigeria, Islamic law guides inheritance practices and, women inherit only half of what their brothers inherit and often, under social pressures, relinquish even that land. Customary laws also discriminate against women and women can only obtain use rights to the land through their husbands. Furthermore, land is almost exclusively registered in men's names.

---

18 USAID. (2010). Country Profile Property Rights and Resources Governance-Malawi.
19 Peterman, A., Quisumbing, A., Behrman, J., & Nkonya, E. (2010). Understanding gender differences in agricultural productivity in Uganda and Nigeria.

Yet on the other hand, Feder and Noronha[20], writing on land rights systems and agricultural development in sub-Saharan Africa, project slightly different findings. They argue that almost half of the plots owned solely by women were obtained as gifts; this may be land that they acquired from their husbands or the community upon marriage. It is noteworthy that they claim to own this land since they are not allowed to own land under customary laws and they obtain access to land through their husbands.

As Levin[21] points out, there is considerable ambiguity surrounding the legal definition of Swazi Nation Land. In his study on land tenure in Swaziland, he charts a history of depressed peasant farm production, exploitation - particularly of women - and forced removals on Swazi Nation Land, with the tacit support of those in power. He argues that, in the abstract, 'communal tenure' may have allowed for democratic involvement. In the tribal context, however, it has proved a misnomer because it conceals the power relations which underlie it and controls land use and allocation.

From the above review, the myriad forms of land tenure systems in Africa complicate the notion of land ownership and make land ownership statistics difficult to compare across, and even within, countries. However, the predominance of patriarchal systems relegates women and children to minority positions, ensuring that women only have access to land and related natural resources through their spouses or male relatives.[22] Central to the understanding of gender relations is a focus on the ways that development, the market, the state, culture, global forces and multiple regimes of property rights affect land use practice and access to land.[23]

The weakness of women's property rights in Kenya has been noted in the past as a problem rooted in both statute and customary law. "The position of women in relation to matrimonial property is also extremely weak. Customary law in relation to the property rights of women seems to be out of step with the present economic

20 Feder, G., & Noronha, R. (1987). Land rights systems and agricultural development in sub-Saharan Africa. The World Bank Research Observer, 2(2), 143–169.
21 Levin, R. (1997). When the sleeping grass awakens: Land and power in Swaziland. Johannesburg: Witswatersrand University Press.
22 Adamo, A. (2005). *Globalization, Gender and Land Tenure in the South: A Literature Review*. DRC: Ottawa.
23 Carney, J. (1996). Converting the Wetlands, Engendering The Environment: The Intersection of Gender Within Agrarian Change in Gambia. In *Liberation Ecologies: Environment, Development and Social Movements*, Peet, R. and Watts, M. (Editors), London and New York: Routledge.

structure and this has the effect of weakening the economic power of women,"[24] there is a common theme that cuts across cultures: women are socially, economically, and politically excluded from structures that enable them to assert equal rights to food security.[25] From the above review, there is a knowledge gap with regard to the historical and cultural understanding relating to gender and land use in Kenya. Therefore, this study attempts to establish the extent to which women's land rights were secure among the Kisii.

Eniola and Akinola[26], tackling the issues of "the social legitimacy of land rights," posit that customary traditions are a stumbling block in realizing women's property rights, as women are seen to be incapable of exercising control over landed property. Based on the above principle, the devolution of property is patriarchal. Land ownership follows the bloodline and is based on the belief that men, as permanent members of the family, will perpetuate the fathers' dynasties while women are expected to marry and cease to be members of their fathers' families.

Despite the enactment of gender-free laws in many African states, women have been consistently denied access to land in many parts of the continent, particularly in rural areas. Gender roles are manifested in social rights and entitlements in a form which denies women equal economic and political empowerment and, in particular, the right to own land. The consequence of gender discrimination in land ownership is women's lack of access to land which constitutes a major source and means of wealth creation and economic empowerment, hence women's vulnerability to marginalization or poverty.

Cagatay[27]'s study on trade, gender and poverty explicates that women are more vulnerable to poverty due to a lack of ownership and control of land, access to credit and income earned through work in the labour market. However, he does not identify the relationship between gender discrimination in land ownership

---

24 Elin H & Sandra F. J. (2009). On the Edge of the Law: Women's Property Rights and Dispute Resolution in Kisii, Kenya. *Law & Society Review* 43(1): 9-60.

25 Ikdahl, I. (2005). Human Rights, Formalization and Women's Land Rights in Southern and Eastern Africa. In *Studies in Women's Law*. Oslo: Institute of Women's Law, University of Oslo.

26 Eniola B., Akinola A. O. (2019). "Women rights and land reform in Africa: Nigeria and South Africa in comparison," *in The Trajectory of Land Reform in Post-Colonial African States: The Quest for Sustainable Development and Utilization* eds Akinola A. O., Wissink H., editors. (Cham: Springer   International Publishing.

27 Cagatay, C. (2001) Trade, Gender and Poverty' United Nations Development Programme.   Washington DC: UNDP Project.

and women's poverty. Besides, the study lacks the basis on how traditional beliefs and cultural practices, gender discrimination is also encouraged by statistical discrimination or social identity susceptibility in ways that some studies have noted influence women's productive outcomes. Such a discriminatory regime affects not only the structure of opportunities open to a social group discriminated against, like Nigerian women, but also shows that social meanings and status are assigned to those groups as their identities.

According to Loury[28], discriminatory regimes not only categorize individuals and establish category-specific rules, but they also invest in those categories with social meaning and create narratives to justify discrimination. The social identities created consequently influence behaviour which remains persistent even if efforts are made by legislation and policies to attenuate their effect. The discriminatory regimes in the context of this work are the traditional beliefs and cultural practices which nurture gender discrimination in the life of the girl-child until womanhood.

In her work analyzing the correlation between gendered land ownership and the gendered path of the agrarian transition in South Asia, Agarwal[29] finds that women's limited access to ownership and control of property contributes to the gender gap in economic well-being, social status and empowerment.[30] She further shows that women's ownership of land serves as a prevention against domestic violence. Agarwal further avers that women's ownership of land leads to improvements in women's welfare, productivity and economic empowerment. And this has been reiterated in studies commissioned by Kieyah, Joseph and Nyaga.[31] As noted by United Nations Habitat[32], owning land assets improves women's productivity and ability to earn a living; women's ownership of land assets contributes to economic development and well-being. Studies of Agarwal and others[33] in other regions also reveal that

28 Loury, M. (2002). The Anatomy of Racial Inequality. Cambridge: Harvard University Press.
29 Agarwal B. (1997) Bargaining and gender relations: within and beyond the household. *Feminist Economics*, 3(1): 1–51.
30 Agarwal, B. (2003). Gender and Land Rights Revisited: Exploring new Prospects via the State, Family and Market. Journal of *Agrarian Change*, 3: 184–224.
31 Kieyah, Joseph and Nyaga. (2009). Land Reform and Poverty in Kenya. GDN_ UNDP_ KIPPRA   Working Paper 17.
32 United Nations Centre for Human Settlements (Habitat), Nairobi. 1999. Women's Rights to Land, Housing and Property in Post-Conflict Situations and During Reconstruction: A Global Overview.
33 Ibid

women's exclusion from landownership puts women at a greater risk of health, poverty and violence.

In Kenya, like many African and Asian countries, social conflicts arise from competition for status and resources between social groups such as ethnicities, clans and communities. As land is a key resource, which provides social status to those who own it, the competition for land in Kenya often takes the form of social conflict, rather than competition between individuals. This is because land and social relationships arising from it are closely connected to kinship and identity. Therefore, contested ownership of land or rights to use land is often propagated in terms of lineage, clan affiliation and ethnicity.

Pre-colonial Kenya had a system of customary land tenure in which land was owned by clans according to culturally and socially accepted hierarchies and rules of access and use. Any disagreements were resolved by dispute resolution fora in which the elders applied rules that had been handed down from previous generations.[34] The customary rules on land gave women secondary access to land, dependent on their relationships with male relatives. Therefore, they could not inherit land in their own right.[35] This implies that customary systems of land tenure only remained viable for as long as there were members of the community who recognized and observed them.

On the position of women in agricultural production, Omwoyo[36] asserts that they played a central role but the recognition of their importance declined with time. In the pre-colonial period, he points out, women played an important role in food production and hence enjoyed a proportionate measure of autonomy in agricultural production. He argues that colonialism, capitalist exploitation and European ideas about appropriate economic and domestic roles for women destroyed the economic independence and traditional forms of social authority exercised by women. Omwoyo shows that the female gender cannot be ignored, especially when investigating the interaction between the systems in precolonial, colonial and post-colonial societies.

---

34 Ojienda, T. (2008). Conveyancing; Principles and Practice. Nairobi, Kenya: Law Africa (K) Publishing Ltd.
35 Hakijamii, GI-ESCR and FIDA, (2016). Joint Shadow Report to the United Nations Committee on Economic, Social and Cultural Rights, 57th Session.
36 Omwoyo, S.M. (1997) "The Colonial Transformation of Gusii Agriculture" M.A.Thesis, Kenyatta University: Nairobi

Gender relations in the ownership and control of land, with specific reference to the Gusii, are important as a focus of this research because women in Gusii tend to have less social capital than men due to the patriarchical nature of the community and are therefore more vulnerable to infringement upon or loss of their property rights in land conflicts.

In their study *On the Edge of The Law: Women's Property Rights and Dispute Resolution in Kisii*, Henrysson and Joireman[37] suggests that customary systems are a better avenue for resolving women's legal disputes over land ownership due to women's negative experiences with formal dispute resolution systems. However, Rose[38] finds that the most positive assessments of women's property rights in customary ownership systems note the necessity for women to negotiate their social relationships in order to sustain access to land through changing life circumstances. As Lastarria-Cornhiel[39] points out, difficulties in ensuring women's access to and control over land have been noted as a problematic feature of customary institutions of dispute resolution, though this study does not highlight women's responses on their access to land, ownership and control. Hence, the need for this research.

Ndege's[40] study on evolving land tenure and agricultural systems says that, when the Gusii arrived in their current cold and wet highland home, they set about clearing the dense forests for cultivation. This was done by kinship groups known as *amasaga*. As the land was hilly and shaped into ridges divided by river valleys, each *risaga* would occupy a ridge or a series of neighbouring ridges, and so the basis of land ownership was communal, determined by the *amasaga* that a person belonged to.[41]

In indigenous Gusii land tenure, gender has always been a factor in land ownership and use. The irony is that, although traditionally women cultivated the land and tended the crops, doing the hardest work on the land, they had the fewest rights to land control and

---

37 Henrysson, E. and Joireman, S.F. (2009). On the Edge of the Law: Women's Property Rights and Dispute Resolution in Kisii, Kenya. *Law & Society Review* 43(1), 39-60.

38 Rose, L.L. (2002). Women's Strategies for Customary Land Access in Swaziland and Malawi: A   Comparative Study. 49 Africa Today, 123-149

39 Lastarria-Cornhiel, S. (1997). Impact of Privatization on Gender and Property Rights in Africa *World Development, 25*: 1317-1333.

40 Ndege, T.M. (2006). Evolving land tenure and agricultural systems, in J.S. Akama and R. Maxon   (2006). *Ethnography of the Gusii of western Kenya: A Vanishing cultural heritage*. Lewiston, NY: Edwin Mellen Press.

41 Ibid

ownership.[42] Relations between family members, including gender relations, were governed by a strict code of conduct called *chinsoni*. This operated within each homestead, headed by the family patriarch, *omogaka bwa omochie*. Subordinate to him were his wives and children, including married sons and their wives and children. Each wife of the patriarch had her own house, yard, and adjacent land for cultivation. This meant that married women had access and control over small pieces of land within their husbands' homesteads, as it was a wife's duty to cultivate the land and feed her husband and children. *Chinsoni* dictated a strictly hierarchical order, with the father at the top and his wives and children in subsequent levels of authority. It was unthinkable for a wife to disobey, openly and otherwise, her husband in any matter. Likewise, children would obey both their parents. Indeed, even the arrangement of houses within a Gusii homestead was intended to reinforce this hierarchy.[43]

As Nyanchoka[44] puts it in her study on the law of succession act and Gusii customary law of inheritance, despite the hard work that Gusii women performed on the land, contributing to the food security of their families and clans, their status in Gusii society remained subservient to men, condemned to a life of hard labour. This was further reinforced by polygamy, which ensured that men were at the top of the social hierarchy. As Gusii women could not own land, they were under complete control of the "owners" of the land, the men. Their subjugation was total, as the land was the entirety of the Gusii mode of life: it provided food, shelter, goods for trade, and status.

Monyenye[45] also found that a woman's access to land in Gusii society ultimately depended on her relation to the man who controlled the land, and by extension to the kinship group that owned it. Ochieng[46] found that under the Gusii communal land ownership system, land tenure rules were based on kinship. These rules were universally understood, and obeyed by everyone, to the extent that no one dared to interfere with land that was temporarily left fallow.

42 Hakansson, T. (1998). *Bridewealth, Women and Land: Social Change mong The Gusii of Kenya*. Uppsala studies in cultural Anthropology. No. 10. Uppsala: Amquiest and Wilsell International.

43 LeVine, S. (1979). *Mothers and Wives: Gusii Women of East Africa*. Chicago: Chicago University   Press.

44 Nyanchoka, J. (1984). The Law of Succession Act and Gusii Customary Law of Inheritance. M.A.   Thesis. Nairobi: University of Nairobi.

45 Monyenye, S. (1977). *The Indigenous Education of the Abagusii People*. M.A. Thesis. Nairobi: University of Nairobi.

46 Ochieng, W. R. (1974). *A Pre-colonial History of the Gusii of Western Kenya, c. 1500-1914*. Nairobi: East African Literature Bureau.

The key rules in Gusii land ownership were: respect for ancestral spirits, existing boundaries, and eyewitness testimony of elders. As the Gusii are a patriarchal society, the male line of succession needed to remain unbroken. Women's claims to land were entirely based on their matrimonial links to families and lineages.

Women in Gusii, like most African women in customary tenure systems, had only secondary or user rights to their husband's land. Different from the foregoing studies, this current study aims at understanding how women responded to such kinds of subordination. Additionally, the foregoing literature is vital to the researcher as it provides knowledge of how the land was administered in the pre-colonial period. However, it is evident that in indigenous tenure systems, women were invisible, but little attention has been paid to women's responses to their rights to land access, use and control.

The Impact of Colonial Land Policies on Gender Relations

This section focuses on the impact of colonial land policies on gender relations from 1920 to 1970 to create an understanding of women's responses to land rights, ownership, access and control in Kisii. Njoki[47] maintains that African women in the past and even, to a significant extent, the present were and are responsible for finding water, sowing seeds, tilling, harvesting, caring for the animals, keeping the home in order, feeding the family, caring for the children and so on. When colonialists moved into Africa from Europe, they claimed the land that had been cared for and cultivated by these women. The women were suddenly alienated from what had, for a long time, defined them and their role in society. This had a huge impact on their economic situation as well as their access to food. However, more than this, it also made these women more dependent on the men in their societies, which led to a sense of male supremacy and dominance, and a loss of the female identity, to some extent.

Musalia's[48] study on gender relations and food crop production in Kiambu District, Kenya, in the 1920-1985 period found that the colonial control of the land meant limited access to available terrain, which implied that women had less diversity in terms of the types of soils available and the crops that could be cultivated. The amount

47 Njoki, W., (2003). Embu Women, Food Production and Traditional Knowledge (online) Available at www.amazon.com
48 Musalia, M. W. (2010). Gender relations and food crop production: a case of Kiambu district Kenya, 1920-1985

of land made available to them was drastically less than before, limiting their agricultural yield significantly. Musalia found that the colonial government was biased against African women because it had a preconceived idea of what an African woman was supposed to do. After all, they were guided by the Victorian ideology that relegated women to the domestic domain. It is this preconceived idea of the place of women that made colonial authorities ignore African women's role in active economic production. Further, the colonial government also wanted women to continue to engage in domestic production to subsidize or cater to the rural reproduction of male labourers.

During the colonial period, states formulated economic policies, largely informed by the colonialist's cultural experiences, which had differential effects on various categories of men and women and, therefore, had implications on gender relations. Consequently, the African and European forms of patriarchy intermingled to form a new system of patriarchy.

Tignor[49], in his study on the colonial transformation of Kenya, found that the most outstanding aspect introduced by European patriarchy was the separation of private and public domains assigned to women and men, respectively. This compartmentalization of life was aimed at making the ideology of capitalism work in Africa. The newly-introduced individual land tenure system destroyed women's access and young men's rights to land inheritance. As well, land consolidation reduced landholding that could be put under cultivation. This, in turn, affected food crop production, greatly altering gender relations of production. The independent government did not deviate from the colonial policy on agricultural production. It continued to give attention to exportable products, for instance, coffee and tea, but with the continual scarcity of land, the Kikuyu of Kiambu moved into horticulture. All these agricultural developments impacted gender relations. The gender analysis here is thus paramount in our study as it will help in giving the most appropriate theoretical perspective to the study.

Like conjoined twins, colonialism and capitalism became sources of women's oppression, especially in economic production. In his study, Throup[50] examines the economic and social origins of Mau

---

49 Tignor, R. L. (1974). The Colonial Transformation of Kenya: the Kamba Kikuyu and Maasai from 1900-1939. Princeton: Princeton University Press.
50 Throup, D. (1988). Economic and Social Origins of Mau Mau 1945- 1953. London: James Currey.

Mau paying particular attention to Kikuyu agriculture after the Second World War. The author argues that problems associated with agriculture, especially land ownership and deteriorating soil fertility, contributed significantly to the outbreak of Mau Mau. However, Throup does not give gender relations considerable attention. It is, however, the contention of this study that policies introduced during the war and the whole of the colonial period had differential impacts on men and women not only in Kiambu District but also in Gusii, which is the focus of this study.

Trinh and Minh-ha[51] posited that the gendered division of labour in developing countries is the outcome of a long history of colonialism. Under colonialism, women's traditional contributions to food production were undermined in favour of exportable crops, such as coffee, and the extraction of raw materials, such as minerals. Men workers were favoured in this work, but they were paid barely enough for their subsistence, let alone the subsistence of their families. As such, women's family members had to provide food for themselves and their children. However, with good land confiscated for cash crop plantations, they also lived at a bare survival level. All this notwithstanding, African women employed their agency and initiative against any oppressive measures,[52] and hence transformed gender relations.

Trinh and Minh-ha further note that women were greatly affected by the alienation of land experienced by most Africans. Nonetheless, women appear to have been driven to become more economically dependent on men. In Tanganyika, male migration nearly halved the male population in some communities such that there were nearly twice as many women as men in those communities. Consequently, the removal of males from African society led to the destruction of the African family. Households no longer had fathers, brothers, uncles and nephews thus leaving a void that the male used to occupy. Male participation in traditional roles in ceremonies, rites and rituals became badly distorted.

51 Trinh, T. Minh-ha. (1989). Woman, Native, Other: Writing Post-coloniality and Feminism. Bloomington: Indiana University Press. This led to an intensification of domestic patriarchy, reinforced by colonial social institutions. The first socio-political effect of colonialism was the concept of the Victorian woman which the colonisers brought with them. The colonialists came with the belief that women were to remain creatures of the private domain. Women were to preoccupy themselves with domestic issues and leave the 'real work' of ruling and running the nation in terms of politics and economics in particular to the men. Male migration profoundly affected women especially in rural areas.

52 Presley, A. C. (1986). Labour Unrest Among Kikuyu Women in Colonial Kenya in Women and Class in Africa (eds.) Robertson Claire and Berger Iris New York, London, Africana Publishing Company.

As colonialism progressed, African patriarchs and the colonial government to a certain extent, attempted to restrict the movement of women in a bid to control their sexuality. As Zeleza[53] explains, 'colonial policy pushed men into migrant labour leaving women stranded in the rural areas with an increasingly onerous workload. These women had little chance of wage employment in towns where opportunities to earn money existed.' As a result, more women migrated to urban areas but were met with stiff opposition in the form of disapproval of African patriarchs in particular. Both the patriarchial system and colonial officials disliked female migration because they felt it came with collateral responsibilities.

Walker[54] avers that the bias against African women was generally in British Africa because the British viewed women from a European perspective. In particular, the British were influenced by the Victorian idea of an "ideal" woman as one confined at home with little or no participation in production. On the other hand, African patriarchs were particularly concerned with controlling women's movement and thus, sexuality for many reasons. First, they wanted to retain the purity of their clans. When women moved away from home, the patriarchs had less control over whom the women married or cohabited with. Thus, African males wanted to keep women under their noses to ensure endogamous marriages by women.

Second, African patriarchs discovered that if women left home and got married in new areas of residence, the groom often did not pay the necessary bride wealth. Since there was no social pressure on couples in urban areas to raise bridewealth, African patriarchs began losing a great deal of income in the form of unpaid bride wealth. African patriarchs became preoccupied with controlling female mobility for these reasons. The colonial administration also became concerned because some African men left their employment early due to domestic problems that arose in the form of accusations of adultery and wives leaving them for other men. This caused the colonial administration to assist the African labourers to secure their families by allowing them time off to visit their homes (initial) mutual benefit.

---

53 Zeleza, T. (1992). The colonial Labour system in Kenya. An Economic History of Kenya (eds.) Ochieng' W.R. and Maxon R M.
54 Walker, C. (1990). Gender and the Development of Migrant Labour System c. 1850-1930. Walker Cherryl (ed) Women and Gender in Southern Africa to 1945. London: James Currey.

In Zimbabwe, McClendon[55] found that the administration passed ordinances and laws such as the 1926 Adultery Ordinance which applied to married women and the 1929 Native Affairs Act, which applied to prostitutes, in an attempt to, 'assist the *kraal* native to control their women'. However, it must be noted that the colonial administration was not very serious in their attempts to control the movement of women due to the observation that the men were more productive when they had their wives or female companions around. Nonetheless, rural women's mobility was constrained, thus limiting the social freedom they used to enjoy. In the past, women participated in activities such as trade and visiting their relatives that required substantial movement. Colonialism caused some women to lose the freedom they once enjoyed.

In Tanzania, Hyden[56] observes that in 1963, the role of traditional chiefs was abolished, clearing the way for the rural revolution, *Vijiji*, which saw two-thirds of the rural population resettled via administrative fiat into nucleated villages. However, the collapse of the rural economy in early the 1970s led to the formulation of the New Agricultural Policy in the 1980s, and the Economic Recovery Programme, heralding a process of liberalization. Despite these changes, women were not given priority in the newly formulated land policies.

Due to the Victorian concept of women held by the colonialists and embraced by the African male, women were excluded from the new political and administrative system. In the past, many African societies had a dual-sex political system which allowed for substantial female representation and involvement in governance and administration. The position of Queen Mother, seen across Africa in Ghana among the Akan, Egypt, Uganda, Ethiopia and Rwanda to name a few, gave women prominent and visible political authority in running the nation.

However, the chauvinist and misogynistic colonial officials made no provisions for such women's participation in the initial administrative design. It is often only with women's protests as was the case of the Aba women's war and the actions of Mekatilili wa Menza, that a meagre number of woman's positions were created in the colonial setup Walker C. (1990). This marginalization of women

55 Thomas V. M. (1995). Tradition and Domestic Struggle in the Courtroom: Customary Law and the Control of Women in Segregation-Era Natal. *The International Journal of African Historical Studies* Vol. 28, No. 3, pp. 527-561.
56 Hyden, G. (1980). Beyond Ujamaa in Tanzania: Underdevelopment and an Uncaptured Peasantry. London: Heinemann.

led to an erosion in the position and influence of women in society. As this new status quo was maintained, African men actually began to believe that women were incapable of leading the nations. This erroneous opinion is still held by many Africans to this day and is reflected in the paltry number of women in parliament and ministerial positions.

In Kenya, the Government[57] pointed out that there was a need for sovereignty over land occupied by indigenous Kenyans and legislation of laws to protect their expropriated interests whereas destroying the customary arrangements. This came in three phases; first, the colonial government on December 13, 1899, expropriated all productive land not formerly held by the Sultan Arabs. This was followed by the colonial government promulgating an ordinance in 1908 in the ten-mile coastal strip formerly held by the Sultan Arabs requiring individuals with interests in this land to make a claim thereof. Lastly, the colonial government created native reserves to facilitate simpler and more efficient control and administration of 'natives'.

For instance, some parts of Laikipia, Rift Valley, and Mau Escapements were apportioned to the "White Settlers" by the colonial Government for industrial farming activities on the theory of "wasteland". Some of the indigenous communities (the natives) that were living on such lands were consequently turned into squatters through some technical resettlement schemes. A lot of people who lost their lands were forced to live in designated locations with home guards that would ensure that the former would not create any undesirable disturbances.[58]

1954 saw the 'Swynnerton Plan' to ensure the 'Intensification of Agriculture' to destroy African land tenure systems and ensure conversion to systems of individualized tenure arrangements.[59] Its effect was the delegitimization of the customary land order, legal systems and structures. The plan also introduced individualized and absolute titles to land.[60] The plan placed women in a precarious economic state. For instance, men were accorded absolute rights over land through the registered land statutes. Particularly, the

57 Government of Kenya, (2002). Report of the Commission of Inquiry into the Land Law System of Kenya on Principles of a National Land Policy Framework, Constitutional Position of Land and New Institutional Framework for Land Administration. Government Press, Nairobi, Kenya.
58 Ibid
59 Swynnerton, R. J. M. (1955). A Plan to intensify the Development of African Agriculture in Kenya. Nairobi, Kenya: Government Printer.
60 Ibid

Registered Land Act (RLA), which actualized the Swynnerton Plan, insulated the rights men gained through the adjudication, consolidation, and registration process by vesting them with absolute ownership of the land. Consequently, the proposed policy failed to acknowledge even the derivative rights of women to land.

The establishment of absolute ownership, validated by the Registered Land Act, destroyed a married woman's ability to claim and protect her interests or rights to matrimonial property.[61] In communal land tenure systems, women had significant indirect access and rights to use communal resources through their roles as household managers. With the new land 'regime', women were further excluded when land tenure was individualized and invariably adjudicated and registered in the names of heads of households or men. Without legal and social/communal protection, women were placed at risk of suddenly becoming landless.

The wars for independence were caused by the question of rights over land[62] which had been unjustly apportioned to the "White-Settlers" by the colonial regime. The British did not take sufficient regard for customary land tenure and particular rights to land proprietorship meant for the African population.

Esese,[63] focusing on the role of social economic, ecological and political factors in agricultural production among the Wanga, with attention to the role of land tenure system in agricultural production and change, analyzed land ownership, crop production and livestock keeping through an integrated approach. Although his work ends in 1945, it is vital to our study for it gives information on the type of land-related issues in Wanga which will be compared to those in Gusii.

The interplay between the system of land ownership and crop production cannot be well analyzed while ignoring gender and labour relations in a given society. Since gender relations are the distinctive social relations between men and women, research works in gender relations during the colonial and post-colonial periods can therefore not be ignored in this study. Stichter[64] found that, among

61 Okoth-Ogendo, H. W. O. (1989). Some Issues of Theory in the Study of Tenure Relations in African Agriculture, 59 Africa 6.

62 Newsinger, J. (1981). Revolt and Repression in Kenya: The "Mau Mau" Rebellion, 1952-1960. 45 Science & Society 159.

63 Esese, D. (1999) "Kenya's Economic Policy Since 1945" in Aseka, M. (Ed.) (1999) The Political Economy of Transition: A Study of Issues and Social Movement in Kenya Since 1945. Nairobi: eight Publishers.

64 Stichter, S. (1975-76). Women and Labour Force in Kenya, 1895-1964. In Rural Africana 29

the Abagusii, it is women who were primarily responsible for food production, household management and the nurture of children.

Ndeda[65] shows how colonialism was discriminatory to African women and how women were overburdened in the reserves in the absence of their labour migrant male folk. Here, women became the sole agricultural producers in the reserves. They planted, weeded, harvested, stored and managed their food harvests in the absence of men. Her work offers more insights into gender relations within the Gusii context on how gender labour relations have impacted the system of land ownership, access and control.

Omwoyo[66] analyzed the organization and transformation of agriculture among the Gusii of Western Kenya in the colonial period. He demonstrated that the dynamism and innovativeness of Gusii indigenous agriculture showed its efficiency and productiveness. He further demonstrated how colonial penetration modified and marginalized Gusii's indigenous agriculture. Nonetheless, he attributes this transformation to colonialism. His work is relevant to this study in that it recognizes the impact of land ownership on crop production from gender lenses. Moreover, Omwoyo[67] points out that the women in Gusii adopted several approaches to counter the impact of coffee production on labour relations. First, they deliberately intensified their labour. As they were forced to undertake the duties of their absent husbands, offer their labour in coffee farms, and perform their designated domestic chores, women had no alternative other than to work a little more and longer than before. Second, they used the working parties more than before. The working parties went around soliciting for jobs to do in rich farmers' coffee holdings to be paid cash.

Third, they sought employment locally in the rich men's coffee *shambas* as individuals. This meant working for their employer in the morning hours and working on their holding late in the afternoon. The fourth strategy employed by the women to cope with their continued marginalization from the cash crop economy was to increase the production of profitable crops within their reach. Such women established vegetable gardens and were often seen selling

65 Ndeda, M. (2002) *'Women and Development since Colonial Times'* in Ochieng, R (Ed.) *Historical Studies and Social Change in Western Kenya.* Nairobi: East African Educational Publishers

66 Omwoyo, S. M. (1992) "The Colonial Transformation of Gusii Agriculture" M.A.Thesis, Kenyatta   University: Nairobi.

67 Omwoyo, S. M. (1997) 'Women and Agricultural Production among the Gusii c. 1875-1963, The Eastern Africa Journal of Historical and Social Sciences Research, Vol .2 No.1.

these in marketplaces on appointed market days. Lastly, women formed small-scale cooperatives or merry-go-round groups to raise the required capital.

The present study benefits from this work when investigating gender relations and labour changes during the colonial period.

Maxon[68] notes that private land ownership was brought to Gusii in the early 20th Century by the British colonial administration. It was a consequence of the colonial administration's unequal land policies, in which the settlers expropriated land by force, to the detriment of Africans, and designed to facilitate European modes of production (for commercial purposes). He further postulates that the effect of this on women's economic status was to move them from a position of self-sufficiency to one of relative dependency resulting in the loss of their socio-economic power. As more land was reserved for cash crops, women became increasingly reliant on cash to buy the food they could no longer produce and turned their labour to cash crop production, the monetary benefits of which were reserved for men.[69]

Nasimiyu[70] assessed the change in land tenure, innovations and the introduction of cash crops in Bungoma between 1902 and 1960. She argues that the changes brought about by agricultural innovations, the introduction of cash crops and changes in land tenure and crop production reduced women to a state of dependency on men. She further adds that women ended up becoming the providers of labour with no security. Her work establishes that women continued to perform their traditional agricultural chores and at the same time participated in the new colonial system of production. Although her work tackles the pre-colonial and colonial periods, she majored in the production process while this study deals with both the system of land ownership and crop production.

Fortmann and Riddell[71] lament that colonialism had profound effects on African tenure systems by introducing the notions of individual and state ownership of land in a bid to promote economic development. Okoth-Ogendo[72] claims that the Torrens title system

---

68 Maxon, R. (2003). *Going Their Separate Ways: Agrarian Transformation In Kenya, 1930-1950.* London: Associated University Presses.
69 Nasimiyu, R. (1985). Women in the Colonial Economy of Bungoma: Role of Women in Agriculture, in G.S. Were (ed.) W*omen and Development in Africa, 56-73.*
70 Nasimiyu R. (1985). Women in the Colonial Economy of Bungoma: The Role of Women in Agriculture 1902-1960. *Journal of Eastern Africa Research and Development No. 15.*
71 Fortmann, L. & Riddell, J. (1985). *Trees and Tenure: An Annotated Bibliography.*
72 Okoth-Ogendo, H. W. O. (1989). Some Issues of Theory in the Study of Tenure Relations in African Agriculture, *59 Africa 6.*

based on statutory registration and ownership of individually demarcated plots was introduced to replace pre-existing customary notions of land ownership. However, still, men dominated in land rights, and women had no place. This current study aims at examining women's responses regarding this.

Leys[73] asserts that the latter has, however, persisted and has been informed in practice by the introduced system. Thus, Bentsi-Enchill[74] avers that the defects of African systems of land tenure have arisen from the fact that these systems have been left to informally adapt to changed circumstances.

Tanui[75] observed that land reform was also seen as a strategy through which the political status quo would be preserved and enforced. The agitation for land among the African population challenged the cornerstones of colonialism by calling for the restoration of stolen lands. Land consolidation and registration were therefore seen as an asset that could be used to reward loyalists and punish the agitators. She further notes that the adjudication process itself was premised on the patriarchal nature of African societies and on customary practices of land ownership and inheritance which did not allow women to own or inherit land.

In addition, she investigated the impact of changing relations in access to resources due to negative political, cultural and social factors which influenced gender relations of production in Kenya and the Nandi district in particular. Her study has shown that political, social and ideological factors interacted in a complex manner and over time influenced gender access to land, control over labour and produce in the Nandi society. This study benefits from her work by investigating women's responses during land consolidation in the study area.

The colonial government passed the Forfeiture of Lands Ordinance, 1953; its invocation resulted in many Mau Mau fighters and supporters being forced to forfeit their land as a punishment for their alleged terrorist activities. The reforms came via the recommendations made by R. J. M. Swynnerton[76]:

73 Leys, C. (1975). Underdevelopment in Kenya: The Political Economy of Neo-colonialism 1964-1971. Nairobi: East African Education Publishers.

74 Bentsi-Enchill, K. (1966). Do African Systems of Land Tenure require a Special Terminology? 9 J. AFR. L. 114-139.

75 Tanui, P. (2005). The Impact of Differential Gender Access to Resources in Agricultural Production: The Case of Nandi District, 1954-2000. Ph.D. Thesis, Kenyatta University.

76 Swynnerton, R. J. M. (1955). *A Plan to intensify the Development of African Agriculture in Kenya*. Nairobi, Kenya: Government Printer.

"Sound agricultural development is dependent upon a system of land tenure which will make available to the African farmer a unit of land and a system of farming whose production will support his family at a level ... comparable to other occupations. He must be provided with such security of tenure through an indefeasible title as will encourage him to offer it as security against such financial credits as he may wish to secure."

The gist of land reform was the individualization of titles. The process would start with adjudication in which ownership of fragmented parcels of land would be ascertained. Downs[77] studied Kenya's land tenure reform particularly the misunderstandings in the public creation of private property. He affirmed that land reform adversely affected women's land rights. Women were neither represented in the adjudication committees nor did they participate in the adjudication committee meetings.

Further, Okoth-Ogendo[78] found that the patriarchal setting overlooked the strong socio-economic status and positions of power that women enjoyed in traditional African societies by giving precedence to individual ownership of land vested in male heads of households without reserving any rights for women. This literature gives the researcher an understanding of how women were undermined in their land usage rights, but also their responses to oppression by men.

Among the Taita of Kenya, the system of tenure and agrarian reforms introduced in the late colonial period and continued under independence, legitimized and made permanent existing inequities in land distribution with the effect that women's ability to make independent decisions in agriculture was jeopardized.[79] The registration of titles almost exclusively in men's names ensured that women did not participate in any credit or loan facilities owing to their lack of collateral and had to rely on their husbands for money to invest in food crop production. Finally, the destruction of African institutions like the *ahoi*, *athami* and the *jodak*, which ensured that everybody had access to land, and the deliberate efforts

---

77 Downs, R. E. (1988). The Kenya Land Tenure Reform: Misunderstandings in the Public Creation of Private Property, in *Land and Society in Contemporary Africa*, 98.

78 Okoth-Ogendo, H. W. O. (1975). The Adjudication Process and the Special Rural Development Process. Unpublished Occasional Paper no. 12, Institute of Development Studies, University of Nairobi.

79 Flueret, A. (1988). Some Consequences of Tenure and Agrarian Reform in Taita, Kenya, in R.E. Downs & S.P. Reyna (eds.). *Land and Society in Contemporary Africa*.

of the colonial administration to create a landless class through individualization of titles not only adversely affected the rights of women to land ownership but also vicariously affected the rights of women to access to land.

Downs[80] found that the wives of the landless, having no traditional social organizations to rely on for access, found themselves sorely dependent on limited cash resources for their survival. With the introduction of cash crop farming, a money economy was brought into play and land use patterns and objectives were transformed. Increasingly, it became more profitable in terms of acquiring money, to grow cash crops instead of food crops. One weakness of this study is, it doesn't show how women benefited in this context.

Leys[81] reports that in the Sessional Paper No. 4 of 1981, the Kenya government acknowledged that the country was facing serious food shortages after experiencing famine in the late 1970s and early 1980s. Even though domestic production was viewed as the best way forward to address the crisis, a specific policy was not formulated on how to approach the main food producers - women. Moreover, the government did not concede to the fact that both men and women contributed differently to food production. The government also continued to give more focus to grains especially wheat and maize ignoring other food crops.

It can be argued that this policy was tantamount to a continuation of the colonial policy. It will be noted that the colonial government was keen on expanding maize production both for export and subsistence while ignoring traditional food crops since they did not have a market value that could boost the colonial economy. It was only after spells of food shortage that Africans were encouraged to grow drought-resistant crops like cassava. The present study seeks to find out if the women in Kisii waited upon the government's encouragement to produce food.

Agrarian land tenure reforms facilitated further limitations to land access as land previously used for food crops was planted with cash crops. Women, therefore, lost the right of ownership of land and also lost access in terms of control of land use. The reforms, therefore, resulted in the deterioration of women's land rights. They destroyed the social structure through which women's economic power and

80 Downs, R. E. (1988). The Kenya Land Tenure Reform: Misunderstandings in the Public Creation of Private Property, in *Land and Society in Contemporary Africa, 98.*
81 Leys, C. (1975). Under-development in Kenya: The Political Economy of Neo-colonialism 1964-1971. Nairobi: East African Education Publishers.

stability were guaranteed and maintained and introduced a new structure which neither reserved nor guaranteed any rights for women in return for what they had lost. From the above analysis, the researchers do not show the significance of women in the agrarian sector and land tenure reforms. Furthermore, Maxwell and Wiebe[82] affirm that it is on this basis that there is a lack of gender-sensitive and integrated research on land tenure and food security. Therefore, there is an increasing interest to investigate the implications of gender relations in land tenure systems with a particular focus on Gusii.

Kitching's[83] class and economic change in Kenya with attention on Central and Nyanza provinces advances the argument that both ownership of land and access to off-farm income caused differentiation. He concludes that increased women's agricultural labour was significant in the agricultural expansion in Kikuyuland. Kitching's work is significant to the current study for he examines the impact of colonial economic policies on what was Central Kenya.

Kitching argues that both ownership of land and access to off-farm income caused differentiation. He concludes that increased women's agricultural labour was significant in the agricultural expansion of Kikuyu land Kitching's work is significant to the current study since he examines the impact of colonial economic policies on land ownership and access in Central Kenya. A similar study with gender interest will be explicated in Gusii.

In Western Kenya, Makana's[84] metropolitan concern, colonial state policy and the embargo on the cultivation of coffee by Africans in colonial Kenya: the example of Bungoma District, 1930–1960, revealed that the widespread involvement of African peasant households in the cultivation of high-value cash crop – coffee - in Kenya dates back only to the mid-1950s. However, this late inclusion of African households in coffee cultivation did not imply their lack of enthusiasm to cultivate the crop from an earlier date. On the contrary, European settlers and some officials of the Department of Agriculture thwarted the aspirations of African households to cultivate coffee by declining permission to do so. The overall view

82 Maxwell, D. and Wiebe, K.; Land Tenure and Food Security: Exploring Dynamic Linkages; Development and Change; 30(4):825–849; 1999.

83 Kitching, G. (1980). *Class and Economic Change in Kenya: the making of an African Petite Bourgeoisie*. New Haven and London: Yale University Press.

84 Makana, N. (2009). Metropolitan Concern, Colonial State Policy and the Embargo on Cultivation of Coffee by Africans in Colonial Kenya: The Example of Bungoma District, 1930–1960. History in Africa, 36, 315-329. doi:10.1353/hia.2010.0007

was in favour of the continued imposition of an embargo on African coffee cultivation. Makana demonstrates that when colonial state policy shifted due to metropolitan and local pressure in favour of African household involvement in coffee cultivation, the African peasants proved themselves to be efficient cultivators of the crop. The major weakness of this study is that it does not show how both men and women we involved in coffee production, thus, the need for the current study.

Throup[85] finds that the population explosion that took place in Gusii, which is the focus of this study during the colonial and post-colonial periods, resulted in increased land fragmentation. Before independence, in the late 1950s, a single household's (12 people) plot of land was less than 2 hectares (2 ha) and maize replaced finger millet as the main staple crop. The increasing popularity of cash crops also contributed to the decline of food production, to the extent that by the end of the 1960s, food crops only accounted for 25% of cultivated land in Gusii.

There is no hesitation that colonial periods dramatically transformed gender relations in the land. The resolution imposed by the colonial system aimed at intensifying agriculture and introducing cash crops with emphasis on male-controlled agriculture was a primary determinant of Gusii women's loss of status and power in land and agriculture. The result of colonial private enterprise was the restructuring of gender roles. The introduction of cash crops for export brought about greater gender segregation in labour tasks with men increasingly becoming agricultural managers. It is essential to understand that given the labour division, Gusii women were the backbone of rural farming.

*****

The foregoing literature on colonial land policies and their impact on issues relating to gender were useful to this research as it enabled the researcher to compare the traditional land tenure system with the modern land tenure system and as a consequence interrogate how the land laws introduced during the colonial periods impacted on gender in ownership and control of land.

Gutto posited that women had virtual control and monopoly of crop production which led to them having rights to land they controlled for the maintenance of their households.[86] Women's status in their

---

85 Throup, D. (1987). "The construction and destruction of the Kenyatta state," in The Politcal Economy of Kenya. Michael G. Schatzberg ed: Praeger
86 Gutto, S. B. O. (1975). Gutto, Land and property rights in modern

agricultural productive tasks was secure under the traditional land tenure system until the colonial land policies introduced legislative programmes designed to replace the traditional land tenure system. One may cautiously conclude, therefore, that land tenure systems in Sub-Saharan Africa particularly Gusii cannot be blamed for the Agrarian crisis.

Despite these results, there is pressure on the countries of Africa to pursue land tenure reforms. In the meantime, little attention is paid to the gender consequences, including the disruption of social order, that accompany these reforms. Most studies on land continue to focus on the implications of the reforms for agricultural production and ignore gender relations to land rights and ownership. Most of the above studies ignore gender struggles around the control of land and their relation to changing tenure systems. It is this gap in the literature which this study was designed to fill by focusing on gender in relation to land ownership and control in Gusii. This study takes the standpoint that land is only significant in so far as it lends itself to human use and presents certain opportunities for human utilization. It sought to demonstrate a fresh approach to the disposition of land, and women were the main players, within the individualized tenure system in Gusii, Kenya between 1920 and 1970.

Land Tenure in Relation to Gender in the Post-Colonial Period

This section focuses on gender rights in relation to land and ownership in the post-colonial period to create an understanding of women's responses to gender relations and land rights. Chigbu, Paradza, and Dachaga[87] on differentiations in women's land tenure experiences and implications for women's land access and tenure security in Sub-Saharan Africa, aver that the study of gender is essential for grasping tenurial and structural transformation and the organization of land rights globally, as gender relations shape women's tenure security status.

---

constitutionalism: Experiences from Africa and possible lessons for South Africa in Wanjala.
87 Chigbu, U, Paradza, G and Dachaga. W. (2019). Differentiations in Women's Land Tenure Experiences: Implications for Women's Land Access and Tenure Security in Sub-Saharan Africa.

After the colonial period, Lele and Meyers[88] found that in the post-independence period in most African countries, including Kenya, there were substantial increases in agricultural productivity, especially in the smallholder sector. Agricultural GDP grew at annual rates between 5.4% in 1967-1973, including land tenure reform. Adoko and Levine[89] posit that land distribution, formalization of individual land rights, and subsequent land transactions frequently vested titles to land in the head of the household only. These were most often men, according to patrilineal custom, and this vesting shifted the traditional concept of what it meant to have rights to land. Therefore, the man as an individual, rather than as the responsible representative of his family, has become the person with all the authority to use, sell, and control land.

In countries such as Nigeria, Zimbabwe and Ghana, national laws and policies were formulated to empower women in land ownership, access and tenure security. However, in Nigeria, a report by the Federal Government of Nigeria[90] documented that the Land Use Act and National Gender Policy were formulated, and while advocating for women's property rights failed to identify differences in women. These laws, which are central to land and women's issues in the country, ignored the different circumstances under which women experience land tenure insecurity.

In Ghana, the Draft Land Bill[91] was criticized for not containing clauses that explicitly protect women's customary and spousal land rights, especially where customary rules discriminate against women's tenure rights. A simple search for the term "women" in the Ghana National Land Policy[92] and the Draft Land Bill[93] returns

88 Lele, U and Meyers, L. R. (1989). Growth and Structural Change in East Africa – Domestic Policies, Agricultural Performance and World Bank Assistance, Washington D.C., World Bank. Managing Agricultural Development in Africa (MADIA) Discussion Paper No. 3
89 Adoko, J, & Levine, S. (2005). "A land market for poverty eradication? A case study of the impact of Uganda's Land Acts on policy hopes for development and poverty eradication." Land and Equity Movement in Uganda.
90 Federal Government of Nigeria (2008). National Gender Policy Strategic Framework-Implementation Plan) Federal Republic of Nigeria 2008–2013; Federal Republic of Nigeria: Abuja, Nigeria.
91 Government of Ghana. (2016). Draft Land Bill. National Land Policy; Government of Ghana: Accra, Ghana.
92 Ekejiuba, F. (1995). Down to the Fundamentals: Women Centred Hearth-Holds in Rural West Africa. In Women Wielding the Hoe: Lessons fromRural Africa for Feminist Theory and Development Practice; Bryceson, D., Ed.; Berg: London, UK,; pp. 47–61.
93 Gray, L.; Kevane, M. (1999). Diminished access, diverted exclusion: Women and land tenure in sub-Saharan Africa. *Afr. Stud. Rev. 42:* 15–39.

no results, let alone providing for differentiations in women's land issues.

Yemisi and Aisha[94] opine that women in colonial and post-colonial periods contribute tremendously to agricultural output but unfortunately they hardly, until recently, benefited from agricultural incentives and innovation because of economic suppression and social and traditional practices which undermine the constitutional provisions on the equality of men and women. The authors further lament that gender discrimination, rather than ignorance, is the reason for the lack of women's participation in agricultural programmes and projects.

Boserup[95] maintains that food production is mainly done by women in subsistence agriculture, with little contribution from the men. This notion is buttressed by Pala[96] who observes that the percentage of work done by women farmers far outweighs that of men in Kenya. Similarly, in Ghana, for instance, smallholdings kept by women provide about 80% of the total food production in the country. Despite this recognition, women are not given any consideration in land rights, ownership, access and control. The current study, therefore, fills this gap by seeking women's responses on gender relations and land rights in Gusii.

In Zimbabwe, Mushunje[97] noted that the 1999 Draft National Land Policy of Zimbabwe sought to address gender issues in the country's reform, but with little success. It also failed to address women's differentiation in land issues. In all of these countries (Ghana, Nigeria, and Zimbabwe), the failures to address differential problems in women's land tenure lie in the fact that these laws (and policies) address land tenure inequalities from the perspective of men-and-women differences while ignoring inter-gender differences in land tenure. This is the reason why this study focused on women's responses to land rights, ownership, access and control.

---

94 Yemisi I. O, & Aisha M. A. (2009). Gender issues in Agricultural and rural development: The role of women. In *Humanities and Social Sciences journal,* 4(1): 19-30.

95 Boserup, A. (1970). Women's Role in Economic Development, London: George Allen and Univin.

96 Pala, A. O. (1976). The role of African women in rural development research priorities. Discussion Paper No. 203.

97 Cousins, B, Winer, D & Amin, N. (1992). Social Differentiation in the Communal Lands of Zimbabwe. Rev. Afr. Political Econ., 19, 5–24.

Chigbu, Paradza and Dachaga[98]'s study in three sub-Saharan African countries confirmed that women are highly differentiated groups in their land access and tenure security experiences. This implies women are highly differentiated in their land tenure experiences within any system or sub-system of society. Makura-Paradza[99], while examining women's land rights vulnerability in Zimbabwe, concluded that the role of patriarchy was sometimes overemphasized in studies of women's land rights vulnerability in the developing world. Chigbu[100] in Nigeria showed that the land challenges women face are sometimes due to the suppression of women. In creating the Sustainable Development Goals (SDGs) agenda, the global community envisaged the critical role that securing land rights for women would play in the pursuit of gender equality and ending poverty in the world. However, this appears difficult to achieve in Sub-Saharan Africa without an adequate grasp of women's responses to land tenure security.

Staudt[101] in studying women and labour in agricultural production acknowledges that agricultural production has its historicity of change and gender relations of production. Using a gendered approach to study agriculture, she focuses on the implications of labour differentiation, incentives and struggles over resources for agricultural development. She argues that while many factors are attributed to the decline in food production in Africa, it is impossible to understand the food crisis without understanding the demands on women's agricultural labour and women's stake in securing some return for that labour. Staudt further argues that male out-migration places more work on rural women without individual access to the productive resources affecting production. She states that political arrangements favour men at the expense of women even though they are the majority of the food producers. Her arguments are enriching to this study. The impact of political arrangements on women's accessibility to land, ownership, control and usage was examined.

98 Chigbu, U, Paradza, G & Dachaga. W. (2019). Differentiations in Women's Land Tenure Experiences: Implications for Women's Land Access and Tenure Security in Sub-Saharan Africa

99 Makura-Paradza, G. (2010). Single Women, Land and Livelihood Vulnerability; Wageningen Publishers: Wageningen, The Netherlands.

100 Chigbu, U. E. (2019). Masculinity, men and patriarchal issues aside: How do women's actions impede women's access to land? Matters Arising from a Peri-rural community in Nigeria. *Land Use Policy*, 81: 39–48.

101 Staudt, K. (1976). Agriculture Policy, Political Power and Women Farmers in Western Kenya. (PhD. Michigan University).

On the Akan of Ghana, Tsikata[102] states that women's labour was used both in colonial and independent periods to transform Ghana into a cash crop-producing state. She argues that pre-capitalist gender relations did not change with the introduction of capitalism, but increased the interests of certain groups of African men. The assertion here is that there is a complex historical linkage between capitalism, patriarchy and the state, which needs to be understood. This argument on the linkage is relevant to the study of Gusii especially in relation to the attempt by Gusii men to control women's movement during the colonial period.

Carney and Watts'[103] work on rice growing among the Mandinka of Senegambia traced the subtle and accumulative change in domestic household relations. The expansion of rice growing by the government caused intra-household struggles over access and control over land and labour. Due to the high demand for rice as the staple food, women were forced to put more labour into its production. Stress was further put on labour with the introduction of groundnuts as a man's cash crop since it made men neglect the growth of millet and sorghum, crops they previously grew to complement their subsistence in their households. The introduction of groundnuts as a cash crop, therefore, transformed the gender division of labour from task to crop-specific gender roles. The authors further argue that any state programme, aimed at increasing rice production among the Mandinka, ignited struggles over access and control over household resources including land. Carney and Watts, maintain that gender-based struggles over property labour and conditions of work were significant in the debate over agricultural intensification.

Over the years, such struggles not only in Ghana but also in all of colonial Africa shaped, and continue to shape, the character and the trajectory of gender relations in land access, use and control. The study of the Mandika shows that there was a correlation between gender relations and food crop production. Accordingly, changes in food crop production impacted gender relations. At the same time, the changes in gender relations continue to affect food crop production.

The findings of the study supplemented the current study by examining women's responses to gendered decisions regarding

102Tsikata, D. (1997). Gender Equality and the State in Ghana: Some Issues of Policy and Practice. Engendering African Social Science (ed). Ayesha M.Imam, Amina Mama, Fatou Sow, Codesria Book Series.
103 Carney J. & Watts, M. (1991). Disciplining Women? Rice mechanization and the Evolution of Mandika Gender Relations in Senegambia. Signs vol. 16 (4).

food crop production in Gusii, They further assert that household relations, especially conjugal, are affected by outside factors. For example, the organization of households around patriarchal power derives support from the state both through the bureaucratic demands of the state organization and through the devolution of power to men by state-run development schemes. Borrowing from the authors, our study examines how external factors influenced gender relations within the household. The issue of Gusii's patriarchal power as it colluded with European patriarchy is discussed.

Bryceson[104] discusses the dynamic interaction between peasant food production and commodity production under conditions of increasing penetration of capital. The author asserts that increased commodity production had a direct link to the serious food shortage and even famines experienced in colonial Tanzania. The decline of food production was, therefore, a consequence of colonial policies that were aimed at restructuring African economies to boost the colonial economy. The study of Gusii examined the effects of gender relations in land rights and ownership to ascertain whether women's responses were considered in decision-making processes related to land access, its use and control.

Bryson[105] (1981) asserts that though African women are the major food producers, they have been excluded from land ownership in the post-colonial period. He argues that ignoring women's land rights only worsens the food situation. Consequently, a historical investigation on individual access to land is imperative for a proper understanding of one's ability in land access, control, ownership and usage.

Gellen[106] shares the same sentiments and sees this problem to be rooted in history and the oppression of women that was "reinforced by discriminatory ideological and systematic practices inherent in development policies". Therefore, he calls for an examination of land policies both in colonial and post-colonial periods to ascertain their influence on gender relations to land access, control, ownership and usage, which is the focus of this study.

104 Bryceson, D. F. (1980). Changes in peasant food production and food supply in relation to the historical development of commodity production in pre-colonial and colonial Tanganyika. The Journal of Peasant Studies. 281-311. Routledge
105 Bryson, J. C. (1981). Women and agriculture in sub-Saharan Africa: Implications for development (an explanatory note). *Journal of Development Studies, 17:* 29-46.
106 Gellen, K. (1994) "Unleashing the Power of women Farmers. Africa's Vast, Hidden Resource holds key to development" African Farmer, April.

Mackenzie[107] examines agriculture in Murang'a District and pays attention to what she calls the politicization of soil conservation as a means of isolating Kikuyu agriculture from the wider political economy. He argues that changes that occurred in agriculture were not only class-based but also gendered. The study is essential because it is based on the same academic interests in gender, a factor that encouraged the interaction of information between the two regions.

Like Mackenzie, Davison[108] argues that gender relations to land in Africa have been modified over time by internal conquest and power struggles and by major intrusions from abroad. Studying land registration in Mutira and Chwele divisions in former Central and Western Provinces respectively, Davison asserts that the implementation of the Swynnerton Plan from the mid-1950s affected food production and caused tension in gender relations, especially at the family level. This was because land registration negatively impacted food crop production, which was a woman's sphere. Further, the household was impacted as the unit of production specifically addressing land policies and how they affected women's usufruct rights. She maintains that women's rights to land have been compromised over time by land policies that tend to favour men. Changes in the land tenure system influenced the mechanisms of decision-making in terms of the amount of land to be put under food crop cultivation. Davison maintains that the less land an individual had, the more it was devoted to food crops and the bigger the land one had, the less was devoted to food crop production. Davison's study concurs with Tanui's study on the impact of differential gender access to resources on agricultural production in the Nandi District -1954-2000.

Njiru[109] dwelt on the effects of tea production on women's work and labour allocation in the Embu District. She examined the gender division of labour and its impact on gender relations among smallholder tea farming households of Embu District. Her study found that agricultural activities before the adoption of commercialized tea production in the area initiated social-economic differentiations among households. These differentiations have been

107Mackenzie, F. (1990). Gender and Land Rights in Murang''a District, Kenya Journal of Peasant Studies, Vol. 17(4).
108Davison, M. J. (1987). Without Land we are nothing. The Effect of Land Tenure Policies and Practices upon Rural Women in Kenya, Rural Africana, 27.
109Njiru, E. (1990). Effects of Tea Production on Women's Work and Labour Allocation in Embu District. M.A. Thesis, Nairobi University: Nairobi.

intensified by tea production. Consequently, labour prioritization for livestock, food production and other household activities are in acute competition with that directed to tea production. She found that, although tea production has increased women's workload generally, it has brought some advantages for some; most tea-producing households have relatively more incomes than before, and better housing, clothing and other amenities in their houses. Her work is vital when assessing gender differentiations after land reform.

Njogu[110] points out that most of the farmers in the tea-producing areas devoted most of their land to tea production at the expense of food. In this research done in Kirinyaga, she found that tea-producing households gave priority to food whenever they received their money. The reason is that these households did not get enough food through home production and therefore had to purchase from the market. These changes in crop production that are a result of diminishing sizes of farmland can be understood intensively if the interplay between the system of land ownership and crop production can be put under intense examination.

Njoki[111] on Embu women's food production and traditional knowledge, noted the participation of Embu women in the food cycle, their traditional techniques of food processing and how the techniques were informed by indigenous knowledge. She focused on the involvement of women in food crop production. The study indicates that Embu women are involved in the food cycle all year round. The activities included clearing the land, planting, weeding, harvesting, food preservation, distribution, cooking and storage.

Among the Embu, crop cultivation was organized by gender. Men cultivated cash crops such as sugar cane, yams, and bananas. Women grew several kinds of potatoes, cassava, millet, vegetables, and legumes, such as cowpeas, pigeon peas, garden peas, kidney beans, white beans, and lentils. Women cultivated maize when it was used for home consumption. However, when maize was cultivated as a commercial commodity, it became a "male" (cash) crop and as such, both husband and wife cared for it. Njoki's study is valuable to the present one for it deals with the issue of women and food production in Embu. It, however, does not deal with the interplay

110 Njogu, E. (2002). Household Food Security and Nutritional Status of Children in Tea and Non- Tea Producing Households in Ndia Division Kirinyaga District. Unpublished Thesis: Kenyatta University.
111 Njoki, W. (2003). Embu Women, Food Production and Traditional Knowledge (online) Available at www.amazon.com

between gender relations and the system of land ownership access and control, which the current study covers.

Bulow[112] is perhaps the only study that comes closer to the present study. He examines changes in gender relations among the Kipsigis of Kenya and argues that both men and women have different cultural ideas about gender, and this subsequently transforms production relations. He maintains that, to understand how gender relations are transformed and how production relations are influenced, there is a need to understand the pre-colonial setting. She asserts that the complementarity and reciprocity between men and women that existed in pre-colonial Kipsigis society have been replaced by women's structural economic dependence on men, the latter's fear that women may try to be 'bigger' than men. Bulow presents gender as an important category that helped structure production relations among the Kipsigis in the pre-colonial period.

Heyer[113] notes that both matrilineal and patrilineal systems reflect culturally embedded norms which give men land entitlements not generally open to women. This may be seen not only relate to inheritance but in the division of labour, decision-making, control of income, livestock, and access to credit.

In pre-colonial Kipsigis society, the gender division of labour made men and women mutually dependent regarding the exchange of products like labour and other services. However, colonialism brought a change in the gender division of labour and hence production relations with regard to the introduction of maize as a cash crop. Women only lost male labour inputs. As well, as the main producers of food crops, they no longer worked as autonomous producers but rather as unremunerated family labourers on their husband's farms. Bulow's work is of significance to our study because it gives a departure in examining the changing gender relations and land rights and ownership relations and how they have been affected in the post-colonial period in Gusii.

Kanogo[114] demonstrates Kikuyu women's understanding of their environment to meet their day-to-day subsistence needs. She argues that colonial policies marginalized women, especially with the alienation of land. Kanogo found that women have, over time, lost rights to land access. She does not, however, show how this has

112Bulow V. D. (1992). Bigger than Men? Gender Relations and their changing meaning in Kipsigis society, Kenya. Africa 62 (4).

113Heyer, J. (1975). The Origins of Regional Inequalities in Smallholder Agriculture in Kenya, 1920-1973" *Eastern Africa Journal of Rural Development 8*, 143.

114Kanogo, T. (1989). Kenya and the Depression, 1929-139 in Ochieng' W.R. (ed) A Modern History of Kenya 1895-1980 Nairobi: Evans Brothers (Kenya) Limited.

altered gender relations in food crop production or what has been the response of women.

Abbot[115] in her study of the socio-cultural and economic change of the Kikuyu community in Kagongo in Nyeri District in the 1950s found that household relations had been affected. She concentrates on the effects of cash crops on women but omits the issue of gender relations in land rights and ownership. The extent to which gender relations are considered in land rights and ownership and control is necessary not only in Gusii but in the rest of the country.

Muchoki[116], on the other hand, writes on the organization and development of Kikuyu agriculture in Kiambu between 1880 and 1920. He investigates the internal dynamics and innovative changes that characterized Kikuyu agriculture in that period. He analyses how the Kikuyu agricultural system functioned to understand how it was transformed during the period under study. Muchoki's study is valuable to the present one for it deals with the issue of pre-colonial agriculture in Kiambu. It, however, does not deal with gender relations of production which the present study targets. Muchoki's study ends in 1920 when Kenya became a British colony. Great historical change in gender relations of production was certainly experienced with the entrenchment of the colonial economy, especially between 1920 and 1970.

It is thus evident from the three clusters of literature reviewed above that while several studies have addressed Gusii gender relations and land rights, none has specifically dealt with women's responses and the changing gender relations in Gusii. Therefore, there is a need to examine how gender relations have been altered and what effect this has had on land rights, ownership and control. Specifically, what changes have occurred with regard to gender relations and land access, ownership control and usage as an important aspect in women's empowerment because previous historical studies have not tackled gender as an important analytical category? The study is equally important to gender studies bearing in mind that they are not well grounded in Kenya's academia.

115Abbot, S. (1974). Full-time Farmers and Weekend Wives: Change and Stress among Rural Kikuyu Women. (PhD, Thesis, North Caroline University).
116Muchoki F. M. (1988). Organisation and Development of Kikuyu Agriculture 1880-1920. (M.A. Thesis, Kenyatta University).

Contextual Framework of the Study

The Property Rights Theory

Furubotn and Pejovich[117] assert that property rights define the nature of sanctioned human behaviour. Such sanctioned behaviours allow people the right to use resources within the 'class of non-prohibited users'. Property rights are 'the rights of individuals to the use of resources supported by the force of etiquette, social custom, ostracism, and formal legally enacted laws supported by the state's power of violence or punishment'. Barzel[118] distinguishes economic concepts of property rights from legal concepts of property rights, viewing the more relevant concept of property rights to be economic rights. The foundation for the property rights theory was also formed by Coase.[119] The 'classical' form of the property rights theory focuses on the historical and institutional context that shapes and changes property rights. In the study, the focus was given to how the theory applied to women's land rights and control. The theory asserts that when rights are well defined and the cost of transacting is zero, resource allocation is efficient and independent of the pattern of ownership.

Rights in land include more than the right of ownership, but also utilization. Property rights have important economic implications in that many different people can hold parts of the rights to a property. The actor who owns a part of the property rights of a resource is called the residual claimant. All economic activities including trade and production are exchanges of bundles of property rights.[120] Attributes to which rights are not assigned by formal or informal contracts or resources, with unclear property rights, are said to be in the public domain.

Kim and Mahoney[121] attempt a balanced theoretical approach in considering the economic aspects of property rights as a complementary concept within the legal framework that allows such property rights

---

117 Furubotn, E. G. & Pejovich, S. (eds) (1974). The Economics of Property Rights (Cambridge, MA: Ballinger).
118 Barzel, Y. (1994). 'The Capture of Wealth by Monopolists and the Protection of Property Rights,' International Review of Law and Economics, 14(4), pp. 393-409.
119 Coase, R. H. (1960). The problem of social cost. *Journal of Law and Economics 3:* 1–44.
120 Farjoun, M. (1998). The independent and joint effects of the skill and physical bases of relatedness in diversification. *Strategic Management Journal,* 19: 611–630.
121 Kim and Mahoney (2005). Resource-based and property rights perspectives on value creation: the case of oil field unitization. *Managerial and Decision Economics,* 23: 225–245.

legal protection and third-party enforcement. In relation to this study, property rights theory provided the basic economic incentive system that shaped resource allocation. Different specifications of property rights arose in response to the economic problem of allocating scarce resources, and the prevailing specification of property rights affects economic behaviour and economic outcomes.[122]

Property rights here are a social construction, essentially a system of relationships, which implies that many perspectives and interpretations of what constitutes property exist at a particular time. Land tenure arrangements, for instance, shape and are shaped by relationships among people and between people and the physical world. The meanings that people assign to a property are constantly changing, primarily in terms of what the dominant classes expect of property and what their fellow citizens consider to be allowable uses of the property.

The research on women and property tends to privilege the instrumental value of access to the property for women as a pathway to economic autonomy that is an enabling condition for social and political agency. In securing access to and control of property, this becomes an asset that is tradable for access to social and political capital in decision-making by effectively enhancing the bargaining power of the individual with property, at the household, community or wider society level.

In this study, the theory was used to analyze the relationship between indigenous land tenure systems and gender relations in Gusii, establish the effects of colonial land policies on gender relations in Gusii, and gender rights in relation to land right and ownership in the post-colonial period in Gusii. Despite its utilitarianism in explaining property rights, this theory is biased toward men's power and authority to control resources, and it is silent on women's response to land rights, access and control, which occasioned the employment of the Agency Theory for complementarity.

Agency Theory

The agency theory was propounded by Stephen Ross and Barry Mitnick[123]. Ross is responsible for the origin of the economic theory of agency, and Mitnick for the institutional theory of agency, though the basic concepts underlying these approaches are similar. The

---

122 Ibid
123 Mitnick, B. M. (1975). The Theory of Agency: A Framework (1975). In: Barry M. Mitnick, The Theory of Agency Cambridge University Press.

agency theory is a presupposition that explains the relationship between principals and agents in business. Agency theory is concerned with resolving problems that can exist in agency relationships due to unaligned goals or different aversion levels to risk. Agency theory is concerned with analyzing and resolving problems that occur in the relationship between principals (owners) and their agents.[124] The theory rests on the presumption that the role of an institution such as the family is to maximize the wealth of (benefits for) their owners (family members)[125].

The agency theory, however, holds that most institutions operate under conditions of incomplete information and uncertainty. The agency theory advocates that the purpose of the principal-agent relationship is to minimize the potential for agents to act in a manner contrary to the interests of owners.[126] Similarly, agricultural arrangements, where the agents receive a share of the crop (e.g. sharecropping or share tenancy) are inefficient, as agents only get a fraction of their production, which demotivates them and discourages them from exerting greater effort.[127]

According to the theory, the productivity gap in agriculture can also result from differences between men and women in their capacity to exercise 'agency', that is to make effective choices and transform these choices into desired outcomes[128]. It has been established that there can be a negative correlation between property rights and women's agency. An analysis of intra-household labour allocation suggests that female household members devote disproportionally more time to diversified farming than men who focus on less time-consuming crop storage and marketing activities.

Kabeer[129] argues that, concerning gender relations, the agency is the ability of a woman to define her goals and act on them. The woman may not act, or create an underlying shift in power relations, but is able, through direct decision-making processes or indirect means,

124 Eisenhardt, K. M. (1989). Building theories from case study research. *Academy of Management Review 14(4),* 532–550.
125 Blair, M. M. (1995). *Ownership and Control, Washington:* The Brookings Institutions.
126 Jensen M.C. & Meckling, W. H. (1976). Theory of the firm: Managerial behavior, agency costs and ownership structure. *Journal of Financial Economics 3(4),* 305-360.
127 Marshall, A. (1890/1956). *Principles of Economics.* 8th ed. London: Macmillan.
128 World Bank. (2012). World Development Report: Gender Equality and Development. Washington, DC.
129 Kabeer, N. (1999). "Resources, agency, achievements: reflections on the measurement of women's empowerment." *Development and Change.* 30(3): 435-464.

to step out of routine behaviours to try to change her environment or outcomes. In this study, agency theory was used to examine women's responses in relation to gender, land ownership and control under the indigenous land tenure systems and gender relations in patrilineal societies in Gusii. The study further sought to explore women's responses to the effects of colonial and post-colonial land policies in relation to gender land relations. The interface among the variables of land policies, gender relations and land access/ utilization over the pre-colonial, colonial and post-colonial periods is summarized by the following conceptual framework.

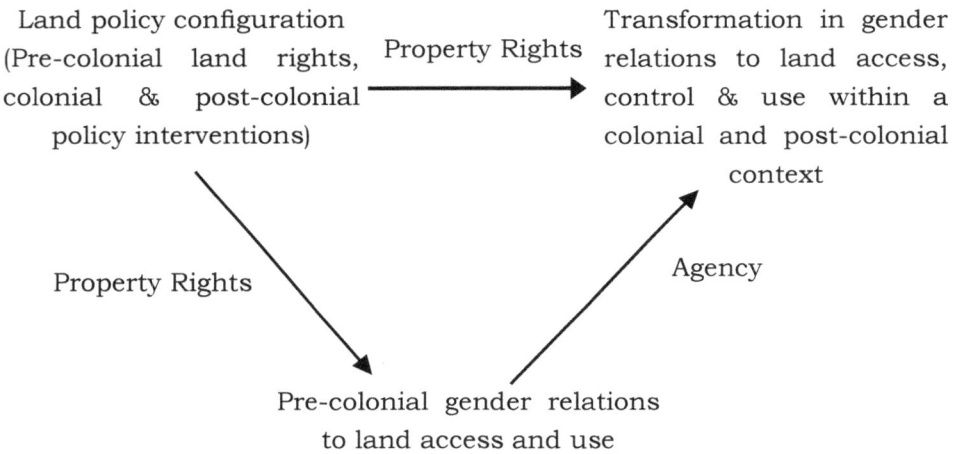

Conceptual Framework

Land policy configuration (Pre-colonial land rights, colonial & post-colonial policy interventions)

Property Rights

Transformation in gender relations to land access, control & use within a colonial and post-colonial context

Property Rights

Agency

Pre-colonial gender relations to land access and use

Figure 1.1 Conceptual Framework

Land policies, as an independent variable, influence gender relations in terms of access, control and ownership of land in Kisii. Hence, alterations in land policies significantly impact gendered land access, ownership and control. That, in turn, triggers multiple transformative responses from Gusii women.

Conclusion

Chapter two identifies existing gaps through a comparative literature review which occasion the theories to be applied in this study. Basically, the study applies two theories, the property rights theory and the agency theory. Also, the chapter provides a framework how the study will be laid out in subsequent chapters. The chapter also provides a review of pre-colonial, colonial and post-colonial land tenurial usufruct and the control of utilization of land coming out explicitly.

Chapter Three

Gusii Indigenous Land Practices, Initial Colonial Land Policies and Their Impact Upon Gender Relations in The Pre-Colonial Period, 1850-1920

Introduction

This chapter discusses indigenous land tenure and gender relations in Gusii land and the impact of initial colonial land policies on gender relations. In an attempt to understand the relationship between indigenous land tenure and gender relations, the chapter details various aspects of indigenous land tenure systems, the interaction between gender and land tenure, and how these interactions shaped land reform and tenure in Gusii specifically and Kenya in general. The chapter further examines the concept of land among the Gusii, modes of land acquisition as well as the customary land tenure systems in relation to gender relations of production.

In the chapter, it is argued that the indigenous land tenure system among the Gusii was flexible and dynamic. This dynamic nature provided for relatively egalitarian access to land by both men and women during the pre-colonial period. The indigenous land tenure system was anchored on the principle that land was owned communally and was handed down from the ancestors to the present and future generations. Therefore, although men remained the custodians of the land, there existed clearly laid down customary laws and norms that guided how the land was handed down to the next generation. Rules and regulations equally guided the community on women's access to land which ensured that women were able to utilize the land to produce food that fed their families.

The chapter further argues that customary land tenure systems and norms provided avenues for resolving critical land use issues. For instance, childless women or those women without sons were not disinherited from family land since there existed special arrangements that allowed them to access and use the land. Land issues were resolved through councils of elders either at the village or clan level. This chapter thus lays the historical foundation against whose backdrop the analysis of the effects of colonial land policies on land access, control and ownership in Kisii County is undertaken in subsequent chapters.

The Gusii Concept of Land

Land tenure in any society should address three-pronged issues concerning the owner(s) of the land, their interests in the land, and the land that holds the interests.[1] Therefore, land tenure is the interest that people have in the possession, utilization and transfer of land. It is also the concept of people, time and space concerning land. However, this concept was not strictly defined, and consequently, there may be occasions in which it overlapped, such as when different people contested possession of the same space of piece of land at the same time.

In Gusii, the rights that an individual had over land were not absolute because they had to be balanced with the rights of others, and the individual's obligations to the broader society. For example, the temporal aspect of tenure determined the duration of one's rights over land, and; one individual could only exercise ownership and utilization rights to land over a specific period, exercised over a definite physical space. However, due to the overlapping aspects of land tenure, different persons could exercise different rights over the same space at different times as observed by Musa Ondiba[2] and supported by Louis F. and James R.[3] who maintain that different persons can exercise different rights over the same piece of land both at the same time and/or at different times.

Consequently, in the Gusii community, as is the case in other African communities, land ownership entailed various community interests and indigenous land was frequently held by different persons simultaneously. However, while most customary laws recognized a measure of individual control over the broader interests, the paramount title was vested in the society. Thus, the rights one person had to the land were subordinate to community rights.[4]

Persistent struggles over land were often symbolic and were constituted within the realm of cultural values, norms and

1   Okoth-Ogendo, H.W.O. (1991). *Tenants of the Crown: Evolution of Agrarian Law and Institutions in Kenya*. Nairobi: African Centre for Technology Studies (ACTS Press).
2   Musa Ondiba 85, Nov.2019
3   Louis, F & James, R. (1985). *Trees and Tenure: An Annotated Bibliography*
4   Krishan M. Maini. (1967). *Land Law in East Africa*. Nairobi: Heinemann.

perceptions that were embedded in the ideas of morality and patriarchy that, in turn, shaped material resource struggles over land.[5] Understood this way, land had multiple meanings that went beyond the understanding of it as being only a material resource which sustained people's livelihoods. The land was also an important symbolic cultural resource which was characterized by diverse socio-cultural dimensions, and in most societies as demonstrated by the Gusii, it was always bound up in patriarchal ideology.

Symbolic meanings of land were socially constructed and manifested themselves as cultural norms, idioms and stigmas that were meant to perpetuate gendered identity and inequitable gender relations. These cultural values were constitutive forces that had real influence in "ordering" life, including gendered property relations and gendered struggles over land.

Among the Gusii, as was the case with most other agrarian communities in Africa, the land was the sole source of livelihood. It is from the land that people got food and sustained their livestock and other livelihood activities. Among the Gusii, mixed farming practices-oriented land to be divided into two spheres such as crop growing land (*endemero*) and grazing land (*oborisia*). It was for this reason that all those who moved to new land had to clear the forest and make the land habitable for use in mixed farming. The land was also an area of residence. It was in the occupied land that various families and clans made homesteads. Existing land or homesteads were either identified with families or clans. Thus, land was identified with family patriarchs such as o'Nyakundi (Nyakundi's land or home), bw'Orang'o (Orang'os land or home). Alternatively, land was also identified by clan names such as Bomachoge or Bobasi (the land of Machoge or land of Bobasi clan) respectively. In this regard, no one was to occupy another person's land or another clan's land except when allowed by family or clan heads, also except in cases of attacks or conquests where families and clans were forcefully evicted by enemy groups from other clans.[6]

The land was and still is the residence of the ancestral spirits. It was generally believed that ancestral spirits dwelled in the areas where they were buried. This justified the fact that the land belonged to the ancestors who had handed it over to the contemporary

---

5   Moore, D. (1993). Contesting Terrain in Zimbabwe's Eastern Highlands: Political Ecology, Ethnography and Peasant Resource Struggles, in *Economic Geography 69*, 380-401.
6   Moronya Omaore; 85,October 2019

community. It is no wonder, therefore, that communally owned land was also referred to as ancestral land *(oboremo bw'echisokoro)*. In this regard, the Gusii had special places or territories where ancestral spirits dwelt. As Orang'o[7] explains it was the duty of the living to take care of the ancestral land and hold it in custody for future generations. All the patriarchs in the community, therefore, held the land as custodians because it had been handed down to them by their ancestors, and they were supposed to hand it to the next generation.

It is from the land that the community derived a sense of property ownership. If one considered himself wealthy, then he had to have specific tracts of land that were under cultivation. The more land one had under cultivation, the richer one was perceived to be. This was also related to the number of wives and children a man had who provided the labour that enabled him to cultivate large pieces of land. The polygamous wealthy owners of large pieces of land gained considerable prestige and were the very people who were typically made clan elders and community leaders

Land among the Gusii, like most African communities, was seen as a territory or jurisdiction belonging to clans and communities. These were areas that the community had total control over and jealously fought to protect against any intrusion, conquest or destruction. Clans, therefore, kept fighting off enemies from the forceful occupation of their territory. As group discussions in Kitutu Chache and Nyaribari put it, the clans kept fighting and displacing each other in the process of expanding their territory. For instance, at some time, the people of the Nyaribari clan were evicted from the current Kitutu territory to their current homeland. The interviewees from the Kitutu and Nyaribari clans ascertained:

> The fore-fathers of the Abanyaribari were originally living together with the Abagetutu and the two clans formed part of the bigger Gusii clan of Abasweta that had moved from the Kano Plains and settled at Marani-Nyagesenda area in the current Kitutu Chache region. However, the patriarchs of Kitutu and Nyaribari had a major altercation as the elder wife of Nyaribari had abused and degraded the patriarch of the Kitutu. It was an abomination for a woman to abuse a patriarch. A fight ensued and the Nyaribari people were driven out. They ran away and eventually took refuge in the current Nyanchwa-Ekerore area near the present Kisii Town. The vanquished Nyaribari men came together and started clearing the virgin land in the new area. The Nyaribari eventually

spread and occupied empty lands in Nyaura and Nyabitunua in the present Nyaribari Chache Constituency.[8]

From the interview, the Gusii are naturally patriarchal and the patriarch decided in the public domain matters appertaining to land. Despite Abagetutu and Abanyaribari being brothers, land as being ancestrally determined drove them into separation and the ancestors guided the Abanyaribari to not only a land that they were to settle in but also land that would accommodate their expansion. However, the interview revealed the traditional/ancestral position of women in matters of land as being subordinate to that of men, especially in the public domain.

Among the Gusii, the concept of gender relations in land tenure was shaped by their history and culture. For instance, it is evident that when the Gusii moved from the Kano Plains to the cold, wet Gusii highland region, their herds had already been depleted by Maasai cattle rustlers. Furthermore, the remaining livestock could not survive the cold weather conditions. Also, the dense forest in the highland region meant that there was less open grassland on which to graze the livestock. However, notwithstanding the changes in environmental and climatic conditions, Monyenye[9] indicates that the Gusii continued practising mixed farming which included the rearing of livestock and growing of subsistence crops such as finger millet and sorghum. A point Akama agrees with when he notes:

> The people migrated to their present homeland, the Gusii Highland region, from the Kano Plains. However, despite the change in landscape, many features of the Gusii people's ownership and usage of land remained. In the flat Kano Plains, the Gusii were majorly cattle keepers, which was their main source of livelihood and also represented a measure of socio-economic status. Gusii people continued to keep cattle, alongside subsistence farming. They also continued to regard cattle as a main source of wealth and prestige and were highly regarded particularly in the payment of bride price.[10]

The gender matrix in the social land equation as demonstrated by Akama while emphasizing the aspects of mixed farming, was the introduction of the parameter of the utilization of livestock not only as a measure and store of value but also as a means of acquiring wives through dowry. In return, the women were to

---

8   Group discussions in Nyaribari and Kitutu, December 2019
9   Ernerst Monyenye (Age 67; 20, December, 2019)
10   Akama, J. S. (2017). *The Gusii of Kenya: Social, Economic, Cultural, Political and Judicial Perspectives*. Canada: Nsemia Publishers.

prove their worth of the livestock they were traditionally exchanged for by working on the land for subsistence production and being biologically productive. Therefore, at marriage, Gusii patriarchs transformed their livestock (measures/stores of value)[11] into forces of production and reproduction on the clan land.

In essence, in the high-potential highland region, a unit of land could support a much higher population than the same amount of land in the Kano Plains where the Gusii had moved from. Equally, the variable ecological conditions enabled the people to practice mixed farming. The production of crop and animal products helped in framing the household (through marriage/dowry then reproduction) and improving nutrition (women and their children working on the family land) in the households. With improved nutrition, women reproductive span lengthened and strengthened as Nyanchama indicated "due to improved nutrition, the age at which women got married went down and the number of children they gave birth to rose. This led to increased demand for wives and children to provide requisite labour." This reaffirmed the silent, but dominant, place of women in Gusii land tenure, which was traditionally relegated to the periphery. Neigus David[12] argues that it was economically unprofitable not to have more children to fulfil existing cultivation to extend cultivation onto fertile unoccupied land.

In this social and ecological context, the Gusii needed more labour (the Gusii woman stamping her authority in matters of land tenure) to cultivate and produce more food in two seasons per year; at the beginning of the year, long rains (*omwaka*) and the last half of the year, short rains (*omwobo*). The two growing seasons were made possible due to highly reliable rainfall in most parts of the year. Furthermore, the main subsistence crop *wimbi* (finger millet) required intensive women labour in [preparation of the land] weeding, harvesting and threshing[13]. In this context, men were traditionally tasked to marry many wives to increase the size of their families and thus human labour for farm production.[14] According to Monyenye[15], the economic competitiveness of wives eventually brought down the average age at which women were married in the

---

11   Miriam Nyanchama; 89, Nov 2019
12   Neigus, D.L (1971). Conflict over Land; A study of Expansion and Inversion in Gusii Society. Thesis, Harvard College
13   South Kavirondo Administration Report, KNA DC/KSl/1/4 1933-1938
14   Ongaro, W. A. (1988). *Adoption of New Farming Technology: A Case Study of Maize Production in Western Kenya*. Ekonomiska Studier 22. Department of Economics. Gothenburg School of Economics, Gothenburg.
15   Ernest Monyenye (Age, 67; 20, December, 2019)

Gusii community. The tender age at which the women got married is interpreted as dual; first, the women longed to get out of their families and family land where they were regarded as daughters to be freed from their brothers' conditionalities in exercising their silent land rights of access through their husbands. Second, the Gusii men knew that the younger the lady the more energetic she was and, therefore, the more productive she would be on the land. Equally, the younger the woman was, the higher the chances of bearing more children compared to older women. More children in turn translated to more hands to work on the family land. From this perspective, the maximization of lineage became an important social factor and, indeed, one of the ideological principles fostering the rapid growth and expansion of the Gusii community.

In addition, environmental and economic conditions promoted the development of social institutions that were consonant with the accelerated rate of population growth in light of the highly productive and unoccupied land in the highland region. Thus, the surplus production of food was invested in population growth and increased consumption. As Nyabaro[16] noted, "It was economically unprofitable not to have more wives and children to fulfil the human labour requirements of existing cultivation in expansive land and to extend cultivation into fertile and unoccupied lands" His views are shared by Coontz [17] in his book, *Analysis of population theories and economic interpretation*. This in essence echoed the productive and reproductive core of women in the Gusii community.

With many wives and children to provide labour, the people expanded the area under cultivation to retain a high per capita productivity and consumption level. As the demand for more productive land for cultivation grew, clans and sub-clans clashed in the continual struggle to secure more land while maintaining control over land already held.[18]

Over time, due to the increasing population, the pressure on land escalated exponentially. Over time, most of the cultivatable land was brought under use and the increase in population led to a rapid reduction of the amount of land available to each family. Onyangore asserts that:

---

16 Okioma Nyabaro (Age,57; 10, December, 2019)

17 Coontz, S. (1957). *Population Theories and Economic Interpretation*. London: Routledge and Kegan Paul.

18 Hakansson, T. (1988). *Bridewealth, Women and Land: Social Change among the Gusii of Kenya*. Uppsala Studies in Cultural Anthropology No. 10. Uppsala: Amquiest and Wilsell International.

Usually, clan land is located on ridges and is divided into strips, with each strip of land running from the top of a ridge to the bottom of a valley (where streams are often found). Such a land strip would contain several homesteads. The land usage within such a strip was and is still based on the principle that every male had hereditary rights over farmland. However, due to the increasing population, there was more demand for land, leading to conflicts and out migration.[19]

Although every patriarch struggled to secure more labour through polygamous marriages and having more children, the residual effects were largely visible in the heredity of the family land by the sons of the family. With the exponential population increase among the Gusii, the available land could not match the needs of the population and this caused concern in families. As documented by Neigus[20], an individual wealthy polygamist had a great deal of influence in the community. He would be among the first members of the clan to experience land pressure on his large family and to instigate action to gain more land with support from numerous sons who made a great part of the warrior force.

The foregoing attitudes of the Gusii about land during the pre-colonial period, coupled with the intervening variables informing these attitudes generated multiple modes of land acquisition as described below.

Modes of Land Acquisition

It should be noted that, to a certain extent, some aspects or manners in which the Gusii acquired land have already been touched on. However, specifically, the Gusii had three major modes of traditional land acquisition, namely, occupation, capture and inheritance. Acquisition of land by occupation and capture was the most involving and taxing as it, at times, could cost people's lives. In the early days of Gusii settlement in the area, occupation as a traditional mode of land acquisition involved clearing the forest and setting up a new homestead or homesteads. However, as the population density escalated, this option only remained operational on the frontier and marginal lands, particularly the areas between the Gusii and their neighbouring communities such as the Luo, the Kipsigis and the Maasai.

---

19   Thomas Onyangore; 59 10th Dec 2019
20   Neigus, D. L. 1971, Conflict over Land, 172

The earliest form of land acquisition was through occupation. This happened when men went hunting or grazing animals and discovered new fertile lands which doubled up with an abundance of pasture and reliable rainfall. They then schemed on how to occupy their newly found land. During the occupation, some kinship groups (*amasaga*) would collaborate on a venture, to hold, clear, settle and cultivate the fallow lands. In this mode of traditional land acquisition, Gusii women played a pivotal role in the occupation of new lands by clans or families as narrated by Omaore:

> There was this concept of *egiateko* (that is upheavals such as famine, disease or attack) then, people could move to new places. The settled land was divided by rivers and people occupied different ridges. The land was acquired by occupying unsettled land (*borabu*). Men built houses and settled, and then called other relatives for security purposes. They married wives to settle and give birth to more children. Such a mode of land acquisition gave special status to men.[21]

As evidenced by Omaore's narrative, when *egiateko* struck, the most affected were the women and their children. As such, the women induced pressure on the men for the need for a new place for settlement which was a frontier they had probably seen in the course of their daily duties like fetching firewood. This happened because they were the ones who worked on the land and therefore, they had the knowledge of which land was productive and would cushion their children and family from *egiateko*. In addition, when Omaore, talks of the land being acquired by occupying the unsettled land, it follows that in traditional Gusii culture, a place could only be considered occupied and habitable if women were present and working on the land, thereby creating the concept of a home which intricately nested in the woman among the Gusii. This, however, happened under the guardianship of men as evinced when Omaore rightly observed that men only constructed houses. As Onyango narrated in agreement:

> Some kinship groups occupied existing bushy and forested land and placed boundaries by planting indigenous trees such as *emeroka, emetagara* or *ebirachuoki*. They could then build houses that were grass thatched and constructed fences around them using thorny tree branches. This was for defence from marauding wild animals and probable adversaries. They regularly kept monitoring any intrusion on boundaries. In case of any intrusion, the people fiercely defended their boundaries

21   Peter Maangi Omaore. 84, Machoge Nov 2019

using traditional weaponry such as bows and arrows, knives and spears. They used iron hoes (*ebisiria* – plural or *egesiria* – singular) for cultivation. The forests were cleared by men through *risaga* (cooperative work) over beer (*ebusa*) and other inducements, while the women did the tilling of the virgin land.[22]

The centrality of women in the land occupation is well underscored by Onyango in his verbatim submissions when he indicated that other than constructing the grass-thatched houses, the remaining responsibilities were the preserve of women. If men were to help women with taxing responsibilities like forest clearing, they would do so upon being corrupted by their wives through what Onyango terms inducements. The study noted that the fences constructed as Onyango puts it, were to ward off animals, wild and /or otherwise, from the subsistence plots put in place by their wives.

In addition, new land would occasionally be discovered in the process of undertaking other livelihood activities such as fetching firewood, grazing livestock or animal hunting expeditions. According to Omandi:

> Land was acquired through occupation. Men went hunting and, on their way, they could get good land and occupy it. They would then build houses and construct fences on the land. After that, they could call their neighbours and show them the boundaries and sub-divisions using landmarks such as special trees and unique landmarks. Any intruders from the broader kinship would be stopped by witnesses who were mostly neighbours. Those who persisted could fight and whoever won took over the land. People could then identify the most fertile land and clear the forest using the labour of strong men. They also used fires to clear the chaff. They made hoes out of iron that women used to plough the land.[23]

The forested fertile lands identified by men during grazing and hunting as explained by Omandi, were to be corroborated by the women on firewood fetching missions. It therefore follows that, in the land occupation acquisition mode, the occupants were women and more so, marked their presence through subsistence agriculture and reproduction in the Gusii community. Furthermore, misfortune would make people move to new frontiers as articulated by Ombogo[24]. Whenever people were attacked by diseases, they moved in order to occupy new land. Those with grown-up sons

---

22   Musa Onyango, 79, Oct 2019
23   Kepha Omandi, 62, Dec 2019
24   Ernest Ombogo (Age, 75; 28, January, 2020)

could invade the lands of those without sons and forcefully evict them. Also, whenever people quarrelled, they would disperse and settle in new places. In addition, people sometimes occupied land by ceding some of the grazing lands. Thus, wherever people grazed their livestock, that area could eventually become their land. Fear of attacks from hostile neighbours made people belonging to the same kinship come together and occupy a specific piece of land as a group for security.

Capture was the second model of traditional land acquisition in Gusii. The capture process of acquiring land, often, involved the use of force against the neighbouring communities and men were at the forefront in this form of acquisition. Therefore, men got full rights to the land they captured, while women were treated as tenants[25]. Further, as explained by Maobe,[26] in acquiring land through capture, one had to be strong to take over the land and be able to defend it. Land boundaries were marked using indigenous trees, and sometimes rivers and ridges made natural boundaries. The owners had to defend their land boundaries from intruders such as members of the other clans. In this socio-economic situation, the weaker groups were only to get unproductive and rocky places where nobody was interested or they would be pushed away to look for alternative land. For instance, Ababasi were pushed by Abanyaribari and Abamachoge to the hilly part of Gusii they currently occupy because they were unable to defend themselves against the aggressive clans.

Once settlement of the captured land was established, people could acquire specific strips of land (*ekenyoro*) which they sub-divided among themselves. This account concerning the processes of land capture and settlement is also shared by Bosire[27] who noted that land was acquired by young men who would attack and capture the land of neighbouring kinships or clans on the advice of elders. After the land had been acquired by the men, it was the responsibility of the women to till the land and grow crops for the sustenance of their households. As a consequence, the initial acquisition of land qualified the men to be its sole owners. Hence it was taboo for a woman to acquire land through capture. Even when a woman was widowed, she was supposed to be allocated land by men of

25 Ndege, T. M. (2006). Evolving land tenure and agricultural systems, in J.S. Akama and R. Maxon (2006). *Ethnography of the Gusii of western Kenya: A Vanishing cultural heritage*. Lewiston, NY: Edwin Mellen Press.
26 Joshua Maobe; 70, 22, December, 2019
27 Samwel Bosire; 75,November 2019

her husband's lineage. However, young widows with sons were protected while in most cases those without sons didn't qualify to get land for cultivation. Apart from the individual wife's land, a man kept for himself a special plot called *emonga* for his production. This was particularly used for security in times of hunger. Note that the *emonga* was typically tilled and maintained by one or more of his wives or his children.

Inheritance was the last model of traditional land acquisition in Gusii. Under this model, land was acquired through capture or occupation was simply passed down by clan members to their male descendants, as expounded by Moseti Omandi;

> The Gusii acquired land according to clans, and settlement was done according to kinship ties. People moved in groups for security purposes, so that in case of attack, they could defend themselves. The clans that settled in an area could also be subdivided into sub-clans and families all occupying the clan land. The regions that were occupied had specific patriarchs that were the custodians of the land. The patriarchs could then hand over the land to younger generations of men mostly at a family level.[28]

Deductively, land inheritance was an elaborate but clear process in the Gusii community. This ran from the clan to the sub-clans to the patriarch to the household to the family and the male siblings as demonstrated by Moseti Omandi. This lineage was punctuated by the land sub-divisions which guided the principle and purpose of inheritance. In particular, among the Gusii, territorial land or specific clan units were the basis of political, social and economic organization. Clan elders were charged with the responsibility of ensuring that every member of the clan had access to land as well as ensuring that there was law and order in the processes of land acquisition, ownership and usage. In these indigenous legal processes, the elders usually selected one leader among themselves as their spokesman. Where territoriality and kinship coincided, one can characterise the kinship or the lineage system as constituting a specific mode of production. In such cases, the lineage or kinship groups were the corporate land-owning groups. Such groups held unified territories and new lineages grew as a result of population growth. Over time, and as the need arose, the existing lineages could further expand their land holdings through conquest or absorption of weaker or smaller lineages.[29]

---

28 Moseti Omandi, 79, Dec 2019
29   Kitching, G. (1980). *Class and Economic Change in Kenya: the making of an African Petite Bourgeoisie*. New Haven and London: Yale University Press.

Land inheritance was well structured as the Gusii were and still are a patriarchal society. Land was and still is passed to the next generations as younger men inherit land from their fathers[30]. When the sons inherited land from their fathers, they were expected to follow a well-defined set of customary land laws. Group discussions with the broader Bonchari clan revealed that the sons who inherited the land also inherited the rights of access and control over the land that was previously enjoyed by their fathers. In this manner, men retained dominance over land, from generation to generation, since ownership and control of land were essential to earning a livelihood in agrarian societies. This mode of land acquisition was well described by Onyango using his inheritance as he narrated:

> This land where I live with my family was acquired through inheritance from my father and grandfather. It was my late father who gave me the land before he died, and I have lived here for many years. My father informed me that the whole land where we are currently living with my brothers plus members of the extended family was originally owned by his grandfather and other members of their lineage. The grandfather and members of his kinship had moved from the current Sengera Manga region and traversed all the way to acquire the land here at Riokindo where we are now living. They had to clear the bushes and trees to make the place habitable and suitable for crop production. After clearing the land and constructing houses, my grandfather eventually allocated his portion of the kinship land among his sons including my father. It is important also to note that my grandfather, my father, and many of the older members of my lineage died and are buried in this very land and as such the spirits of my departed ancestors are domiciled here. As tradition demands I am holding this land in trust for my sons and grandsons, and this ancestral land cannot be sold to outsiders.[31]

The evidence by Onyango reveals that control of land in Gusii was centred on the family and clan level, and individuals like Onyango did not have exclusive rights to control, dispose or allocate land in their private capacity. More importantly, every person within the family had a right to use the family land, and competing rights of usage were mainly determined within the family or the wider kinship setup. As represented by Onyango, the land was allocated through inheritance to the male head of each household. The

---

30 **Editor's Note:** it is possible that things may change in the future following the passing of Constitution of Kenya 2010 that guarantees equal rights of inheritance for both sons and daughters.
31 Zachariah Onyango, 70. Dec 2019.

patriarch could then allocate the land to different 'houses' within his homestead (each house constituted of a wife and her children).

Upon the death of the patriarch, his sons would inherit the land, based on the amount that had been allocated to each wife for cultivation, during the life of the patriarch. Therefore, while the land belonged to the father, it was transmitted to the sons through the patriarch's wives. However, when a patriarch died among the Gusii, his wives would act as trustees of the land on behalf of their sons, especially if the sons were young and/or were not married. Thus, the sons themselves only obtained control and use of the land upon marriage, which was considered a sign of maturity. It was noted that the firstborn and lastborn sons were allocated comparatively larger pieces of land; the firstborn because he automatically became the head of the household upon the death of his father, and often took care of his younger siblings if they were still minors[32]. Equally, the lastborn son would receive a larger portion because it was culturally expected the lastborn son cared for his parents during their old age.[33]

As stated earlier, the land that was acquired and/or inherited was settled by the members of the kinship. The patriarchs always sub-divided the kinship land among each other, and the women were allowed to cultivate the land and grow crops for family sustenance in their husband's share of the land. Thus, each wife of the patriarch was given land where she grew crops that were harvested and stored in her specific store. Orang'o narrated:

> Women did most of the digging, weeding and harvesting, as well as preparing crops for storage, whereas men built stores for their wives to store food and feed their families. Lazy women were discouraged and made to abandon such unbecoming behaviour through ridicule and proverbs such as *"Moserengeti ore eero, ngetiro ke mogondo"* (The lazy talk a lot in the sitting room but farm work is an uphill task for them). Men also fenced the land and sometimes undertook farm work on a specific need basis, such as virgin land that required energetic and muscular men to till.[34]

---

32 Editor's Note: additionally, there were considerations of land allocation based on 'need'. Typically, the eldest son would have a home of his own and likely with more grown children than the younger sons and hence needed more land for cultivation to meet his family's needs.

33 Ibid.

34 Joseph Orang'o, 85. Nov 2019

In Gusii, it was the responsibility of the women to participate in the tilling, weeding and harvesting of food crops. The festivity seasons aside, Gusii women were first required to contend with the demanding tasks of harvesting food crops through the processes of drying, threshing, sorting, winnowing and storing the final product.[35] However, some of the harvested food was stored in the patriarch's special store and was used in times of need. Each wife was supposed to contribute a percentage of their harvest to the patriarch's special store. They respected the patriarch's word and this helped solve family disputes including disagreements in the sharing of available food during times of famine. Also, the younger wives respected the senior wife of the homestead because she was considered the matriarch of the home and the age mate of the family patriarch.

Sometimes there were elements of envy among wives, especially if the husband favoured one wife over the others. This caused a lot of friction in the family. Such disputes were settled by kinship elders who were also polygamous, therefore, were able to understand such delicate matrimonial situations as explained by Omaore Moronya.[36]

According to traditional law, the senior wife was given slightly bigger land than the other wives. Also, men made sure that they did not marry from lazy families *abanyancharanchara* (people or families that are associated with hunger). This explained why, before marrying, a man's family sent a 'spy' (*esigani*) to investigate the kind of family they intended to marry from to ensure that it was a family of hard workers. In addition, some women were generally hard-working but were extravagant and misused their farm produce. Such women did not command much respect in the homestead and the whole kinship.

Monyancha[37] noted that unmarried daughters used to be taken care of by their families but were not given land which was a reserve for the sons. Women who had bad character such as being always rude or disrespectful to their husbands were usually unaccepted in the whole family or clan. Furthermore, when sharing land among wives, husbands sometimes gave a troublesome wife unproductive land to till. This was supposed to 'keep her busy.' Hence the saying; *"Mokungu omobe aegwa boremo bo kenyambi nabwo akorema*

35   KNA DC/KSl/1/6, South Kavirondo District Annual Reports, 1944

36   Omaore Moronya 89. 12th Dec 2019

37   Henry Monyancha 65; 28th , December, 2019

k'obwata omotwe." (a troublesome woman is given the tough and unproductive land where she can feel the pinch and change her unbecoming behaviour).[38]

The socio-economic distinctions between men and women were rigid and were strictly enforced in the clan system. In this regard, as Onyango explained, "the Gusii homestead through the concept of *egesaku* was used to denote the distinction between the descendants of a man, either a living man or a departed patriarch, whereas *enyomba* (house) denoted the matrifocal unit of a wife within a polygamous family".[39]

Also, women were supposed to be given land through their grown-up sons. This made it very crucial for all the married women to ensure that they had sons to be able to access the land. Apart from ensuring that they got married to access land, women also struggled to give birth to sons to ensure the security of land access through the sons. Therefore, barren women tried all means to get children especially sons by consulting herbalists, healers, seers and/or even witch doctors. Those with daughters only would also try the same means to see if they could get sons of their own through whom they could be assured of access to the land beyond old age.[40]

Those who never got sons at all could use their daughters' dowry to 'marry another woman' to beget sons for them.[41] Also, childless wives were allowed to get a lady who had a son or sons to enable them to access the family land. Widows who were denied land by their in-laws could report to *etureti* (a clan-based informal court) which would come and order the in-laws to give the widows the requisite land. In addition, those widows who were chased away by the members of *etureti* (sub-clan) for one reason or the other, could move away from their departed husband's kinship and could eventually be given land by their maternal relatives[42]. In the broader context of the Gusii community, therefore, inter-clan land conflicts were resolved by a higher-level Council of elders referred

---

38   Chief Chuma Agwata;85,Nov 2019
39   Zachary Onyango; 70, Dec 2019
40   N. Thomas Hakansson; 1991, Grain Cattle and power: Social Processes of Intensive cultivation and Exchange in Precolonial Western Kenya, Journal of Anthropological Research vol. 50 No. 3 pp 249-276. University of New Mexico, 58-60
41   Editor's Note: in a strict sense, a woman without a son paid dowry for a woman who became her 'daughter-in-law' and made arangements for someone who could be her nephew in the family tree to beget children with the young woman. Those children were seen as grandchildren of the woman who had no sons.
42   Kerubo Ondabu (Novembr, 2019) Oral Interview at Bomachoge

to as *Abakumi*. This was the highest court of the land similar to the modern-day Supreme Court.

Unmarried sons were not given land, and it was seen as a very bad omen when a grown-up son died without a wife or children. Such a son was buried in his mother's compound as a sign of 'communal regret'. Also, an unmarried woman who died in her natal home was buried outside the family homestead as a sign of showing that she did not belong to her place of birth since she was supposed to have been married into other clans. On special and very rare occasions, women who never got married and had children were given land near their homes but far from the family homestead, Such homes eventually grew to become clans of their own. A good example is the Abanchari clan which is named after a daughter called Monchari who was given land near her parental home, married a man from Luo land and founded the Abanchari clan.[43]

The evolution of the pre-colonial Gusii land tenure system was therefore a direct outgrowth of these three modes of land acquisition as detailed above.

Customary Land Tenure System and its Implication on Gender Relations in Pre-colonial Gusii

Land tenure is the allocation of the available community land resource among individuals in the community. It is the way individuals have access to the land including the conditions under which community land is held. The land tenure system has undergone tremendous transformation among the Gusii. These transformations have seen the Gusii modify their environment in relation to land utilization. This was reflected in the Gusii customary laws and rules that govern the allocation and utilization of land. This indicates Gusii's adaptive and innovative nature to the Gusii highlands.

The abundance of land in pre-colonial Gusii implied that the human factor would be the most important variable in determining land usage. Reflecting this were such elements as alliance relations, client-ship linkages, rights to people and labour, and the competence to organize these labour resources as observed by Nyakwara.[44] Features of the social and agrarian organization strongly coincided with principles of land tenure and land rights among the Gusii and were determined by the status enjoyed within the community, as

43   Group discussion with Abanchari elders, Nov 2019
44   Zablon Nyakwara ; 85, Nov 2019

well as meeting a host of social obligations of other households/ family members. Land was thus vested in the Gusii community, with the underlying principle of Gusii land tenure, during the pre-colonial era, being the rights to access and use land for both men and women.

Land as a natural resource, was crucial to the existence and livelihood of humankind. Since time immemorial, the Gusii exploited land for their overall sustenance. From the beginning, in pre-historic agrarian societies, land was a key livelihood resource just as it is among the Gusii. Asiago Nyang'aya[45] explains that humans have established social systems and hierarchies based on age, gender, and class to implement land appropriation and distribution, in order to guarantee their overall subsistence, a view shared by Hanna. S. and Jentoft S.[46] This helps to explain the nature of the indigenous land tenure system in Africa in general and among the Gusii in particular, where the majority of the population is still agrarian.

As noted earlier, gender relations of production regarding land ownership, access and production were culturally specific and characterized by differential power relations between women and men. Furthermore, power relations were continually being negotiated, contested and resisted in various ways. Consequently, multiple and different co-existing domains of difference produced different outcomes, that influenced women's and men's access to resources. Access, control and ownership of natural resources such as land were negotiated within and between the household, and therefore, gender-household relations remained a focal point through which relations of production were constructed.[47]

As already stated, under the Gusii land tenure system, ownership and control rules were based on kinship. These rules were universally understood, and obeyed by everyone, to the extent that no one dared to interfere with land that was temporarily left fallow.[48] Ancestral spirits of departed relatives who had once lived on the land were greatly feared and respected. If anyone was wrongfully dispossessed of their land, they were required to swear an oath in the name of their ancestors who had once lived on the land in

45 Asiago Nyang'aya; 95, Dec 2019
46 Hanna, S. and Jentoft, S. (1996). Human Use of the Natural Environment: An Overview of Social and Economic Dimensions. In Susan S. Hanna, Carl Folke and Karl-Goran Maler (eds.): *Rights to Nature: Ecological, Economic, Cultural, and Political Principles of Institutions for the Environment.* Washington D.C. Island Press.
47 Ibid.
48 Ochieng, W. R. (1974). *A Pre-colonial History of the Gusii of Western Kenya, c. 1500- 1914.* Nairobi: East African Literature Bureau.

question. It was believed that the ancestors would come to the aid of their descendants, by causing harm to false claimants of land, either through sickness or death. Therefore, it was almost unthinkable for someone within the clan to make a false claim of ownership of land, as the retribution of the ancestors was assured.[49]

Fencing of land was also a strictly observed customary rule among the Gusii. The land of particular homesteads or clans was demarcated using a hedge made of the *omoroka* plant. There was also a ritual that was performed during fencing in which the heads of the family and other members were shaved, and the shaved hair was buried under the roots of the *omoroka* plant at a particular location of the fence, known only to the members of the family/kinship group. The Bogetutu elders noted that this ritual guaranteed ownership of the land for all future generations, and was particularly feared by all outsiders. It was also used to resolve land disputes, as the hair would be dug up to prove that the claimant of a piece of land was indeed the rightful heir.

Eyewitness testimonies of clan elders were used to resolve land disputes that dated back to a time when the land was first settled and/or bequeathed to a succeeding generation. An elder who had witnessed the initial settlement/bequest would swear an oath invoking the name of the ancestors that the land in question was the rightful property of a particular person/family. This was particularly important in resolving disputes within families and/or clans over the ownership of land. In traditional Gusii society, members of the extended family lived together, so children grew up knowing their uncles, grandparents, and even great-grandparents. Thus, in the event of a land dispute between brothers or cousins, older generations could testify as to who was its rightful owner.[50]

Therefore, in the Gusii patriarchal society, the male line of succession needed to remain unbroken. Thus, it was crucial that deceased men were buried on the same piece of land where their ancestors were buried, as ancestral spirits had to be connected to a physical or a specific geographical location. This explains the continued Gusii attachment to ancestral land, and their reluctance to sell it. However, the requirement of burial on ancestral or clan land does not apply to women, especially if they were unmarried. Indeed, the Gusii culture seems to display a high level of indifference

---

49   Ndege, T. M. (2006). Evolving land tenure and agricultural systems, in J.S. Akama and R. Maxon (2006). *Ethnography of the Gusii of western Kenya: A Vanishing cultural heritage.* Lewiston, NY: Edwin Mellen Press.
50   Ibid.

as to where women are buried, because they are still perceived as outsiders, whose main social role is to help build bonds between different lineages and or clans.[51]

Among the Gusii, land rights and access were governed by well-articulated customary laws, and the land was never privately owned but communal and individuals only worked on the land to meet their daily obligations and utilities through planting food crops to nourish their families[52]. Therefore, in Gusii, social and gender relations continued to structure land access, control and ownership. Under the customary land tenure system, control of resources followed clearly defined gender-segregated patterns based on traditional norms that operated in such a way that limit the rights of women to land.

In this regard, women's access and control over productive resources, including land, was determined by clearly structured male-centred kinship institutions and power relations that tended to restrict women's land rights in favour of men.[53] In many social settings, women had to strategize more skilfully and fight to access, use and control land as noted by Moronya.[54] Socio-cultural situations such as widowhood, divorce, women's resistance to marriage and other life-cycle changes created uncertainties that were to be negotiated carefully. Consequently, the rules governing land rights were rooted in male-dominated, kinship-based institutions and traditional authority structures that discriminated against women. Women's right to inheritance was further undermined by the system where women would also be inherited as part of the property of a deceased man. In consonance with the scenario obtaining within the Gusii community, a report from a Committee which investigated the system of land tenure in Western Kenya in 1934 noted that:

> A woman does not own land. A girl who is married cannot come back to claim any clan land. When a man dies his wife is inherited together with her cultivation, by the heir. If the heir is a son, he inherits his father's property and provides for his mother.[55]

51   LeVine, S. (1979). *Mothers and Wives: Gusii Women of East Africa.* Chicago: Chicago University Press.
52   Moseti Omandi; 76, DEC 2019
53   Tengey W.2008. 'Gender relations, rural women and land tenure in Ghana: A communication nightmare', in FAO, Land access in rural Africa: Strategies to fight gender inequality. Proceedings of FAO-Dimitra Workshop: 'Information and communication strategies to fight gender inequality as regards land access and its consequences for rural populations in Africa', 22-26 September. Brussels: FAO.
54   Bitutu Moronya 85, south mogirango, Dec 2019
55   KNA DC/NN/10/ I, Political Association, 1926-1940.

The commission's report evidenced the desolate position of women in Gusii on matters of land ownership, control and utilization. It should, however, be noted that even under these circumstances, a woman enjoyed access to the land allocated to her by the deceased husband and could be able to provide food for her house. In addition, the report noted the traditional vulnerable position of daughters who were yet to get married. Therefore, the dominant avenue for women to acquire land was dependent on their relations with men. In group discussions, women from Gianchere in Nyaribari Chache revealed that women were considered to be temporal members of their birthplaces. Hence, there was no need for them to own land. Men, therefore, could decide which part of their land could be given to which one of the wives. Consequently, existing forms of gendered social hierarchies and other factors of production combined to limit women's land access, ownership and usage.

Traditionally in Gusii therefore, all the land was held in trust by the clan elders who allocated the land to the members of the clan, mainly male household heads. It followed therefore that single men and women had no entitlement to land.[56] The Abanyameyio sub-clan elders in Nyaribari who we spoke to indicated that women's land access was governed by Gusii customary laws depending on the type of marriage one was in. Thus, land was acquired through male lineage, and women could only access it through their husbands and/or sons. As a consequence, once a woman was divorced, she lost the right to access and use the land and returned to her clan. Ondieki Nyamari, however, explained that if a husband died, the wife had the right to use the family piece of land as long as she remained unmarried and lived in the matrimonial home.[57]

In Gusii, socially constructed roles of women and men were integral to the delineation of land access rights. Control over land entailed the power to distribute and redistribute access rights to members of the family or society. This power was determined by the power relations among members of the community. In the Gusii patriarchal set up this role was vested in the elderly male members of the community. Kemuma demonstrated this point in the following terms

Land ownership constituted the overall right to land use and control in Gusii influenced social relations in the community.

---

56   Thorp L. (1997). 'Access to Land: a rural perspective on tradition and resources', in S. Meer (ed.) Women, Land and Authority, Cape Town: David Phillip.
57   Ondieki Nyamari;76, Jan 2020

Although the perception was that the land was owned by the entire community, it was seen that the entity that had control over the land could exercise rights akin to individual ownership to the detriment of other members of the community. In most, if not all cases, it was the men who traditionally had ownership and control over the community land. Equally, the men had the authority to determine how the land would be distributed and utilized.[58]

Based on Kemuma's narration, it is clear that in the traditional Gusii community, the men had an upper hand in decision-making with regard to land ownership and control. This male privilege was exercised by the household heads (the husband/man) by allocating the land to the various houses/women/wives that made up his homestead. Therefore, community ownership could be characterized as proxy and collateral because, in reality, the women needed to hold an association qualification certificate by way of getting married.

Gusii cultural norms determined which rights to land a woman was to exercise freely. For instance, women would have the right to use a specific parcel of land or the right to gather farm produce from it. However, the right to bequeath it through inheritance was negated as this was limited to husbands and sons. In this social-cultural context, a woman's land-related rights were usually tied to her place in her husband's family. Thus land rights were viewed within the broader context of the social-cultural and economic distribution of wealth within the extended family.

It emerges therefore that ownership of land in Gusii was based on family and kinship ties, with a level of family control at the household level. However, in terms of livestock grazing rights, the land usage system was more communal. Land was a communal resource, while cattle were household possessions that were allowed to graze on communal grazing land. Additionally, there were communal rights with respect to access to water and firewood resources. This showed that the Gusii traditional land tenure system was more concerned with control and usage than with ownership in the contemporary sense. Women could use and control land, by communal consensus, but the wider community (family, homestead and clan men) owned the land.

Traditionally, the division of labour was structured by gender and age. Richard Nyatangi[59] asserts that men would clear virgin forests using machetes, while the work of cultivating (using hoes),

---

58   Onteri Kemuma, 71; 20 Jan 2020
59   Richard Nyatangi; 57,Dec 2019

planting and weeding were done by women. Young, circumcised but unmarried youths were in charge of looking after cattle, while uncircumcised boys would take care of sheep and goats. It is thus ironic as observed by Hackanson that although women cultivated the land and tended the crops, thus doing the hardest work, they had fewer rights to land ownership.[60]

As discussed elsewhere in this work, relations among Gusii family members, including gender relations, were governed by a strict code of conduct called *chinsoni*. This code of conduct operated within each homestead, headed by the family patriarch, *omogaka bwa omochie*. Subordinate to him were his wives and children, including married sons and their wives and children. In addition, each wife of the patriarch had her own house and home yard, and adjacent land for cultivation. This meant that married women had access to and control over pieces of land within their husbands' homesteads, as it was a wife's duty to cultivate the land and feed her husband and children.

The physical layout of a Gusii homestead was a real-life demonstration of the *chinsoni* concept, with the husband's house closest to the cattle enclosure at the centre of the compound. The wives' houses would be nearby, each with its small enclosure and granary, and the houses of unmarried sons would be some distance from the others, on either side of the main gate.[61] Omayo[62] observed that "*Chinsoni* was strictly hierarchical, with the father at the top and his wives and children in subsequent levels of authority. It was unthinkable for a wife to disobey her husband in any matter."

On the same account, children needed to obey their parents. Levine[63] notes that the arrangement of houses within a Gusii homestead was intended to reinforce social relations, hierarchy and power relations in the household. This was amplified by Monyenye through the following recollection. The homestead head was formerly the absolute ruler of this group and owner of all its property including land....no one within or outside the homestead could challenge the man's authority and the matter would wait until he died for the adjudication by other elders.[64]

60 Hakansson, T. (1988). *Bridewealth, Women and Land: Social Change among the Gusii of Kenya*. Uppsala Studies in Cultural Anthropology No. 10. Uppsala: Amquiest and Wilsell International.
61 Akama, J.S 2017. The Gusii of Kenya, 38-39
62 Ombuchi Omayo, 62; 11 Nov 2019
63 LeVine, S. (1979). *Mothers and Wives: Gusii Women of East Africa*. Chicago: Chicago   University Press.
64 Japheth Monyenye, 80. 20 dec 2019

Monyenye confirms the authority of the household head and when he allocated the family land, no one among the family members would question why they were given a particular portion and not the other or why they were given this size and not more.

This study noted that, through the payment of bride wealth, women were not only detached from their lineage of birth but were integrated into their husbands' lineage when daughters could eventually get married to the other clans. It was taboo for a daughter to get married within her clan. Formerly, when an infant was born, people could inquire about its gender by asking whether it was "of the cattle pen or outside?"[65] (a boy or a girl respectively). It was thereby implied that the boys were part of the patrilineage where they spring from and, this was symbolized by being inside the cattle pen, while the girls belonged elsewhere (outside the cattle pen). It was observed that although these idioms by themselves may not constitute much significance. However, taken together with other cultural values and ideologies as presented in this study, they entirely complete a picture of Gusii women's ambiguous and peripheral status as daughters and/or sisters. According to Mandere:

> In traditional Gusii, the responsibilities of women included *gokunga*, which meant taking care of the property. In the overall, the man was in control of his family. Thus, "masculinity and femininity" began in childhood. Culturally, a woman moved from her home to a man's home and was supposed to handle the resources that had been handed over to her husband through his lineage.[66]

Mandere indicates that the process of assigning roles and responsibilities in Gusii from a young age was ascribed by the community. The women were, therefore, treated as having roles and responsibilities of economic resource value. Therefore, what a man to a certain extent owned, also a woman owned. However, despite the hard work that Gusii women performed on the land, contributing to the food security of their families and clans, their status in society remained subservient to that of men. This was further reinforced by polygamy, which ensured that men were at the top of the social hierarchy in their respective homesteads.

It is therefore clear from the study that women, in particular, had access and/or usage rights to land. However, they did not control or own the land. This implied to a large extent that, their autonomy in the social and economic realms was circumscribed by their lack

65   Mayer, l.(1975). The Patriarchal Image: Routine Dissociation in Gusii Families. *African Studies* 34:259-281.
66   Mokare Mandere , 75. 28 Dec 2019

of ownership and control over land as intimated by the various women discussion groups.[67] These contentions resonated well with Tambiah's assertion[68] that this was quite significant in taking into account that land represented the vehicle, through which women moved from the reproductive (private and non-work) realm to the productive (public and work) realm. Despite these bottlenecks impinging on women's rights to own/ control land, the Gusii customary land tenure system evolved avenues for the resolution of disputes of land ownership.

The most positive assessment of women's property rights in customary systems was the necessity for women to negotiate their social relationships to sustain their access to land through the changing of life circumstances. This was even though, difficulties in ensuring women's control and ownership of land remained a problematic feature of Gusii customary institutions of land dispute resolution, land use and land control/management. Women who worked hard on the piece of land provided by their husbands and were able to produce a lot of food were highly respected both by their husbands and the community. This is because they were always in possession of surplus food which they could help those in need, and even exchange with neighbours for what they did not have. They made their families prestigious as they at times attracted those who lacked food to work for them to get food thus increasing labour in the home which translated to more food production.

On the other hand, Gusii women who were able to nurture their children from infancy to adulthood especially sons were held in very high regard. They were able to influence critical decisions at the family or even clan level. Their opinions were sought in critical situations like land conflicts. In the background, their advice was sought. Men never made major decisions without consulting them. Their granaries were never interfered with even by their husbands. This is why men had to have their stores within the homestead. Such special women as herbalists, seers, prophetesses, and others who proved themselves worthy of wisdom were consulted in times of need.

The aforementioned customary rules, combined with the Gusii social structure, in which people lived communally in extended family groups, and where kinship links could be established to

---

67 Women group discussions at keumbu,Nyacheki,Kenyenya and Riosiri;Nov-Dec 2019
68 Tambiah, S. (1989). Bridewealth and Dowry Revisited. *Current Anthropology* *30*(4), 413-416.

various other groups, through common ancestry or marriage, combined with the reverence for ancestors, who were considered to be part of the family, ensured that the pre-colonial Gusii people did not have the modern concept of private ownership of land.[69] As Nyanchoka narrates:

> Individuals did have significant, even almost exclusive rights to use land, although these rights did not exclude other members of the family and/or kinsmen. Moreover, even the ancestors had land rights, hence land rights were derived from the ancestors, rather than from mere physical occupation and use.[70]

Therefore, the land was held in trust for future generations just as the ancestors had held it in trust for the current generation. This implied that in the Gusii community, the land was denoted as "ours" as opposed to "mine." Norman Humphrey[71], a senior colonial agricultural officer in his works on the Luhya agrees with this when he notes that ownership resided not in the man alone but also in his ancestors... whose interests had to be guided just as those of the living members of the family, both men and women. These pre-colonial land practices would however begin to experience a shift due to the inception of colonial policies from the late 19th century

Initial Colonial Land Policies

The origin of European interest in land in Kenya can be traced back to 15th June 1895 when Britain established its rule over the East Africa Protectorate, present-day Kenya. This was followed by the physical occupation of the colony where indigenous inhabitants of Kenya were subdued through military conquest or were tricked to let the British settlers acquire or get land to settle. It was the policy of the colonial administration to allow European settlers to occupy and utilize the land for agricultural production which would allow the colonial government to raise money to help settle the construction and administrative expenses of the Kenya-Uganda railway. The colonial administration and the European settlers had different perceptions and orientations as regards overall social and economic development in general, and land use management in particular. As it shall be demonstrated, these colonial conceptions had far-reaching impacts on the socio-economic development of the

---

69   Nyamwaya, D. and Buruchara, R. (1986). Property and land Tenure, in G. S. Were and D. Nyamweya (Eds.). *Kisii District Socio-cultural Profile*. Nairobi: Government Printer.
70   Nyanchoka Omare, 64. 28 Oct 2019
71   Norman, H (1944) The Liguru and the Land: Sociological Aspects of some Agricultural Problems of North Kavirondo. Government Printer. Nairobi, Kenya

indigenous Kenyan people. In particular, it impacted the African conception of gender as relates to property in general and land ownership in particular.

To justify the occupation of indigenous land, the British colonial administration claimed that the land they were acquiring was either unoccupied or sparsely populated and/or completely underutilized.[72] A series of legislations were thus put in place to justify the acquisition of land. In 1890, the Foreign Jurisdiction Act declared that all the unoccupied land with no settled form of government was under colonial control. Also, through the Indian Land Acquisition Act of June 1894, the colonial administration was able to acquire indigenous land by force for railway construction and for other public purposes such as the construction of roads, government houses and offices.

In 1898, the East Africa (Acquisition of Land) Order-in-Council was promulgated. This legislative measure allowed the expropriation of land for European settlement. More significantly, this legislation vested the ownership of all land outside the Coastal strip that was originally under the Commissioner of the East Africa Protectorate to the Colonial Government. Further in 1901, the East Africa Lands Order-in-Council was passed. This colonial law defined Crown Lands as: "All public lands within the East Africa Protectorate which are subject to the control of His Majesty under any treaty, convention or agreement."[73] In other words, this legislation simply transferred all perceived unoccupied African land to the colonial government. Then in 1902, the Crown Lands Ordinance was passed that empowered the Colonial Commissioner to lease or sell freehold land not exceeding 1000 acres to European settlers. The 1915 Crown Land Ordinance made all land, including all the land occupied by the indigenous people, Crown land. It also created Native Reserves for the Africans. The African rights to the Native Reserves that they had been moved to were eventually alienated with the change of Kenya's status from a protectorate to a colony in 1920[74].

The completion of the construction of the Kenya-Uganda railway opened up the interior for European and Indian settlement as it improved transportation into the East African hinterland. This raised the value of land along the railway line and thus forced the Colonial Commissioner, Hardinge to apply the Indian Land

---

72   Sorrenson M .Y. K 1968 Origins of European Settlement in Kenya, Oxford University Press. Nairobi,38
73   Ibid, 63
74   Ibid

Acquisition Act to reserve land of one mile along the railway line for public use. Afterwards, European settlement was particularly encouraged especially by Charles Eliot to make the railway pay.

From 1903, the highlands of East Africa Protectorate (present-day Kenya) had become a centre of attraction for European settlement. In the protectorate, the colonial administration found what they described as, "amorphous, leaderless populations scattered in the highlands of Ukambani and Kikuyu land." The British Foreign Office, therefore, encouraged increased European settlement to bring to an end the Government criticism over huge losses that the colonial administration was making in the control and administration of the East African colony.[75]

Initially, the British wanted to settle Indians in the central highland region because, through their trading activities, they would introduce a money economy to the African communities. Furthermore, the Indians would carry out small-scale farming that white settlers could not engage in. However, when Charles Eliot replaced Hardinge in 1901, he decided to reserve the Central Highlands for European settlement. Supported by the Colonial Secretary, Joseph Chamberlain, who had visited the protectorate in 1902, Eliot went on a campaign to encourage European settlement with the support of pioneer settlers who had already settled in the Central Highland region. As the railway line reached Nairobi, the town became a European frontier centre and the starting point for European settlement towards the western part of the colony. Nairobi, therefore, became what Eliot called "pre-eminently a white man's country."[76] By April 1903, over 100 Europeans had settled in Nairobi and its surrounding areas, and by May 1904, 168 more settlers had arrived from South Africa.[77]

However, the colonial administrators were in blatant contradiction with one another on how to acquire, allocate and use the declared Crown land in Kenya. While the British Government was in agreement with the administration in Nairobi on land acquisition and settlement, it insisted on the consideration of the existing facts on the ground. The colonial administration in Kenya, on the other hand, insisted that the land was almost empty and that it should be occupied by the European settlers. Furthermore, the local administrators, particularly the District Commissioners, were

75 Sorrension 1968, 34
76 R. M. Maxon 1990 Agriculture ; William R. Ochieng (Ed) Themes in Kenyan *History*
77 Sorrenson 1968, 63

lobbying for compensation for the lost African land that had been occupied by the European settlers. Thus, with Eliot as the Colonial Commissioner, most of the land from Ukambani to Naivasha was alienated and given to the settlers. At one-point Sir Fredrick Jackson, the Colonial Secretary, complained that Eliot was offering land in the Rift Valley without making adequate provision for the protection of African rights.[78] Eliot thus denied Africans their rights to their land in favour of European settlers' interests. Further, under Sir Donald Stewart who took over from Eliot, the Maasai were eventually moved to an unproductive Native Reserve to the south of the railway line.

Consequently, between 1907 and 1912, under the Chairmanship of J. A. L. Montgomery, the Colonial Land Commission saw the settlement of whites in various parts of the country. For instance, in early 1907, over 5000-acre leases were surveyed and given out to European settlers. In August 1907, the Rift Valley allotment was completed. Also, towards the end of 1907, the allotment was made around the Sotik area. At the same time in 1910, the Western Kenya allotment was completed, while the Londiani allotment was completed in 1912. In 1915, the Crown Land Ordinance was promulgated. The law defined Crown Land as including "all land occupied by the native tribes of the protectorate and all lands reserved for the use of any members of the native tribe"[79] This legally rendered Africans as tenants at will of the Crown.

Specifically, Gusii had come under colonial rule as part of the British protectorate of Uganda in 1894 with the whole area east of Lake Victoria to Naivasha to the west being part of the Uganda protectorate. The Gusii region, however, remained detached from the colonial administration because it was far from the railway line and most of the people were not engaged in long-distance trade that would have opened up the area to the outside world. Moreover, transportation and communication to the nearest colonial administrative centre at Kisumu were nonexistent. In May 1902, an administrative station was established at Kericho. Also, in 1903, another administration post was established at Kalungu in Luo land. The creation of these administrative centres in the neighbouring areas of Kericho and Kalungu enabled the British to enter Gusii.

According to the Colonial Commissioner, Donald Stewart, "Gusii land was a potential area for European settlement... It was

78   Sorrension, 74
79   Ibid; 189

important to open this part of the protectorate which is well adapted to European settlement."[80] The colonial administration moved in to establish an administrative centre in Gusii. However, first, they had to pacify the Gusii who were accused of raiding the Luo and stealing livestock, an area already under the British colonial administration. In this regard, the British colonial soldiers (the King's Army Riffles {KAR}) swept through South Mogirango, Bonchari and Bomachoge in Gusii confiscating herds of cattle to compensate the Luo. The capture of large herds of cattle from the people of Gusii had immediate social and economic repercussions on the community. As Gesare of South Mogirango recounted, "Mothers were left with no milk for their children, while for some time, men could not marry for lack of [enough animals with which to pay] dowry.[81]

The British soldiers, however, encountered stiff resistance from the Abagetutu Clan under Chief Angwenyi who fought back to recover their cattle. Robert Maxon points out that the hostile encounter of the Gusii community with the British who used excessive force on them could affect future relations as the Gusii remained bitter and resistant to colonial administration long after the conquest.[82] By 1907, an administrative centre had been established at Getembe (present Kisii Town) with Northcote as the first District Commissioner. The DC had, however, to settle scores with the Kitutu of Bogeka area who had been affected most by earlier British attacks due to their persistent resistance to the establishment of colonial rule over their territory and the capture of their livestock by the British soldiers. The Bogeka people of Kitutu were especially motivated by the prophecies of a famous Gusii prophetess, Moraa Ng'iti, who according to Gusii elders never accepted foreigners in Gusii. She openly despises men who never fought to keep the enemy away. Hence, she strongly encouraged Gusii warriors, under the leadership of Otenyo Nyamaterere, to attack Northcote who was leading a contingent of the King's African Rifles soldiers in an expedition to punish the Kitutu people, especially the people of the Bogeka sub-clan[83].

As a prelude to the attack of the Kitutu people in 1908, Northcote started collecting hut tax to raise revenue and encourage the sale of surplus production. This was aimed at promoting the capitalistic mode of production. In this regard, the colonial administration

80   Stewart to Lyttleton June 8 1905:PRO: CO 533/2
81   Gesare Bitengo Gotichaki ,99yrs,Dec 2019
82   Maxon R A, Conlicts and Accomodation ,pg 32
83   Akama,J.S (2018). The Untold Stories: Gusii Survival Techniques and Resistence to the Establishment of British Colonial Rule. Kisii University Press.

insisted on tax payment in cash making the Gusii men sell their cattle, goats and sheep. Live animals were also confiscated from those who refused to pay taxes. These colonial initiatives offended the Kitutu people who decided to retaliate. In January 1908, Kitutu warriors attacked the British soldiers who were under the command of Northcote. The war saw many Kisii warriors massacred by colonial soldiers who had superior weaponry. However, notwithstanding the advanced weaponry of the British soldiers, according to Gusii elders, the Gusii warriors managed to kill over 40 of the King's African Rifles soldiers.[84] Also, the Gusii warriors went ahead and killed several Indian traders and policemen who were based at Getembe station.

In this critical initial encounter, the colonial soldiers were forced to retreat and seek reinforcement from Kalungu, Kisumu, Kericho and as far as the Nandi Station in the north. The reinforced British expedition re-entered Kitutu in August 1908 and by the end of September 1908 they had destroyed several Gusii homesteads, killed many people, burnt houses and granaries, raped women and captured over 5000 herds of cattle[85].

Overall, the loss of cattle in the British attacks made the Gusii embrace more crop farming than before. Also, the breakout of rinderpest in 1908 to 1909 made the situation worse as the colonial officials banned any movement and sale of animals that was a major cash earner for the payment of tax. Therefore, for the Gusii to get cash for payment of tax and purchase of consumer goods, they had to produce more crops for sale.[86] The colonial government encouraged this through the supply of seeds and encouraging the sale of produce by inviting Indian and Arab traders to the area. Thus, new ways of wealth accumulation and consumption were introduced in Gusii[87].

Thus, the eventual suppression of the Gusii marked the beginning of keener interest of the British in the Gusii highland region. The District administrative headquarters were moved from Gaya in Luo land to Kisii Town. Furthermore, more non-government groups, including traders and missionaries started coming to Gusii. The colonial government was now bent on establishing clear political and economic measures to move forward. The colonial administration chose loyal men whom they made chiefs and tasked them with the responsibility of maintaining law and order, arresting offenders

---

84   East African Standard, 25 January 1908, 11.
85   Akama, 2018 The Untold Stories, 35
86   Onyambu Moruga Machoge, 95 yrs, Jan 2020
87   Neigus, Conflict Over Land, 159

and hearing petty cases. However, the appointed chiefs were more associated with white rule and the local population did not appreciate their role. Hence, the Native Ordinance of 1912 provided for the appointment of a council of elders who were able to help mobilize more young men to undertake public works. It also made it easier to abolish *ebisarate* (the military encampments where male youth undertook military training for the protection of the community). These youths who appeared to be a security risk for the colonial administration were forced to go back to their families where it was easier to control them.[88] However, as will be discussed later, this arrangement would upset the social economic life as well as gender relations among the Gusii. Eventually, the colonial government established seventeen councils of elders in different parts of Gusii. Soon, the Gusii started taking both civil and criminal cases to these councils, thus laying the foundation for colonial administration and the entrenchment of colonial judicial systems.

As the British government was establishing its rule over Gusii, the colonial administration adopted a dual economic policy which provided for parallel economic development for the settlers and the Africans. The major resources for development (i.e., land and labour) were used in favour of European development as African productive land was given to the settlers, while the African men were made to work in settler estates. The Gusii, however, were never subjected to major land alienation though many of the Gusii men were taken to work in European farms. This was mainly because of the late conquest of the Gusii, poor transport as the land was located far from the railway line, as well as the persistent Gusii resistance that as Robert Maxon puts it, changed British intention to settle in Gusii,

The colonial government, however, introduced new economic systems of production and a market economy in Gusii. Indian traders were encouraged to reside in Gusii to encourage commercial production while the chiefs were to initiate new forms of economic production through family labour. Consequently, with the availability of productive land, many Gusii men including those who had been displaced with the disbandment of *ebisarate* took to farming to pay taxes. However, many Gusii men were not keen on working away from home. As Makori Riana indicates, this was partly a form of continued resistance to British colonial rule coupled with the fact that many of those who volunteered to work away from home could die and as such could neither be accounted for by the community nor come back home. In 1913, the colonial government started the forced recruitment of labour. Consequently, between 1913 and 1914, the District Commissioner, Spencer, sent over 4,000 Luo and Gusii men out for public works.[89] As will be discussed later, this labour recruitment would eventually affect the gender relations among the Gusii as relates to land usage, access and ownership.

It is worth noting that despite this early colonial establishment in Gusii limited progress had taken place by 1914. The outbreak of the First World War made things worse especially when Kisii became the arena of war between the British and the Germans. The Germans, who ambushed and attacked the Kisii administrative headquarters, forced a hurried retreat of the DC and other colonial administrators from Kisii, leaving the administrative centre deserted. Elders from neighbouring Bonchari and Nyaribari recalled that this allowed the Gusii to loot and destroy the centre, an aggressive act that came to be known by the colonial administrators as 'the sack.'[90] On return after the war, DC Spencer organized a massive punitive expedition against the Abagetutu, Abanyaribari and Abanchari, the clans that mainly took part in the destruction and looting of the administrative headquarters. Over 3000 herds of cattle were immediately captured and a further fine of 16,525 herds of cattle was imposed on the Gusii and the Luo people.[91] Further, over 3000 men were arrested and forced to work on government projects.

The DC who took over after Spencer, W. F. G. Campell continued recruiting more Luo and Gusii young men to work in the Carrier Corps. Around 5,210 men were sent out of the District between 1914-1915.[92] More men kept being sent out of the District to work even after the end of the war. Thus, by 1920 a large number of men were going out to work for wages.

The war also led to an increase in taxes. Both poll and hut tax were increased throughout the protectorate to 5 rupees and the collectors who included the DCs, chiefs and headmen ensured the exploitation of all taxable sources. This forced the people of Gusii to work harder to produce more for sale. By 1920 the tax had been further increased to eight Rupees.[93]

It must, however, be noted that the war period was a period of economic hardship. The Gusii could not sell their products except to

---

89   South Kavirondo Administration Report 1913-1914, KNA:DC/KSI/1/2.
90   Group discussions at Bonchari and Nyaribari, November 2019
91   DC Spencer ,23 September 1914.KNA: PC/NZA/3/65/47
92   SKAR 1914-1915, KNA: DC/KSI/2
93   SKAR 1920, KNA: DC/KSI/1/2.

their neighbours, the Luo. In 1918 drought struck many parts of the protectorate followed by an influenza attack in 1919. However, Gusii was not much affected. This provided the Gusii with an opportunity to produce and sell their surplus to their Luo neighbours. Even with the end of the drought, the effects of the global economic depression kept agricultural development at the bare minimum, especially for those who had begun growing cash crops, because prices had gone down.[94]

In 1919, the Native Registration Ordinance was passed to enable the colonial administration to identify the men according to where they worked and their ethnic background. The men were given a certificate or *kipande* that they wore around the neck and this enabled easy identification of those men who were not working for them to be recruited into the workforce.

These various colonial strategies and plans that were aimed at political, economic and social change in the Gusii community did not augur well, especially with Gusii indigenous religious groups. Particularly, the people turned to *mumboism* to demonstrate their discomfort with colonialism. In the spirit of *mumboism*, a woman named Bonareri started teaching people that their renowned prophet Sakawa would return soon, that black men would rule themselves again, and that white men would leave. Her teachings became so popular and she got a big following from different parts of Gusii that the DC decided to deport her, together with her husband, son and other followers to Lamu on the Coast.[95]

As indicated, Gusii effectively came under colonial rule after the 1908 'punitive' expedition by the DC. The imposition of colonial rule led to the introduction of new crops and adversely affected the indigenous Gusii agricultural systems. It can be argued that while colonial capitalism provided new opportunities for some Gusii to accumulate wealth and expand agricultural output, it in the long run pauperised the majority of the population most of whom were women. In addition, the new mode of production hindered and, in most cases, ruined indigenous patterns of agricultural production, which to some level favoured women as producers and direct appropriators of the food crops.

However, it should be noted that Gusii was a special area, far from the centre, with richly fertile land. However, at the same time, it was difficult to cultivate its hilly terrain. Furthermore, at the time, no

94   DC/KSI/1/2 South Kavirondo Annual District Report, May, 1919.
95   Senior Commissioner's report to police in kisumu, 23 march 1921 ,KNA: Coast 40/922

settlers occupied the Gusii highlands. The only white settlers were in the "buffer zones" of Kericho and Sotik. There was also a small coffee plantation near Kisii Town owned by a European settler. However, the Crown Lands Ordinance of 1902 which declared all African "unoccupied" land as Crown Land affected the buffer zones between the Gusii and their neighbours, especially the Kipisgis. Thus, after 1908, the buffer zone land of Sotik and Kericho was given to the European settlers for tea and pyrethrum growing and came to be the Sotik-Kericho settlement area.

In the early period of colonial rule, the indigenous crops still dominated as the new crops were being experimented with and gradually established. However, over time, the Gusii were influenced by colonial policies to start growing crops for sale over and above the level of pre-colonial production by supplying them with seeds and beginning with chiefs who then would influence their subjects. They were gradually introduced into the money economy and found themselves producing crops both for subsistence and for sale[96].

Furthermore, the introduction of coffee as a cash crop in Gusii played a critical role in the changing patterns of accumulation and social status. For most of the colonial period, most Africans in Kenya were forbidden from growing high-value export crops like coffee, tea and pyrethrum, for fear that competition would lower returns to white settlers and inhibit the availability of cheap labour. It is, therefore, interesting to note that when the high-valued crop, coffee, was allowed to be grown in Gusii, it was mainly 'owned and managed' by men. Though women provided labour in the production of coffee, they were more visible in the growing and management of food crops.[97]

The position of women in the patriarchal Gusii society was increasingly eroded with the introduction of colonialism. Also, changes in socio-economic trends during the colonial era triggered a dramatic shift in the structure of the traditional division of labour between women and men. Thus, as most men opted for migratory labour, the women essentially retained their traditional roles and added extra ones initially reserved for men.[98]

When the colonialists arrived in Gusii, the Gusii were still expanding their occupation to frontier areas, especially towards Sotik and Kericho regions to the east and the Trans-Mara area to

---

96 KNA DC/KSI/1/2 South Kavirondo District Annual Report, 1914.

97 KNA DC/KSl/1/4 1933-1938

98 KNA DC/KSl/ 1/2 South Kavirondo District Annual Reports I 913JI 923

the southeast. As the Gusii population grew, land became a crucial factor of production. Polygamy was encouraged so that men would have more wives with more children who would provide extensive labour to enable them to occupy more land and maintain control of the one already occupied. However, with the arrival of the British in the Kericho and Sotik areas, and their subsequent occupation of the land in these frontier areas, there was a sudden end of the Gusii expansion to these areas. This meant that the households had to hold onto what they had acquired even when family numbers were growing. This increased pressure led to quarrels within and between families and clans as they rushed to grab any unoccupied piece of land within.

Further, the creation of reserves for the African communities saw the colonial governments create boundaries that confined each community to a specific reserve. As already mentioned the British arrived at the height of the Gusii expansion process, a process that could not continue further. Neigus[99], however, notes that with the creation of reserves and administrative boundaries, the Gusii borders became closed and the people were not allowed to settle anywhere outside the territory set aside for them by the colonial administration. The acquired productive lands that were outside the native reserves were reserved for European settlers and cash crop production. Thus, the Gusii now started looking inwards to occupy any land left unoccupied. Omosa indicates that, first, the people occupied boundary land between clans and then moved to occupy grazing land that was communal until there was no more free land to occupy.[100] Men had to subdivide the land they had to give their sons who came of age through marriage. This was the beginning of increased land stratification in Gusii, a process that has continued to the present time.

With this confinement, the Gusii were forced to adopt a more intensive form of cultivation. Fortunately, the good soils and reliable climate allowed for this drastic change. The periods of fallowing were cut by half as they now had two planting seasons; *omwaka* and *omwobo*. The labour input was intensified with women working longer to provide food for their families. Conflicts over land intensified between wives, families and clans. At first, land was seen as a means of production of subsistence and surplus for exchange in the clan setup. This changed as the clan could no longer help in the expansion and protection of land with the limitation of the colonial

99   Neigus, Conflict Over Land
100 Stephen Omosa. Kitutu chache,89.Jan2020

administrative boundaries[101]. Thus, individual households started fighting for their space and this laid the foundation for individual ownership of land, Families now started consolidating their land and protecting it from encroachment by neighbours. The scarcity of land also meant that women's access to and use of land would be limited.

Furthermore, the introduction of a cash economy by the British also came with a new set of exchange relationships. This was done through the introduction of a currency system of trade where people had to buy foreign goods using money, the introduction of taxes that were to be paid in the form of money, wage labour and the introduction of cash crops. All these engendered the Gusii towards working to achieve the results of their labour. The result was an end of group rights to property and the advent of private ownership and individual competition for resources.

As already mentioned, British cultural values were passed on to the Africans in the process of Westernization. One such Western value is the subsumed place of a woman in the homestead. This idea of the Victorian woman was passed on to the African communities changing their initial noble attitudes towards women. Thus, unlike in the African setup where a woman was allowed access to land where she worked and produced food with which she fed her family, the Victorian concept of a woman was simply a home keeper who waited for everything to be done by men. In all aspects, the British eroded the African conception of a woman and imposed their social and cultural values on the Africans. Coupled with the practice of individual ownership of land, women found themselves not being able to carry out their traditional duty of being given land to produce food for their families.

Conclusion

From the foregoing discussion in this chapter, it is apparent that the Gusii greatly valued land as a means of production. The chapter has established that right from the time of settlement or occupation of land, men played a major role in the acquisition of land, clearing of forests for farming and providing the most needed security against intruders. According to trading, this qualified them to be owners of the land not as individuals but as a clan or community. As the land was handed over to younger generations, it came to be known as ancestral land. The Gusii, as was the case with most other African

---

101 Kitching, The making of an African Petite Beorgeoisie

communities, evolved a land tenure system in which ownership was based on egalitarian principles where, while men's rights to own and share land were clear, they only held the land as custodians on behalf of their ancestors and the community for future generations. Women also enjoyed the rights of access and use of the land within marriage for the production of food to feed their families. These rights enabled the community to operate with limited conflicts and promoted sustainability in the utilization of land resources for the overall well-being of the community.

Although both men and women in the community accessed land, after marrying, women had the daunting task of ensuring that their right to access and usage of land was assured by meeting other cultural requirements such as ensuring that they got sons who would perpetuate the ownership of land allocated to them by their husbands. This created the agency in women to ensure that they got sons of their own or by arranging to 'marry' a woman who would bear children for them. Therefore, the only feasible way for a woman to acquire land and property was through her children, especially her sons. It was also evident in the chapter that, without sons, a woman in Gusii had minimal rights to property and would face old age without any economic support or prospects.

The arrival of Europeans and the establishment of colonial rule over Gusii at the beginning of the 20th Century saw the community face major changes socially, economically and politically that disrupted their smooth cultural operations. Most of the changes greatly affected the position, role and economic conditions of women more negatively. The initial expansion of the community was halted with the creation of reserves and administrative boundaries beyond which members could not expand their areas of occupation. This led to increased pressure over limited land resulting in conflicts over land as households fought to acquire more of whatever land was remaining within the reserve and retain that which they had already occupied for themselves. At the family level, women got disadvantaged as land gradually diminished denying them their means of production for subsistence. Thus, the gradual colonial advancement of the money economy and private ownership of land left women with no right to ownership, access or usage of land. This would be more aggravated as colonial policies got more entrenched in the colony as will be shown in the next chapter.

Chapter Four

Colonial Land Policies and Gender Relations In Gusii-Land, 1920-193

Introduction

The analysis in the previous chapter revolved around the effects of nascent colonial policies on the questions of land access, ownership and control in Kisii County. It emerged that the institution of colonial policies in this formative period had the net effect of constricting women's access, control, ownership and utilization of land as this resource became more contested and competitive. The discussion in this chapter is situated within the context of colonial agrarian policies that were instituted and implemented between 1920 and 1939. Key among these were the policies informed by the post-World War I (WWI) economic meltdown that ultimately compelled the official enunciation of the dual policy. The chapter interrogates the major elements of these policies and assesses the extent to which their attempted implementation impacted women's access, control and utilization of land in Kisii County. Further, this chapter details the dramatic effects of the Great Depression on overall colonial agrarian policies in Kenya's rural areas like Kisii that bestowed an enduring imprint on issues of women's access, control and utilization of land. The chapter ultimately addresses alterations or contradictions exhibited in colonial agrarian policies in the wake of African household response to the measures instituted earlier to stem off the negative consequences engendered by the Great Depression on the colonial economy. The chapter measures the impact of these "control strategies" on Gusii women as pertains to land access, control and utilization.

The Post-WWI and its aftermath in Kisii, 1920-1922

With the devastating impact of the First World War, the Colonial Office in London diverted its attention to higher imperial interests beyond the East African colony. This allowed room for the settlers to gain influence in the Colonial State and push for the protection of their interests as the European elected representatives could articulate and defend settler interests at the government policy level. By the 1920s, the settlers had managed to gain the right to elective representation in the Legislative Council, therefore, gaining greater political influence that boosted their economic dominance. The settlers would then push the Colonial State in Kenya to make their demands accepted by the Colonial Office.[1]

The Post-World War I period saw the colonial office in London concentrate more on enhancing the economic stability of the colony. It made the colonial state transform its land use approaches to realize higher agricultural yields. While, initially, the colonial state had focused on settler production and protection of settler interest especially in agricultural production,[2] through the provision of loans, agricultural extension services and guaranteed markets for the European settler producers, it turned out that settler production alone could not sustain the colony's economy. The colonial government, therefore, turned to African production to fill the void due to steadily declining agricultural production by settler farmers occasioned by the depressed prices during this period.

As evidenced in the First World War, the colonial state in Kenya supported settler agricultural production to ensure supplies for the war. The colonial state in Nairobi passed various policies that majorly aimed at spurring settler production. As such, the war period saw important gains made by European settlers. For example, the total export share for coffee and sisal rose from 32% to 57% while the export value of African products remarkably declined[3]. While the colonial office in London concentrated on the war efforts, the colonial state and the men on the spot in Nairobi leaned more towards settler needs to ensure settler agriculture flourished. In the Crown Lands Ordinance of 1915, for example, the colonial office in London had allowed the colonial state under pressure from the settlers, to give an extension of land leases to 999 years, making it convenient and cheaper for settlers to lease land. Equally, the colonial governor was given veto power over land transactions between members of different races thus defining all land occupied by Africans as crown land by 1919, thereby making Africans tenants at the will of the crown.

---

1 Robert Maxon, *The years of revolutionary advance 1920-1929* W. R. Ochieng, Ed, 1989) *A modern History of Kenya 1895-1980; Evans Brothers ,Nairobi*, 74

2 David Anderson and David Throup "Africa and Agricultural Production in Colonial Kenya; The myth of the war as a watershed" A Journal of African History 26 (1985) 329-330, Robert Maxon, 1984, Going their separate ways 57

3   Makana, E.N "Reinterrogating the interface between settler and peasant sectors of Kenya's colonial economy 1901-1929". A paper presented in a workshop on new frontiers in African Economic History, Geneava, September 2012.

At the end of the war, the colonial state embarked on the settlement of the ex-World War I soldiers in the settler schemes that had been set aside in Trans-Nzoia, Laikipia, Nyeri, Kipsigis and Nandi reserves. Governor Sir Edward Northey pushed the colonial state to allow ex-world War I soldiers with resources to settle in Kenya. This led to an influx of European settlers and land agents into the country. These hoped to increase settler production and by extension the colonial economy.

To boost revenue in the colony, the Colonial State raised taxes after WWI to meet increased financial needs. An income tax law was introduced in mid-1921[4] for both Africans and settlers. Through their representatives in the Legislative Council, the settlers repealed the Income Bill and were relieved from tax payments in 1922.[5] While the Africans in the reserves, as illustrated by the Gusii, continued to bear the burden of revenue remittance through increased taxation, the colonial government used the revenue to subsidize the settler economy, especially in the area of agriculture. Settler areas and urban centres that were mainly occupied by the settlers witnessed a heavy inflow of capital. Railway extensions were constructed to connect settler areas to the main railway line for settler accessibility to and from market centres. This was done using African forced labour through coerced recruitment in Kisii and other African reserves.

The colonial state in Nairobi led b,y Governor Northey, strongly supported the settler mode of production at the expense of African agriculture. In the Northey circular of 23rd October 1919[6], the Governor directed that the state shall help the settlers in accessing labour supply by stressing on his administration officers, chiefs, and headmen to use every lawful influence to make or even coerce able-bodied male natives to go to work. This policy was implemented without approval from the colonial office in London. Since the colonial state in Nairobi was under pressure from settlers, the colonial office allowed the colonial state to source for forced labour. The statistics provided in Table 3.1 below show the trend of labour recruitment between 1919 and 1924.

Table 3.1: Units of African Labour In Employment 1919-1924

Year	men	Women	Children	Total
1919-1920	45,005	3,917	4,789	53,711

---

4   Ochieng' W.R 1989, Themes in Kenyan History
5   Ibid.
6   Maxon The years of revolutionary advance 1920-1929 Ed Ochieng W, R. 1989,73

1920-1921	55,939	4,911	6,539	67,389
1921-1922	51,753	4,261	5,935	61,949
1922-1923	54,406	6,609	9,942	70,957
1923-1924	66,993	8,316	11,784	87,093

Source: Colony & Protectorate of Kenya, Department of Agriculture, Annual Report 1924

As can be seen in Table 3.1 above, the Northey Circular led to a steady increase in labour recruitment from 1919 to 1924. To secure regular and reliable labour supply as had long been pushed by settlers, a registration measure was put in place where all men, sixteen years and above, were required to carry an identification document that doubled as a work record. The registration document, popularly known as *kipande,* was put into operation in the1920s, forcing more Africans to join the labour force to boost settler farming.[7] As illustrated by McGregor-Ross, by the end of 1920, some 194,750 Native Registration Certificates were issued which increased to 519,056 by 1924 and 119,7467 by 1931.[8] A substantial portion of these registration certificates went to the Kisii African reserve.

During World War I, the massive recruitment of men to join the war pushed many Kisii men into migrant labour to avoid conscription to the war fronts. This enabled settler farmers to enjoy a regular supply of African labour from Kisii. The supply, however, declined as the war came to an end and the labourers (the Gusii men) started trickling back into the Gusii native reserves. The former labourers would join in the family household farming putting more land under the plough.

Parenthetically, World War I violently disrupted indigenous forms of agricultural production in Kisii, as large numbers of Gusii men were conscripted into military service or carrier corps, and many others were forced into migrant labour which took a heavy toll on indigenous 'human capital.' Almost half of the men returning home from Carrier Corps duties were reportedly not fit for hard work again for a long time.[9] This left the bulk of the family chores, agricultural duties and responsibilities in Kisii to be handled by the women.

The colonial state in Nairobi put in place measures that would

7 Ibid, 72

8 McGregor-Ross, W. (1968), Kenya From Within. London: Frank Cass.

9 Alila, P. (1984). *Kenyan Agricultural Policy: The Colonial Roots of African Smallholder Agricultural Policy and Services.* Institute for Development Studies. University of Nairobi. Working Paper 327.

push Africans into the capitalistic commercial production of grains so that the communities got enough farm produce for subsistence and the surplus for sale. First, the colonial government introduced taxation[10] in 1901 under the Hut Tax Regulations. The hut tax increased from one to two rupees in 1902. By 1903, it had been increased to three rupees. 1909 saw the introduction of the Poll tax which stood at five rupees in 1915 and eventually sixteen shillings (the new currency) in 1920,[11] which had to be paid using money that was previously not in circulation.

Further, western goods were introduced that could be purchased only by using money. Moreover, the cattle that could be sold to get money was rapidly depleted after the outbreak of diseases such as rinderpest, the confiscation of cattle by the colonial administrators, as well as the placement of a ban on the movement of cattle outside Gusii[12]. Equally, the young men who used to carry out raids into neighbouring ethnic groups to replenish their stocks had dispersed after the disbandment of the traditional youth camps (*ebisarate*) and were now at home. The community thus increased the land under cultivation to get surplus produce to be sold to enable them to get money for the payment of tax. The circumstances were such that men also took to grain farming as an alternative to raise money to pay taxes.

However, the start of the 1920s saw Gusii suffer the double tragedy of drought and locust invasion, especially in South Kavirondo District and the Northern parts of the district[13]. This affected the production of both maize and finger millet in the Gusii region and other parts of the South Kavirondo District.

The years 1918 and 1919 saw Kenya experience one of the worst famines. The rains failed in many parts of the country resulting in famine in many African areas. This forced the Colonial Government to import food to avoid starvation[14]. At the same time, the country suffered the worldwide influenza attack that killed many people and shook the world economy. Between 1919 and 1922 Kenya suffered a depressed economy as farmers were hit by the collapse of prices of their agricultural produce both internally and externally[15]. In South

10 David L. Neigus 1971, Conflicts Over Land 57-60
11 Makana, E.N "Re-interrogating" 6.
12 Gavin Kitching 1980, *The Making of an African Petite Borgeoisie*, Yale university Press, London
13 Great Britain, Kenya Land Commission Evidence and Memoranda vol 3 1934 ,2272
14 Maxon R.M. The years of revolutionary advance, Ed Ochieng W. R 1989, 72
15 I. D. Talbot,1974, The Kenyan Flax Boom, *Kenya Historical Review* 2, 62-3

Nyanza, which Kisii was part of, for example, businesses closed down as the Asians closed shop and business ground to a stop[16]. In the mix, settler cash crop exports were severely affected as prices for coffee and tea went down by over 50 percent[17]. The fall in prices forced the settlers to cut down on African labour and wages. This made Africans unable to pay taxes, thus plunging the economy into greater economic challenges.

The effects of the mini-depression led to African protests against high taxes, low wages and land alienation that culminated in the formation of political associations such as the Young Kikuyu Association, the East African Association and the Young Kavirondo Association. The Gusii did not join the political movement till November 1945 when the Kisii Union was formed, both as a trade union and a political association led by John Kebaso of North Mogirango[18]. This was because of the late arrival of the colonialists and the fact that the Gusii did not experience land alienation to the extent that it happened elsewhere, as will be discussed in Chapter Five.

Consequently, although women's land rights, control and usufruct in pre-colonial Kisii were relatively insecure to the extent that they only had usufructuary rights and did not enjoy the rights of ownership or disposition, the advent of the colonial state demand for increased agricultural production and expanded land use after 1922 saw the security they had in the utilization of land eroded gradually. Eventually, these rights were extinguished with the passing of legislation which failed to recognize the user rights that the Gusii women enjoyed previously. From the onset, the colonial state was pressing for the alienation of more land for European settlers on a freehold arrangement. However, as much as most of the early European travellers and adventure seekers had observed, they had found large tracts of land without people, consisting of forest country which was full of antelopes and lions and other wild animals. That notwithstanding, the study maintains that this African land in Gusii had its rightful controllers, users and owners[19] who were by right/rite the Gusii women.

Furthermore, the principles of obligation and responsibility under the indigenous African Kisii land tenure system guaranteed

16 SKAR 1918-1919, 1919-1920, 19201921, 1922, KNA; DC/KSI/1/2
17 Ibid.
18 Robert M. Maxon,1984, Conflict and Accomodation in Western Kenya' 125-127
19 Ochieng, W. R. (1974). *A Pre-colonial History of the Gusii of Western Kenya, c. 1500- 1914.* Nairobi: East African Literature Bureau.

women's access to land and control over food crops. The colonial intrusion instilled conflicts and contradictions between foreign-type agricultural production and the Kisii traditional agricultural economies of affection.[20] In the 1920s, the rights of Gusii women concerning ownership, control and use of land were further interfered with, by the introduction of capitalist production and reproduction for gendered gains. In particular, more colonial land reforms negated and progressively reversed the existing Gusii traditional order and eventually introduced male domination in land ownership and income-generating agriculture.

According to Nasimiyu[21] since the production of cash crops and subsistence crops were directly linked to the access to land, women in Gusii and other reserves were in the colonial period confronted with a whole range of handicaps in fulfilling their role as primary producers. This study affirms that the lack of control over land and all that went with it in Gusii became a major cause of women's economic dependence and marginalization. Without land, Gusii women were reduced to a state of dependency with no sense of social and economic security. The more land was reserved for commercial crops in Kisii, the more women became increasingly reliant on a cash-oriented domestic economy. The Gusii women could no longer produce sufficient food as their labour was transformed and reallocated to commercial crop production, the monetary benefits of which were the preserve of men.

Narrating her experience, Moraa Nyakundi observed that when her father went for migrant labour, they were left with her mother to work extremely hard on their piece of land, just like her stepmothers, for sustainability in the household. However, when the father came back from work, he made the wives surrender part of the land they had been given as their share to be added to the father's already existing *emonga.*[22] The father then planted his maize for sale to enable him to pay taxes. This meant that the women's land for food production was reduced as there was no more land for expansion. Clearly, this created a conflict between the Gusii traditional system of agriculture and the colonial one in the 1920s. This conflict contradicted the norm as women in Gusii became disempowered.

20 Munro, J. F. (1968). *The Machakos Akamba Under British Rule, 1889-1939: A Study of Colonial Impact.* Ph.D Thesis, University of Wisconsin.
21 Ruth, N. (1985). Women in the Colonial Economy of Bungoma: Role of Women in Agriculture, in Women and Development in Africa 56-73 (G.S. Were ed.)
22 As previously defined, emonga was an exclusive piece of land for the homestead patriarch.

Also, the family members, especially women, had to spare some days to work on their husband's *emonga* from where they received nothing. This became the coronation of the capitalistic mode of production in Kisii and the exploitation of the Gusii women's labour.[23]

The study noted that when the Gusii started experiencing the impact of colonial land policies, issues relating to engendering land use were mild given that land was increasingly being subdivided in the 1920s to 1930s.

The 1920s also saw new opportunities for Gusii men. First, a larger number of them, having come out of the youth camps *(ebisarate)*, found it necessary to go for wage labour to get money for payment of taxes. This, in reality, allowed women unilateral access to and control of the land back home as the men were out selling their labour for wages. By 1922, for example, over three hundred Gusii men were recruited to work outside Gusii.[24] However, it is important to note that most Gusii men liked working not far from home so that they could return home when they earned wages to invest the money through their women in agriculture and other productive activities. This explains why Gusii men never liked working in railway construction or as squatters in settler farms far away from their homeland.

The Dual Policy and its attempted implementation in Kisii

The mini-depression following WWI hurt the colony's finances. By 1922 the colonial state had a deficit of six hundred thousand dollars[25] with Governor Northey having spent increased revenue on expanded administration and support of European settlers in agricultural activities. On the other hand, African production was never completely crushed by the lack of colonial support. On the contrary, African production in most districts as exemplified by Kisii increased. The districts were able to produce a surplus for the local markets in urban centres, settler farms and neighbours who sometimes suffered from drought. The Colonial Office in London, therefore, pressured the Nairobi colonial state to balance its budget. In 1922, Sir Humphrey Legget, Chairman of the East African branch of the London Chamber of Commerce, sent a report to the Colonial

23 MoraaNyakundi 90, Bomachoge 12th December 2019
24 Robert M. Maxon 1984, Conflict and Accomodation In Western Kenya The Gusii and the British,1907-1963, Fairlegh Dickinson University press London. 79
25 Robert Maxon,The years of revolutionary advance. ED Ochieng W. R.1989, A Modern History of Kenya 84-85

Office maintaining that reliance on the European settler mode of production was costing Kenya dearly. He noted:

> *"...the solution to Kenya's problems was to stimulate African production by spending more on the reserves while reducing the load of African taxation..."*

This marked the official state recognition of the vital role of African reserves, Kisii included, in the colonial economy. Legget recommended African production of low value alongside settler bulk, high value and capital-intensive production.[26] The Colonial Office in London with W. C. Botommley as the head of the East African Department at the colonial office was thus convinced that African taxation had to be reduced, their mode of production stimulated and expenditure on their production increased. Under pressure from the Colonial Office, the Colonial State under Northey reluctantly endorsed the idea of government resources being partially used to support African production[27] which occasioned his exit as governor.

In July 1920, the transformation of the East African Protectorate to colony status enabled the colonial office in London to have a grip on the colonial state and reengineer the interests of the African natives as evidenced by the recall of Northey and the coronation of Coryndon to execute the Dual Policy. This happened after the colonial office in London had lost sight of the colonial state in Nairobi as the colonial office concentrated on the war efforts. The short lapse of metropolitan control over Nairobi created a vacuum that was filled by the white settlers who used their dominance to manipulate the man on the spot in Nairobi to their advantage. In June 1922, Northey was recalled, and Coryndon replaced him in Nairobi. Coryndon conceived and adopted the policy that came to be widely accepted as the Dual Policy where African production in reserves and settler production would develop complimentarily.[28]

The Dual Policy was adopted by the colonial office in London to straddle settler agriculture with African peasant agriculture, especially in reserves like the Kisii native reserve.

Despite the popularisation of the Dual Policy in 1922, the policy never boosted African production. Instead, for the rest of the period, settler production for export was favoured by the Colonial State. Even when there had been calls for African bulk production in the

---

26 Ian R. G. Spencer.1981, The first World War and the origins of the Dual Policy in Kenya,1914-1922, *World Development* 9, 742
27 Robert Maxon Modern History of Kenya, 81
28 Ibid,89

reserves, this never came to pass. Settler agriculture, therefore, expanded in the second half of the 1920s. In 1926 to illustrate, African produce only accounted for £470,750 out of a total agricultural export value of £2,211,665 and in 1927-28 alone their exports exceeded two million pounds.[29] The settlers' increase in number and production led to increased demand for African labour which also reduced African production caused by the labour drain. Moreover, land purchase was subsidized especially during the period of the mini depression to make it affordable to the settlers. The increased white settlement also meant increased demand for African labour.

In Gusii, just like in other African reserve areas, the colonial state had not done much initially to promote African agricultural development. However, over time, the Gusii realized increased production of grains out of their responsive measures as they put more land under agricultural production. This led to the occupation of empty lands and frontier land to the East of Sotik while the South of the current Trans-Mara region was also not spared.[30] This expansive utilization of land led to increased production, especially of grains, thus promoting the production and sale of surplus produce. These changes greatly impacted land tenure systems and gender relations in Gusii to be discussed herein.

The expansion of farmland under cultivation could later be enhanced by the colonial government's introduction of better farm implements such as iron hoes and oxen-drawn ploughs as well as quality seeds.[31] Therefore, the 1920s saw the Gusii increase the production of grains such as finger millet and sorghum, which became their commodities of trade with their neighbours, especially the Luo and the Kipsigis. This prompted the Nairobi-based colonial state to seek to improve the quality of African production in the Kisii native reserve. This was achieved through the introduction of quality seeds and improved production techniques such as the understanding of soil fertility and climate patterns as well as ecological zoning in the region.

With regards to marketing, the state-owned marketing cooperatives provided the settlers with an edge over the Africans which prompted the Gusii women to resort to local and black markets within the area

29 Department of Agriculture Annual Report 1929, 651
30 David L Neigus Conflicts over Land; A study of Expansion and Inversion in Gusii Society. Thesis,Harvard College, 1971; 46-50
31 Robert M, Maxon 1984,Conflicts andAccomodation. 57

and the neighbourhood. The cooperatives practice regulated prices of agricultural commodities where they offered extremely low prices for agricultural produce originating from African reserves like Kisii.

Initially, Africans were seen and treated essentially as a source of cheap labour. They also produced much of their food requirements in the reserves and often realized surplus for sale, hence subsidizing the colonial economy. The 1920s saw a lot of pressure exerted on the Gusii to produce more grain which included finger millet, sorghum and maize[32]

Once the market economy had picked up in Gusii, men and women were presented with new opportunities and choices to improve their livelihoods and those of their families. One such opportunity was engaging in formal education. The introduction of formal education in Gusii started in the early 1920s with the establishment of missionary schools such as Nyanchwa in 1918 and Nyabururu in the 1920s.[33] The few men who acquired formal education found it easier to get jobs in the colonial system where they were appointed to work as administrators and clerks.[34] Others could be absorbed to work in the settler agricultural fields as supervisors and office secretaries. Later on, the Gusii men started demanding better formal education in government schools that were deemed to provide quality education compared to missionary schools.[35]

Also, the Gusii's increased interest in education was because of the enhanced efforts and campaigns by the church missionaries and government officials. Thus, the chiefs and village headmen stressed the importance of formal education to their people. However, from the very beginning Gusii girls and women, as was the case in other African reserves, were excluded from formal education. Inevitably, this marked the beginning of new gender roles in the labour market and property rights in Gusii. Particularly, women were required to stay at home and carry on with domestic chores as men's new roles were shaped based on formal education, employment and migrant labour. The educated men used their salaries to engage in commercial maize growing.[36] Mokeira Omari exemplified women who were left behind as their male counterparts progressed in education. She vividly recounted how two of her younger brothers were taken to school at Nyanchwa in 1924 while she remained at

32 Department of Agriculture circular.22-31 October 1932. KNA: PC/NZA/3/2/106
33 SKAR 1923, KNA: DC/KSI/1/2
34 Focused Group Discussion at Bonchari, November 2020
35 R. M. Maxon. 1984, Conflict and Accomdation,84.
36 Musa Ayako, 85.Nyaribari Chache,jan 2020

home to take care of her other younger siblings. The brothers later got employment as clerks in European demonstration farms and earned money for personal development while she remained at home helping her mother with farm work as her father worked in Kericho.[37]

To promote the native African agricultural economy in Kisii and other African reserves, the colonial state prepared grounds for the capitalist enterprises in the Gusii region and other African reserves. The colonial state through the chiefs in the Gusii region pioneered the enterprise. The chiefs were the first to engage in modernized mechanized farming and formed the majority of the people who owned grain grinding mills.[38] Furthermore, the chiefs used their positions to influence access to land, labour and improved seeds as their farms acted in most cases as demonstration farms. The colonial state also supported the agrarian transformation of the chiefs through whom they promoted the capitalist agenda.

In 1924, the colonial state introduced the Local Native Councils (LNC)), a strategy in which African development in African areas/reserves like Kisii would be secured without necessarily using resources from the central government.[39] The Council assisted Kisii women farmers and traders in improving their agricultural productivity and marketing. The Council became the source of capital financing Kisii women for agriculture, and business as well as being the source of salaried employment in the native African area of Gusii-land.

Intending to entrench its rule, in 1923 the colonial government established a system of location-based tribunals that handled civil cases in the native reserves like Gusii-land.[40] These tribunals at the location level replaced the indigenous African Councils of Elders (*chitureti*; singular: *etureti*) that existed in the pre-colonial and early colonial periods. With the creation of the colonial court system, the people in the native reserve of Kisii quickly adopted and accommodated this new system of litigation with a little customization. In this regard, most of the subsequent District Commissioners observed that the people in the Kisii reserve area loved litigation and wasted their time and resources in the courts instead of utilizing the resources for economic and agricultural

---

37 Mokeira Omari 94, Kitutu, January 2020
38 South Kavirondo Administration Report, 1928, KNA: DC/KSI/1/3
39 Kitching, Economic Change, 188.
40 Robert M. Maxon1984. Conflict and Accommodation. 87-88

development given the productivity profile of the area.[41] Between 1924 and 1926, the colonial state established a Local Native Council (LNC) in every District, headed by the District Commissioners. In Gusii, a Native Council was established in 1925.[42] The local members of the Native Council, such as Chief Musa Nyandusi, used their positions to push for local/women gains[43]. With time, however, the Local Native Council was used to push for the needs of the community such as advocating for quality government education and the provision of medical and agricultural services which explains the Musa Nyandusi High School as a remnant legacy.

The Great Depression and its Aftermath in Gusii, 1929-1939

The great depression of 1929 was a result of changes and volatility in the world market system. It started with the collapse of the Wall Street stock market in New York in the United States of America. This led to a worldwide economic downturn that began in 1929 and lasted until 1933, colonies included. Prices of primary commodities dropped sharply in Kenya, just like in many other colonies. Further, the depression disorganized the primary commodity production and export trade of the white settlers in Kenya. The depression sparked fundamental changes in economic and social institutions and macroeconomic policies. In particular, the great depression caused drastic declines in production, severe unemployment, and acute deflation in most parts of the world, with far-reaching implications on Kenya's agricultural economy.

The great depression also affected the prices of settler crops which sharply declined. The settler monopoly of commercial production for export was now under threat. In Kenya, the fall in export prices coincided with the fall in government revenue. By 1934, for example, the value of the country's export dropped to levels they were in 1922-23.[44] Maize which was largely produced in Kisii was hard hit as its prices fell by half while coffee prices fell by forty percent. It ushered in an increased need to further expand agricultural production in the African native reserves like Kisii and to exploit other natural resources. Furthermore, the colonial state placed increased attention on the African reserves with the intent to increase agricultural production and supply of requisite colonial

41 South Kavirondo Administration Report, 1929, KNA: DC/KSI/1/3
42 South Kavirondo Administration report 1926, KNA: DC/KSI/1/3.
43 Robert Maxon: In (Ed) W. R. Ochieng, 1989, Modern History of Kenya, 97
44 Tabitha Kanogo, Kenya and the Depression1929-1939, W R Ochieng,1989, 115.

commodities. Consequently, more land was put under the plough in the Kisii African reserve than was the case hitherto. As such, land became a more contested resource with major implications on gender relations in Kenya and particularly among the Gusii, owing to the agricultural utility of the area. Ochieng' illustrates that by the mid-1930s, about one-fifth of all usable land in Kenya was under agricultural control and utilization[45] which the study believes the lead area was Gusii.

In the 1930s, migrant labour had become popular with Gusii men. The effects of the great depression made many Gusii men move out to maximally utilize the available land in their localities as many more moved to Sotik and Kericho tea estates as an alternative to agricultural production. In 1936, eighty percent of the 2813 men working in the tea estates came from Gusii[46]. Other Gusii men went to neighbouring South Kavirondo and Lolgorien regions to work in mining centers.[47] Notably, most of these men worked on a contract basis and kept links with their homeland where they returned whenever agricultural need arose. For instance, when the prices of maize crops improved in 1937, Gusii men concentrated on putting more land under maize production instead of going out for wage labour.[48] As the District Commissioner noted, there was a considerable shortage of labour in South Kavirondo that not even raising wages and other incentives influenced enough Gusii men for the required workforce.[49] Thus, as the production of grains especially maize increased in the 1930s, the Gusii found a ready market for their surplus produce with their neighbours, the Luo, and among migrant labourers, especially in Kericho and Sotik. Particularly, the grains were sold to the migrant workers on settler plantations who provided an alternative market for the Gusii farm produce.

Nevertheless, this study maintains that, despite the turbulent economic times of the day, Kisii produced commodities in Kenya's export for the decade as Gusii agricultural production during the great depression was neither stultified nor crushed. Indications from oral sources are that Gusii's agricultural production increased during the great depression, which can only be attributed to Gusii's

45 David L. Neigus: Conflicts over Land, A Study of Expansion and Inversion in Gusii Society. Thesis, Havard College,1971
46 SKMIR for October 1936, KNA: PC/NZA.4/5/8
47 Robert Maxon Going their Separate Ways,78
48 Orvis, Men "Women and Agriculture"8-11
49 SKMIR July 1937, KNA: PC/NZA/A/5/8

110

response to the prevailing times.[50] This is evidenced by the quantities of maize and *wimbi* (finger millet) produced in Kisii in the 1930s as illustrated by Table 3.2 below;

Table 3.2: Maize & Wimbi produced by the Gusii between 1936-1938

Year	1936	1937	1938
Maize (tons)	689	2378	1226
Wimbi (tons)	631	541	688

Source: SK Ag ARs 1937-39, KNA: AK/2/33

Table 3.2 above reveals that the Gusii production of Maize and *wimbi* was on the increase during the decade despite the turbulent times. In addition, as migrant labour employment rebounded in the 1930s for many men, the increasingly common absence of men began to affect women adversely, as they were required to take on a substantially increased share of agricultural labour.[51] However, as postulated by Kitching, production continued to expand through the 1930s as migrant labour had little negative impact on African agriculture as the Kisii women and their non-migrant men were able to increase their labour time and employ new tools (iron hoes and oxen ploughs) and the introduction of new crops such as maize, groundnuts and exotic trees to increase productivity.[52]

From the early 1930s, Africans were increasingly initiated into the commercialization of life in the reserves. Cash was increasingly used for services and purchases of items such as footwear, utensils, furniture, hoes and ploughs. The more commercialization of rural life grew, the more Gusii women found themselves marginalized. In part, this is because the Gusii men, due to the society's patriarchal nature, collaborated with the colonial officials to whittle down and erode women's legal rights, especially as relates to access and usage of land. This happened through the incorporation of traditional laws that favoured men into a new body of laws drawn up by the colonial state. It resulted in the emergence of new sexist colonial laws.[53] For instance, with the Gusii men, being the ones who got formal education and migrant labour that gave them a cash advantage, it was thus clear from the word go that the colonial state was a male

50 Group discussion with elders from Bobasi and Bonchari, Dec 2019
51 Hay, M. J. (1972). Economic Change in Luoland: Kowe, 1890-1945. Ph.D. diss., University of Wisconsin-Madison.
52 Kitching, G. (1980). Class and Economic Change in Kenya: The Making of an African Petite-Bourgeoisie. New Haven:Yale University Press.
53 Jane, P. (1986). Women's Rights and the Lagos Plan of Action, 8 HUM. RTS Q. 180

world. This was blended with the traditional patriarchal system to produce a structure that to a large extent disempowered Gusii women. As Rhoda explained, Western ideological imperialisms and the introduction of capitalism and subsequent neo-colonialism were the linchpins of gender inequality in Africa as exemplified by the Gusii.[54]

One link between the Kisii pre-colonial and early 1930s colonial experiences was the consistent denial of women's rights for independent access to land and the control of the resources that were produced by a combination of land and labour. As the Gusii tradition showed, the most salient fact about women's access to land was that it typically remained and continued to be derived from someone else rather than existing independently and directly. That is, land rights only accrued to Gusii women as a result of their status within a family as discussed previously. However, the problem lay in the fact of mutability of such status and of the rights they struggled to retain. In the late 1930s, as land got more and more scarce, and given that the unoccupied land was getting exhausted, Gusii women's access to land, use and control were affected even more as more and more men were getting back home to control their ancestral land for commercial production.

It was noted that in a situation where land was in abundance and the social organization ensured that women held important structural positions, women's right to access and use the land was secure. However, as land got progressively subdivided and limited in the 1930s, Gusii women gradually lost the security and power they had initially enjoyed. Their inability to get and own land other than through the status of a wife and the inability to inherit land in the land regulations of the 1930s adversely affected their future land rights and their socio-economic status. The whittling away of women's land rights by the changes instituted by the colonial state was a direct result of their inabilities arising from the customary rules of inheritance and the customary division of labour which had resulted in Gusii women not being able to directly acquire land for themselves. Whitehead & Tsikata noted:

> Most rural African women play a substantial part in primary agricultural production, making the complex of local norms, customary practices, statutory instruments and laws that affect their access to and interests in [the] land very significant not

54 Rhoda, H. (1984). Women's Rights in English Speaking Sub-Saharan Africa, in Human Rights and Development in Africa, 46.

only to them, their dependents and their male relatives, but also arguably to levels of agricultural production[55]

Although Gusii women's land rights in the pre-colonial period were insecure to the extent that they only had usufructuary rights and did not enjoy the rights of ownership or disposition, the advent of European settlement and colonialism in Kisii in the 1930s saw whatever security they had in land being eroded and eventually extinguished with the passing of further colonial legislations in the years to come that failed to recognize the land access and user rights Gusii women previously possessed. Omandi[56] observes that:

> Colonialism stopped further movement to new lands. Land started being partitioned into smaller holdings. Clear permanent boundaries were introduced. Land was initially marked using hills, rivers, valleys and specific trees. However, with the creation of permanent boundaries, clan land remained static as [the] human population within families and clans increased leading to reduced land that can be used for cultivation and food production by the Kisii women.

According to Monyenye,[57] the British never cared much about the Gusii women in the 1930s since they were excluded from any form of public work and had no formal education. Moreover, their traditional role as primary food producers, which gave them mandatory access to land, was sidestepped in the 1930s by the colonial state. Women in the 1930s were no longer to hold the land in custody for their growing sons as commercial agricultural production took over. The commercial agricultural production in the 1930s reinforced the idea of Gusii men as eligible and absolute owners of the land. The colonial authorities found it appropriate to equate the power held by traditional male Gusii elders in the allocation of land to the Western conception of property ownership to the exclusion of Gusii women. The result was the 1930s gender paradox among the Gusii. In such cases, the Gusii women lost the guarantee of the traditional land tenure systems in the mid-1930s which had traditionally allowed them to access and use land for agricultural production. As Monyenye narrates:

> In traditional society, there was no hunger as women always farmed enough land for the subsistence of their children. It is

---

55 Whitehead, A &Tsikata, D. (2003). *"POLICY DISCOURSES ON WOMEN'S LAND RIGHTS IN SUB-SAHARAN AFRICA: THE IMPLICATIONS OF THE RETURN TO THE CUSTOMARY.* Journal of Agrarian Studies, 3 (1-2), 67-112.
56 David Omandi (Age, 55; 21 December, 2019)
57 Ernest Monyenye, (Age 67; 20, December,2019)

until the mid-1930s when women were increasingly deprived of the opportunity to utilize the land that families and the whole community started experiencing hunger and food shortage.[58]

Therefore, it is clear that the colonial state in the mid-1930s, by design, ruthlessly suppressed the indigenous women-friendly mode of land ownership, usage and agricultural production in Gisii which adversely affected Gusii women's participation in economic production and social progress. According to Ong'esa:

> The 1930s colonial land policies stopped free movement to new land. Trends in land ownership changed, as colonial officials were given powers to make decisions over issues of land without considering and consulting Gusii traditional land use. They introduced punitive restrictions to land where the Gusii men became the owners of land as the colonial state handled all matters related to land with only men in Kisii area.[59]

From Ongesa's narrative, it is apparent that the commodification of land entrenched capitalism in the late 1930s among the Gusii. Gusii men started dictating how, when and where land was used; and they also started exploiting Gusii women's labour for their benefit. Furthermore, communal protection of Gusii women's access to land was curtailed with the introduction of exclusive male tribunals in Gusii that were less likely to take into consideration existing Gusii women's plights. At worst, the Gusii women were left to fight for their survival on their own towards the end of the 1930s. In the prevailing situation, some daring Gusii women tried to persuade their husbands to give them a share of the family land.

The Gusii women who were in control of the domestic/subsistence economy swiftly responded by reverting to the growing of traditional sweet potatoes and cassava as alternative crops to survive the locust invasion of 1934. Furthermore, the Gusii women halted the selling of the extra food they had in store as a cautionary measure just in case the famine caused by the locusts was to extend[60]. As they were getting out of these natural calamities, the Gusii women embarked on increased production of finger millet, sorghum and maize for their sustenance of the domestic economy.

While the increased need for migrant labour put more pressure on women's labour time, Kitching[61] suggests that this early period

---

58 Monyenye
59 Elkana Ong'esa (Age, 60; 19, December,2019)
60 Nyachae Ombongi 89, Nyaribari Masaba. December 2019.
61 Kitching, G. (1980). *Class and Economic Change in Kenya: The Making of an*

should be characterized simply as one in which underutilized male labour was absorbed and employed, resulting in large increases in production in Gusii and other African native reserves. Labour was underutilized in part because colonial conquest largely nullified the indigenous juridical, political and military roles that men of all ages played in their societies.[62] Thus, in trying to find out how colonial state policies affected gender relations in food production and land use. Wangari[63] argues that the alienation of more land and the conscription of African male labour played a critical role in the transformation of gender-land relations in most parts of Kenya as illustrated by Gusii. The study affirms that this new development made more able-bodied men go to work as migrant labourers, leaving women in the African reserves with more responsibilities. Functions such as clearing and tilling of virgin land that were previously solely done by men were left to women and children. Norah Mong'ina says she learnt to clear the thick bushes near their home from her mother who had to work for long hours to put more land to crop farming while her father was away working in Kericho.[64] Further, due to the traditional patriarchal setup, women were often unable to exercise their economic and social rights. Hence, women were overburdened with various agricultural tasks in the absence of their able-bodied sons and husbands.

Lonsdale and Berman[65] indicate that the establishment of capitalistic production depended upon the appropriation of African land and labour, a point Ndege[66] concurs with when he notes that, at any rate, the British colonial economic policies in Kenya including land alienation for European settlement, taxation, and migrant/forced labour, export production, railway & road transport and communication, education and health had complex and far-reaching implications on the livelihoods of the Africans in the reserves, especially the Gusii.

African Petite-Bourgeoisie. New Haven: Yale University Press.

62 KNA/DC/KSI/1/1-3 South Kavirondo District Administration Reprt 1924-32, 167.

63 Wangari, M. (1996). Asian Versus Africans in Kenyans; Post-Colonial Economy in the Eastern African Journal of History and Social Sciences Research.

64 Norah Mong'ina, 90, Nyaribari Masaba: November, 2020.

65 Lonsdale, J. and Berman, B. (1979). 'Coping with the contradictions: The Development of the Colonial State in Kenya, 1894-1914,' Journal of African History 20.

66 Ndege O.P. (2006). Colonialism and its Legacies in Kenya. Lecture delivered during Fulbright-Hays Group project abroad program: July 5th to August 6th 2009 at the Moi University Main Campus.

In summary, the interplay between the land ownership system and crop production in Kisii cannot be well analyzed while ignoring gender and labour relations in the area. Among the Gusii, it is the women who were primarily responsible for food production, household management and the nurturing of children. By the start of the 1930s, a large number of Gusii men were out on migrant labour leaving their wives with increased agricultural and household tasks.[67] Despite maximizing their labour, agricultural policies marginalized women not only in cash crop production but also in the provision of formal education. Ndeda[68] asserts that colonialism was discriminative to the African (Gusii) women who were overburdened in the reserves in the absence of male labour. In this regard, the Gusii women became the sole agricultural producers in the Kisii reserve. They planted, weeded, harvested, stored and managed their food harvests both in the presence and absence of men until colonialism contradicted this norm.

This marginalized women in Kisii further as it entrenched gender inequality in the ownership of land. Therefore, this study argues that, while colonial capitalism provided some new opportunities in the Kisii reserve, the Gusii men exploited them selectively in the mid-1930s to accrue and accumulate wealth and expand individualistic agricultural output. It also pauperized a large part of the women population. In addition, the new mode of production hindered and, in some cases, ruined indigenous patterns of agricultural production that were hinged on women.

Traditionally, in a situation where land was in abundance, the social organization of the society ensured that women held important social and structural positions, as women's rights of access to land and control as well as usufruct were to a larger extent secure. However, the promulgation of new land tenure systems and agrarian changes conflicted and contradicted the traditional tenets of the people in the native reserve of Kisii as women gradually lost the security and power they had hitherto enjoyed traditionally.

Equally, the colonial state abolished traditional "cattle camps", (*ebisarate*) by 1937 and most of the grazing areas were replaced

67 Omwoyo, S. (2008). Assessing the Impact of Coffee Production on Abagusii Women in Western Kenya: A Historical Analysis (1900-1963). In C. W. Kitetu (Ed.), Gender, Science and Technology: Perspectives from Africa (156-167). Senegal. African Books Collective.

68 Ndeda, J.M., (1993) The Impact of Male Migration on Rural Women: A case Study of Siaya District c. 1894-1963. Ph.D. Thesis, Kenyatta University

by the growth of male-dominated commercial crop farming. As the Gusii traditional male activities and obligations vanished, Gusii women faced increasingly greater obligations. These supplemented the colonial economic production system, since when labour requirements in European farms fell, the men returned to their families to be provided for by their women/wives. However, this made the procreative labour of women to be devalued by the colonial capitalistic production relations. Less emphasis was placed upon food production and the Gusii women's labour in this sector was uncompensated, while Gusii men's labour in cash crop agriculture assumed exchange value.

The Gusii customary rights of women continued to be eroded by colonial reforms.[69] The result of colonial capitalism was the re-structuring of gender roles to the detriment of the Gusii women. The introduction of commodity production for export in Kisii brought about greater gender segregation in labour in the 1930s with Gusii men increasingly becoming agricultural managers.[70]

Gusii Response to the Colonial Expansion of Economic Space in the 1930s and its Implications on Gender Relations

By 1930, maize had been established as a major crop grown both for domestic consumption and export. However, the poor transport network became a major obstacle for the Gusii women to be able to sell their farm produce in the neighbouring areas.[71] The poor road network made the transport costs very high.

As the Gusii expanded agricultural production, they equally ventured into other non-agricultural activities to support their households. One such income-generating venture was the construction of water-driven grinding mills for grinding grains. Thus, some enterprising Gusii men used the money generated from the sale of maize to buy grinding mills, to grind maize and finger millet, to supplement their livelihood and the paying taxes. By mid-1932, petty African businessmen had taken over what was initially seen as Asian business. Around this time, eleven Gusii men were operating the water-driven grinding mills in different parts of

69 Nzioki, E. (2003). *Why Women's Right To Land?* Ad-Hoc Expert meeting on Land Tenure System and Sustainable Development. Lusaka, Zambia.

70 Davison, J. (1987). Who Owns What? Land Registration and Tensions in Gender Relations and Production in Kenya. In Davison, J. (eds), *Agriculture, Women and Land: The African Experience.*

71 Maxon R, Going Their Separate Ways: Associated University press, Canada. 2010 pg 54

Gusii.[72] This is a clear indication of a people keen on embracing the colonial capitalistic modes of production. By 1935, the Local Native Council had approved sixty-six applications for the purchase and installation of water mills.[73] African entrepreneurship and the rise of a petite bourgeoisie group had started evolving in Gusii.

Meanwhile, African men in Kisii were inducted and coerced into cash crop production for export.[74] As discussed earlier in this chapter, it was the migrant labourers, the educated and the chiefs, all of whom were men, who ventured into cash crop farming because of exposure to financial capability and administrative power bestowed upon them by the colonial state in terms of land use. In the process, Gusii women were banished into subsistence production at the margin of the colonial capitalistic economy. Nyachoti[75] observes that during the colonial period, Gusii women lagged behind men in numerous ways; they had far limited experience with the cash economy for it was the Gusii men who had gained exposure through education and migrant labour while their women had little formal education if any, and minimal technical training in "modern" agricultural methods. Thus, women suffered a serious loss of social and economic vibrance.

The Gusii socio-economic and customary practices became restructured, modified and recast during the great depression times. The changes affected the people's way of life including the way they perceived themselves and their property. For instance, the Gusii households were forced to sell their cattle to pay taxes in cash. In pre-colonial Gusii, it was unheard of that a cow has been sold let alone for cash. But, with the establishment of colonialism and its penetration into the area plus the demand for cash in the mid-1930s, such trading activities became the norm. As the Gusii, like other native communities, were forced to sell their cattle, the value of the cattle as a store of value and a symbol of wealth started fading as they gradually started embracing the cash economy.

Another impact on one of the key pillars of the pre-colonial Gusii society began in the 1930s, simultaneous to and caused by the rise of the Gusii men's off-farm employment. Young Gusii men started gaining increased independence from their elders and

72 KNA: PC/NZA/2/1/22, Minutes of KisiiBakoria LNC Meeting,26-27 Mau 1932
73 Minutes of Kisii Bakoria LNC meeting, may 26and 271932 KNA: PC / NZA/2/1/22
74 Falk M, S. (1996). Changing African Land Tenure: Reflections on the incapacities of the State, The European Journal of Development Research, 10; 2: 33-49.
75 ChumaNyachoti 83, KitutuChache, jan 2020

began to obtain their bridewealth by purchasing cattle [to start families].[76] This was a major shift from pre-colonial Gusii marital arrangements that were majorly transacted with bridewealth from the groom's sister. In this regard, off-farm cash income gave young Gusii men the opportunity to pay bridewealth from their means. Inadvertently, this minimized the role of Gusii elders in controlling marital arrangements in the community. It also meant that the young families deterred the involvement of elders in resolving marital and family conflicts, especially where injustices were vested upon women over the use of critical family resources such as land. Gusii women, therefore, could not seek the intervention of clan elders whenever they were faced with injustices from their men folk like before, especially issues related to access, use and control of the land.

With land getting limited in the late 1930s, employment offered a new and open vista for socio-economic expansion through sons' careers. Initially, education became a means of obtaining profitable employment for sons. In addition, most of the Gusii men invested in businesses and trade. The late 1930s saw the cost of education and the scarcity of land place economic restrictions on polygyny. Through business and wage employment, alternative paths to wealth creation opened for Gusii men and political power became more and more dependent on one's place in the local and national administration. As a result, polygyny as a means of expansion and prestige for Gusii men went on a speedy decline.[77] Also as discussed earlier, the influence of the church, especially the Catholic and Seventh Day Adventist churches, in promoting monogamy led to the reduction of polygyny.

Moreover, the role of women in childbearing among the Gusii, and the high value that the Gusii placed on children affected the Gusii gender relations, land ownership and control towards the end of the 1930s. As sedentary cultivators in fertile, well-watered, and relatively underpopulated land, the pre-colonial Gusii people needed as many hands as possible to work the land. Therefore, Gusii women, the number of wives and subsequently children, were important measures of success and esteem among Gusii men. The high value placed on wives and children in Gusii was further

76 Mose Nyandusi, 93, NyaribariChache January,2020

77 Abbott, S. (1980). Power among Kikuyu Women: Domestic and Extra-Domestic Resources and Strategies. In *Anthropological Papers in Honor of Earl H. Swanson, Jr.* L. Harten, C. Warren, and D. Touhy, (eds.), pp. 8-14. Boise: Special Publications of the Idaho Museum of Natural History.

influenced by the high rates of child mortality that occurred in the area. As such, Gusii families would have as many children as possible, with the negative conscience that some will not survive to adulthood. However, this desire for large families remained even after the arrival of the colonial era and Western medical practices, explaining the population explosion in Gusii.[78]

While the changing economy of Gusii in the late 1930s fuelled rising bride wealth prices, other factors exacerbated the increase[79], such as the large amount of money entering Gusii which was unevenly distributed among cash crop producers who had acquired substantial new wealth during the pre-World War II period. Philip Mayer[80], an anthropological resident in Gusii in the 1930s, revealed that, although large amounts of wealth in circulation could be a legitimate cause for higher bride wealth, there were unfair bargains made by the newly rich members of the community. This, in turn, helped push bride wealth into an inflationary spiral as other Gusii men were forced to demand higher amounts for their daughters. Mayer observed:

> Every father fears being left in the lurch by finding that the bride wealth which he has accepted for his daughter will not suffice to get him a daughter-in-law; therefore, he is always on the look-out for any signs of a rise in the rate and tends to raise his demands whenever he hears of other fathers doing so. This means, in general terms, that individual cases of overpayment quickly produce a general rise in the rate all around.[81]

Moreover, to a limited extent, Gusii women gained increased independence, as Bukh suggests,[82] though often at the expense of increased workload curtailing available options.[83] Furthermore, by 1935, increased production allowed the development of African-controlled retail trade in Gusii-land and other parts of Kenya.[84] As

78 Hakansson, T. (1988). *Bridewealth, Women and Land: Social Change Among The Gusii of Kenya.* Uppsala studies in cultural anthropology. No. 10. Uppsala: AmquiestandWilsell International.

79 Hakansson, N. T. (1994). The Detachability of Women: Gender and Kinship in Processes of Socioeconomic Change among the Gusii of Kenya. *American Ethnologist, 21*(3):516-538.

80 Ibid

81 Mayer, P. quoted in Lucy Mair, *African Marriage and Social Change* (London, 1969), 52.

82 Bukh, J. (1979). *The Village Woman in Ghana.* Uppsala: Scandinavian Institute of African Studies.

83 Guyer, J.I. (1984). *Family and Farm in Southern Cameroon.* Boston: Boston University. African Studies Center.

84 Kitching, G. (1980). *Class and Economic Change in Kenya: The Making of an African Petite-Bourgeoisie.* New Haven:Yale University Press.

people increased agricultural production and increasingly ventured into trade in cereals and transportation of various agricultural goods.

It is also important to note that, by 1939, Gusii men financed almost all land leases.[85] Once leasing of land began, most of the Gusii families leased land more or less continuously, leasing different plots each year as the need arose. Only the sudden loss of a Gusii man's off-farm income or unusually high expenditures would cause a break in land leasing. However, given that leasing was temporary, almost all such land was planted with male-controlled annual crops such as maize. Land leases represented the shrinking of household subsistence, as cash crops expanded and the decreasing fallow periods lowered grain production on the family land. This new trend increased Gusii women's dependence on their men for key cash inputs into agricultural production.

Occasionally, some women would move and acquire land on their own with the support of their grown-up sons. Kwamboka Onyambu exemplified the latter case in the 1930s as the eighth wife of a large polygamous family at a time when boundaries had been fixed between clans and communities. When her husband became aged and she realized that she had to get enough food for her seven sons, Kwamboka moved from the ridge occupied by her husband and went several kilometres away looking for free land to settle. She then came across a piece of land that was previously used by her husband's clansmen as grazing land (*oborisia*) in Erandi area in the current Bomachoge-Borabu region. Kwamboka marked the boundaries for her new land. She then built a home with the support of her sons and thus managed to acquire land for herself and her grown-up sons.

Claiming ownership of the land was not easy for a Gusii woman at the time as men from her husband's clan tried to force her out. However, with the support of her sons, she stayed put. Later, and to enhance her security over the acquired land, Kwamboka convinced two of her co-wives to come and occupy part of the land. This strategic re-alignment and consolidation of family members made men from the clan let her stay on the acquired land. Her community eventually nicknamed her "*Otwoma*" to mean one who pushes her way to achieve what she wants. This was probably in awe due to what Kwamboka had managed to accomplish in terms

85 Kitching 1980: 74-85; and David L. Neigus, Conflicts over land 115

of moving away from the Kisii family homestead and managing to acquire virgin land almost single-handedly for her progeny.[86]

Furthermore, the research interviews and personal communications revealed that many Gusii women constantly expressed suffering from increasing stress, fear, and dissatisfaction with their situation, especially those in non-bride wealth unions.[87] The Gusii women repeatedly emphasized the fear of living under the constant threat of expulsion, social disgrace, and economic depression. Thus, as long as a Gusii man had not paid the essential bridewealth, the woman/wife was open to exploitation and mistreatment to a much higher degree than was the case in a traditionally legal Kisii union. Such a woman, staying in an unpaid bridewealth union, had no attractive alternatives; leaving the man would wilfully expose her both to probable gossip and ostracism for being a 'loose' woman resulting in economic insecurity and increased poverty.

Another transformation during the period of the late 1930s was that Gusii men in migrant labour failed to meet their social and economic obligation in attending to traditional *amasaga*, the agricultural system of organized group labour initiatives, and their wives were also freed of this obligation.[88] Their access to the Gusii group labour became increasingly uncertain considering that it was the men's responsibility to invite their relatives and neighbours to attend his wive's *risaga* farming activities. Only the Gusii women and younger unmarried and unemployed men remained available for *amasaga*. Consequently, in Kisii, mixed-sex labour groups started coming together and agreed to perform certain amounts of work for the provision of a certain amount of beer in which all members would partake. In this regard, group members could negotiate with a Gusii woman (their hostess) over the exact amount of work for an exact amount of beer and food to be given. Thus, both commercialized beer and manual labour had clear market values in the late 1930s. Thus, *amasaga* ceased to function as institutions that provided requisite social function to each household based on need and became based on monetary and market-like transactions towards the beginning of the 1940s.

Furthermore, due to the increasing population, high poverty levels worsened and increased insecurity in the Kisii African reserve. This intensified the initial agitation for the return of indigenous

86 Onyambu Onyambu, 92, Bomachoge. Dec 2020
87 LeVine, S. (1979). *Mothers and Wives.* Chicago: University of Chicago Press.
88 Group discussion with women from Kitutu Chache January 2020.

land particularly in Western (that Kisii was part of) and Central Kenya. Various efforts, including the creation of land commissions to address the rising tension and agitation among the African peoples in the reserves like the Kisii reserve, were mooted by the colonial state marked by the launch of the 1930 Native Lands Trust Ordinance.[89] The Ordinance aimed at setting aside African reserves, and where the need arose, provide additional land for the Africans in the reserves. The law also established a Native Trust Board to manage leases and transfer of land in the native African reserves like the Kisii reserve. However, the Native Land Trust Ordinance was limited to the extent that the Crown could grant leases and licenses to Europeans in the African reserves as exemplified by the Gold mine lease and license in the Kakamega reserve in 1934. In essence, the agitation for land ownership, control and use did not cease with such token and unilateral measures that still preserved the colonial state interests of the indigenous Africans interests.

The 1933 Morris Carter Land Commission was formed to look into the African protests over land and the general feeling that land for Africans in the reserves was not adequate. The commission was tasked to estimate African land requirements and recommend, if necessary, their extension. It was also to establish the extent of settler encroachment on African land. The commission made several recommendations that sought to address some of the grievances in the African reserves. Principally, it was to address the need for more land, the rights to own and use land and other property by the Africans within and without the African reserves like the Kisii reserve. The colonial state crafted and introduced further laws on the assumption that the problems in the Kisii reserve, for example, were due to overpopulation, bad land use and defective land tenure arrangements[90] The state further devised plans to co-opt "civilized" indigenous Africans into the colonial capitalist system where individuals amassed wealth to deal with the "dangers posed to the colonial hegemony".

According to Okoth-Ogendo,[91] the colonial state authorities in Kisii identified the solution to the problem as lying in the individualization of land tenure in the Kisii African reserve, just like in many other

89 Land Tenure, K. Kibwana in William R. Ochieng (ed)1990. Themes in Kenyan History: Heineman Kenya Limited, 235-236

90 Kenya Land Commission Report,1933. Government Printer.Nairobi 287-297

91 Okoth Ogendo H. W. O. 1975 The adjudication process and The Special Development Process. Unpublished Occasional Paper no. 12, Institute of Development Studies, University of Nairobi

native African reserves. This was reflected in 1932 when the Carter Land Commission visited Gusii to gather complaints on the land issues in the area and got no specific complaint from the Gusii women except for the men what the elders termed minor intra-community land quarrels which they stated were internally managed.[92] From the group oral interviews, however, the exclusive composition of men to appear before the commission denied the women a chance to voice their land-related complaints such as limited land for subsistence production. Hence, at the time, the Gusii women were left to suffer in silence regarding land control and use in the area.

The pre-WW II period witnessed the introduction of state policies that sought to create a delicate balance between promoting agricultural production and controlling land degradation in the African reserves, especially the Kisii highland reserve. This was due to the reality that with the disruption of the indigenous African land tenure system, coupled with increased population and intensive use of available arable land on the Kisii highlands necessitated by the competition between Gusii men and their women, the rate of land degradation and soil erosion was alarming in Kisii. The competitive land use policies in the area had divisive implications on gender relations in the rich agricultural zone of Gusii-land.

The capitalistic ethic that had been awakened in response to the state policies adopted during the Great Depression was now being curtailed as the focus shifted to the prevention of what was referred to as "land mining".[93] As late as 1939, while the colonial state had embarked on soil conservation in African reserves, encouragement of land use and introduction of new crops was more significant in Kisii highlands.[94]

The colonial state, on its part, faced opposition from the Gusii when it attempted to acquire land for the establishment of a scheme for the planting of exotic trees as a soil conservation measure. Maxon[95] observes that the Gusii feared that supporting tree planting would mean that they lose their land to the white settlers. In addition, the 1930 Forestry Department report indicated that the Gusii feared losing their land to the colonial state. Therefore, they opposed every effort towards the tree planting scheme, forcing the colonial state

92 Great Britain, *Kenya Land Commission Report* 9London: HMSO,1934), 297
93 Orvis, S.W (1989). Political economy of Agriculture in Kisii:Social reproduction & Household Response to Development Policy. PhD Thesis. University of Wisconsin, Madson.
94 Maxon, M.R (1984) Conflicts and Accommodation, 106
95 Robert M. Maxon 1984. Conflict and Accomodation, 87

to abandon the project in the late 1930s.[96] However, the planting of wattle trees became a centre of focus in Gusii in the later years. Apart from being a cash crop, where its bark was sold for tanning, the tree was also useful for other purposes such as supplying building material, firewood and charcoal, all of which were fringe benefits that accrued to women in Gusii. Besides, the growing of wattle trees needed less labour and, therefore, was convenient to grow hence why Gusii women supported it. With the recommendation by the Colony Economic Department in 1935 that wattle trees can be planted outside Central Province, the District Commissioner of South Kavirondo and the District Agricultural Officer, in particular, started encouraging the Gusii to plant the trees.[97] Furthermore, the Local Native Council financed the purchase of wattle seedlings for planting. By 1937, wattle tree planting had spread in many parts of Gusii with households providing the required labour.[98] The ease of the spread of wattle trees in the Kisii reserve is credited to women's support of the venture.

Bobasi women, through oral interviews, revealed to our study that as they surrendered more land for commercial production, a venture that men were keenly controlling, they found themselves accessing limited land for subsistence production. This forced them to start abandoning the traditional practice of shifting cultivation which eventually led to soil exhaustion and degradation. Given that women would only use the land for food production and were not allowed to own the land, the traditions and practices concerning women's use, access and control over land degenerated further in the 1930s.

As the effects of the great depression began to diminish in the colony and Gusii, in particular, with the fall of prices of crops and locust invasion in the mid1930s, there were marked economic changes. As an effect of the great depression, the settler farmers swiftly moved into the reduction of migrant labour as most white farmers were not making profits from their crops.[99] As a result, the colonial white settlers reduced the planting of crops and were, therefore, not in need of labour to the extent they had previously. Consequently, many Gusii men, who turned up for labour, would

---

96 Colony and Protectorate of Kenya, *Forestry Department Annual Report 1930* (Nairobi: GP,1931), 17
97 Robert M. Maxon1984, *Going their Separate ways: Agrarian transformation in Kenya 1930-1950.* 86-94
98 Ibid
99 Gavin Kitching 1980, Class and Economic Change in Kenya. pg 58.

not be hired. In essence, many Gusii men lost their source of income and this forced them to go back home to share with their wives, daughters and mothers whatever few available resources.

The locust invasion in South Kavirondo, around the same time, had devastating effects on the local people, especially on their Luo neighbours of the Gusii. All crops in Luo land were destroyed, resulting in the outbreak of famine.[100] The Gusii women, who had not been so much affected, got the opportunity to sell their maize to their Luo neighbours, though the prices kept fluctuating.

On the other hand, the colonial state did not relax the taxation requirements,[101] therefore, creating more strain on the Gusii women who were already overstretched. This pressure would eventually result in family conflicts and quarrels over property rights, with adverse effects on the Gusii women.

Conclusion

The chapter set out to give a portrayal of how colonial agrarian policies between 1920 and 1939 impacted land and gender relations among the Gusii. The chapter identified the post-WWI period as one that coincided with the promulgation of policies favourable to the promotion of male-dominated agriculture in Gusii. Thus, in the aftermath of the First World War, the agricultural policies that were introduced favoured and assisted men in Gusii to focus on producing for the market and not for consumption. On the whole, Gusii women were seen and treated, essentially, as a source of cheap labour. They produced much of their food requirements in the native reserves and they often realized limited surplus for sale. However, the Great Depression of 1929-1933 forced the colonial state to direct more attention toward the Kisii Native Reserve as a source of cheap food production. The consequence was that more land was put under the hoe or/and plough to the detriment of soil fertility and conservation as land use became contested between genders and thus straining gender relations in Kisii.

Due to land degradation in the post-Great Depression period, new land use policies aimed at promoting agricultural production and controlling land degradation in the Kisii Native Reserve were promulgated by the colonial state. These had major implications on gender relations in the rich agricultural zones of Gusii, where

100   SKMIR,April 1931, KNA: PC/NZA.4/5/7
101   SKAR1932, KNA: DC/KSI/1/3

men left the women working on the land as they sought migrant labour employment in the European settlements. The increasingly common absence of Gusii men began to affect women adversely, as they were required to take on a substantially increased share of agricultural labour coupled with other household activities, although with curtailed usufructs.

Thus, though the colonial impact on gender relations, in many ways, weakened the social and economic position of Gusii women, it presented them with minimal potential opportunities for the enhancement of their roles in land ownership and usage. The importance of land in agricultural production in Gusii, and the resultant gender-related issues that its utilization raised, became even more manifest as the colonial state navigated the challenges posed by the Second World War. This will constitute the subject of analysis in Chapter Four.

Chapter Five

Gendered Land Use and Women Response During the Second World War, 1939-1945

Introduction

In the previous chapter, it emerged that in the period preceding World War II, the colonial authorities had become alarmed at the damage done to soil fertility as African households in Gusii spontaneously stepped-up agricultural production in response to measures instituted to promote production to mitigate the negative effects of the Great Depression on the colonial economy. The period between 1935-1939 saw the colonial authorities put on premium measures tailored to contain soil degradation and, in a sense, discourage intense land use.

However, the onset of World War II, forced the abandonment of these measures as more emphasis was placed on increased agricultural production with little regard to soil damage. Another facet of colonial policy in the wake of WWII was the unprecedented mobilization of human (men) resources to serve the purposes of the war either as soldiers or as carriers. This chapter measures the extent to which these policies were applied on the ground in Gusii and the effects that they had on women's access, control and use of land. It analyses how the drive for increased agricultural production triggered more intense land use among the Gusii thereby exacerbating competition and contestation over this resource. The chapter argues that this scenario exercised a profound impact on gender relations by further constricting control and access of women to land as a key factor of production.

Further, this chapter discusses the effects of the unprecedented mobilization of human and material resources on women's control, access and use of land among the Gusii. It is argued that this particular aspect of the war had the cumulative effect of increasing the agricultural workload for the women without bestowing any land ownership rights on them.

Human Resource, Military Conscriptions and Land Use in Kisii in the War-time

1939 marked the start of the Second World War which was a defining stage in Gusii on land matters. The women in Gusii found themselves in a contradictory position with the colonial state regarding their participation in the war efforts. Families in Gusii were torn apart with men being forcefully taken to go to war. Also, the colonial state wanted to ensure increased agricultural production in support of the war efforts and in the face of the escalating and glaring soil erosion in Gusii as Anderson & Throup[1] observe. Furthermore, during the Second World War, the colonial state targeted to increase food production in the Kisii African Reserve with little attention to soil conservation as noted by Orvis and Heyer.[2] Agricultural officers, for example, emphasized that all efforts must be made to ensure increased food production, a position held by the Provincial Commissioner (PC) in Nyanza who noted a reduction in the number of agricultural extension officers in the villages.

At the outbreak of the war, the immediate task of the colonial office and the colonial government was to mobilise all potential resources of the colonial empire, both men and material for the war.[3] In Kenya, the British government called for intensified agricultural production. The colonial state cooperated with the settlers more than ever before to ensure increased production.

It should be noted that the start of World War II caused a lot of discomfort among the Gusii youth since many of them had previously been captured for military service as carrier corps during the First World War and the military experience was not encouraging. Consequently, many of the youth decided to escape and work in the tea estates in Kericho, and in the mines in the South Kavirondo District in Luo and Maasai lands to avoid being recruited into war services.[4] Even attempts by the District Commissioner (DC) to assure the youths that they could not be captured and taken to war were in vain. Not even the *Barazas* that were held and even the use of Gusii leaders to provide encouragement messages in local vernacular stations worked.[5]

1 David Anderson & David Throup; Africans and Agricultural Production in Colonial Kenya: The Myth of the War as a Watershed
2 Judith Heyer, 'Achievements, Problems and Prospects in the Agricultural Sector,' in Heyer Judith (et al), (ed), (1976), Agricultural Development in Kenya. Nairobi: Oxford University Press. See Stephen Orvis. (1997). The Agrarian Quesition in Kenya. Gainesville: University of Florida Press. See also North Kavirondo Annual Agricultural Report, 1939. Native Affairs Report, 1939
3 Hrold Macmillan,1967, The Blast of War 1939-1945. London
4 SKAR DC Report 1939-1945, 14a
5 Robert M. Maxon. Conflict and Accomodation,114.

With the outbreak of the war, as noted by Barker, the British embarked on the recruitment of Gusii men in the Kisii Reserve for military utility[6]. Maxon indicates that the recruitment in Gusii started even before the war began in August 1939.[7] The Kisii Native Reserve was a recruitment centre where men were drafted into the military as East African Military Labour Corps and Services. Here they served as service men and women who engaged in support services and they were conscripted as King's African Rifle soldiers.

Thus, during the war period, there was pressure on both land and labour in African areas such as Gusii. Parenthetically, highly productive areas with high population density such as Gusii were a target for the recruitment of men for the war and other essential services. Thus in this regard, the colonial government laid down measures to legalize labour acquisition.[8] The colonial government passed the Emergence Power Defence Act, 1939 at the start of the war, where the government was given broad powers of labour requisition, control of movement and censorship.[9] In addition, the 1940 Defence (Native Personnel) Regulations gave the Colonial Governor power to order the Provincial Commissioners to produce stipulated quotas of workers for military and other essential services for both the state and private contractors who were working for the colonial state. Many of the Africans who were conscripted to join the army or as essential service workers were either captured by chiefs or were tricked to go for military service. The state in Gusii pressured the locals through conscriptions to provide military and service men to aid in the war.[10] More labourers were recruited to work in essential service areas such as the construction of airfields, roads and military training camps. By 1941, 98000 Kenyans from African reserves, like Kisii, had been recruited to the armed force[11].

---

6 Jonathan Barker, (1989). Rural Communities Under Stress: Peasant Farmers and the State in Africa. Cambridge: Cambridge University Press. See also North Kavirondo Annual Agricultural Report, 1940

7 Robert Maxon, "Fantastic Prices" in the Midst of "An Acute Food Shortage": Market, Environment, and the Colonial State in the 1943 Vihiga (Western Kenya) Famine. In African Economic History, No. 28 (2000). African Studies Program, Madison; University of Wisconsin.

8 Wangari, M. (2010). Gender Relations And Food Crop Production: A Case of Kiambu District Kenya, 1920-1985.

9 Zeleza, T. (1992). The colonial Labour system in Kenya. An Economic History of Kenya (eds.) Ochieng' W.R. and Maxon R M.

10 Robert Maxon. (2003). Going Their Separate Ways: Agrarian Transformation in Kenya, 1930-1950. London: Associated University Press.

11 Clayton & Savage. (1974). Government and Labour in Kenya, 1895-1963. London.

However, in April 1942, the colonial government initiated forced recruitment, thus forcing more than six thousand men from South Kavirondo to go out to work.[12] An Essential Undertakings Board was established in the same year to determine the production sectors that needed conscripted labour. This helped to promote increased military services as well as enhanced agricultural production. Plans for conscription were made as reported by PC Nyanza in 1944 below.

Table 4.1: Planned conscription of labour in Nyanza Province 1944

	CK	NK	SK
January	400	200	Nil
February	400	Nil	Nil
March	Nil	200	400
April	Nil	400	400
Total	800	800	800

Source: KNA: PC/NZA/2/12/76

As indicated in the above table, Gusii which was part of South Kavirondo also suffered from the conscription programme.

Eventually, more men started going for wage labour voluntarily as their cattle had been auctioned by colonial administrators for taxation and war support. In May 1943 for example, 12,639 Gusii men were in civil employment as voluntary workers, while 8,269 were on military conscription.[13]

The colonial state, in conjunction with the settlers, went for forceful procurement of labour to work for the settlers. Oral interviews noted that many men were forcefully taken from their villages for war purposes and worked in the settler farms. Peter Orang'o one of the ex-WW11 soldiers says that he, together with his age mates, were forcefully rounded up by colonial policemen under the instruction of their chief Nyakeri at Nyakoora Hills where they were grazing family cattle. The police picked up about eight of them and took them to Kisii town where, later, they were taken to Nairobi Eastleigh for military training before being shipped to Ethiopia for military services.[14] Further, Maxon notes that many men were employed outside the district for non-military service in 1943.[15] The high

---

12 South Kavirondo Administration Report 1942. KNA: DC/KSI/1/4.
13 Registrer of Natives to DCSouth Kavirondo 3rd June 1943. KNA: PC/NZA/3/13/13
14 Peter Orang'o , 97 Kitutu Chache. November,2019
15 Register of Natives to DC South Kavirondo 3rd june 1943

numbers of conscripted men in 1943 coincided with the peak of the famine and the low quantities of maize produced in Gusii during this period.

Notwithstanding the use of force, African men were also cheated that they were being taken for off-farm employment only to find themselves conscripted into the military as narrated in oral interviews with various group interviews[16]. Moreover, other men were taken out of school, while some European employers gave out a number of their workers to join the military. There are those who, however, joined because they were enticed by misleading information. For instance, it was rumoured that those who joined the military could be exempted from paying taxes but were not exempted in the long run.[17] Thus, by 1941, over 98,000 Kenyan men were serving in the military forces in various roles.[18]

Impact of Conscription on Gender

1944 had the highest number of recruits from Kisii which coincided with the peak of the war that required more military men and this explains the 1944/45 famine a position echoed by the 1942 Annual Report which noted that conscripted labour recruitment for essential war services had overshadowed every aspect of normal activities in South Kavirondo.[19] Frankel affirms that the absence of Nyanza males had hindered the improvement of African farming as men were likely to be more agriculturally progressive,[20] a position this study contradicts. According to Maxon, South Kavirondo, Kisii included, provided the third largest male military recruits for military purposes in Kenya.[21]

The conscription into the military took majorly a gender dimension as mostly men were conscripted into the army. As a result, women in Gusii took over the roles of control and land use which guaranteed war supplies to the state. However, it should be noted that the conscription and recruitment of Gusii men into labour outside the Kisii African Reserve in the war period did not result in a labour shortage in the family farms in Kisii as agricultural production in

16 Group interviews at Masongo Nyaribari and Kitutu chache January,2021.
17 Orina Nyakwara 90, Kitutu Chache ,December 2019
18 Shiroya, O, J. E. (1985). Kenya and World War II: African soldiers in the European war Nairobi: Kenya Literature Bureau.
19 South Kavirondo Annual Agricultural Report, 1942
20 Note by Prof. Frankel as reproduced in Hugh Fearn, (1961). An African Economy: A Study of the Economic Development of the Nyanza Province of Kenya, 1903-1953. London; Oxford University Press.
21 Robert Maxon, Going their separate way

the reserve was a preserve of women. Frankel notes that men were likely to be more progressive because of educational opportunities with the additional experience they had gained from the European farms. The complexity of this contention was that their education and skills gained from the European farms could not be utilized for agricultural production for they were away from the farm serving in the military. This socio-economic scenario where men were conscripted by the colonial state to work in the military and settler farms, to a certain extent, re-engineered the female labour power in agrarian production in the area.

With such numbers of men out of Gusii, women boldly took land control and use as their primary prerogative and faced the prevailing situation and handled the colonial state pressures of the day while ensuring family food security. With the absence of the male labour that was crucial for the clearing of the land and the breaking of the virgin land, the state's efforts to expand and increase maize production for the war were hampered as commercial maize production greatly declined while family food production in Kisii remained intact.[22]

The recruitment of the Gusii men into the army gave the Gusii women an opportunity, although limited, to exercise control and use of land which saw the Gusii women invest more time and labour in the farms resulting in more production than the state appropriated for war efforts. The more Gusii men were recruited into the army from the start of the war to the end of the war, the more Gusii women exercised control over and the use of the land, unfortunately to the benefit of the state for war supplies.

Conscription and recruitment of men in Kisii for military, settler and civil purposes restructured the Kisii agricultural labour system and gender relations. The redirection of Gusii male labour had bestowed land control and usufruct rights to the Gusii women and the children,[23] and limited it to household survival and where surplus was realized, it accrued to the colonial state for war purposes. In Gusii agriculture, the absence of the men was largely felt at the start of every production cycle due to the limited capacity of the women folk to clear land for planting in addition to bringing more land to agricultural production. With these limitations, the colonial state was worried that the Gusii may not majorly contribute to the

---

22 Motari Nteng'a 85,Ibacho,Nyaribari Masaba Nov. 2019
23 Hugh Fearn, (1961). *An African Economy: A study of the economic development of the Nyanza Province of Kenya 1903-1953.* London; Oxford University Press.

war demands. The Agriculture Department in South Nyanza did not expect that the Gusii women could produce food crops for the families while being in a position to produce for both commercial purposes and military supplies,[24] a point echoed by elderly women in oral interviews who complained of their mothers taking up the responsibility as their fathers had been snatched by the war.[25] While the state anticipated increased production to support the war efforts, it failed to put in mind the ability of women to produce for both commercial and domestic purposes.

By the mid-1940s, the number of wage labourers from Gusii had increased tremendously. Women and children who were left in the reserves now undertook duties such as taking care of livestock and breaking the groundwork of virgin land, work previously done by men. Perhaps more important, it should be stated that changes in the traditional norms governing access to land were not accompanied by a change in women's formal status. Women still had neither birth rights to their parents' land nor any ascribed rights to it in their status as sisters or daughters. It is only through marriage that they were able to obtain land and their access to basic subsistence even within marriage was increasingly becoming problematic, as land ownership was largely male-dominated.

Thus, in the 1940s, marriage patterns were relatively loosened from the tight grip of tradition and household elders, courtesy of the war dynamics. The colonial impact on gender relations, in many instances, tended to weaken the social and economic position of the Gusii women. Nevertheless, it presented them with potential opportunities for the enhancement of their roles, social status and participation in societal economic progress during the Second World War.

During the war, families were forced to base their control of land and agricultural use on women's labour. As a last resort, to mitigate the 1942 famine, vulnerable households provided farm labour to well-off families in exchange for food rations.[26] Equally, the forceful redirection of the remaining male labour in Gusii to soil conservation

---

24 KNA: PC/NZA/2/1/130. The Special Agricultural Officer writing to the Director of Agriculture

25 Group discussion with women from Nyaura, Nyaribari Chache. 2nd Feb., 2021

26 Robert Maxon. (2003). Going Their Separate Ways: Agrarian Transformation in Kenya, 1930-1950. London: Associated University Press. This is supported by Maore Moronya, 89, Bomachoge Dec., 2012

denied the area the crucial labour power that would have consorted with women's labour to avert the emerging famine.

Consequently, in this period, African labour was reorganized not only in the provision of agricultural produce but also in providing manpower in the construction of infrastructure and participation in the war, and other colonial services. Wartime production directly transformed gender relations because of the re-organization of the land tenure system and labour relations. The consequence of this was an increased inclination towards what would later become an individual-based land tenure system. As many Gusii men joined the war and other forms of wage employment, women were left to maintain and sustain rural production. However, in promoting commercial agriculture, the colonial government targeted men leaving out women who were traditionally in charge of cultivated land. The colonial state believed that compared to men, women were conservative and were neither willing nor able to adopt new methods of cultivation.[27]

Despite the official acknowledgement of the negative impact the withdrawal of male labour had on rural production, nothing was ever done to rectify the situation. The situation continued to deteriorate as more individuals, both men and women, moved out of the reserves for wage employment and formal education.[28] It is no wonder that African production continued to be outdone by settler agriculture, which not only had cheap labour at its disposal but also government-friendly policies.[29] Therefore, the food shortage experienced in 1942-43 was both a result of the war demands and the cumulative effects of discriminatory colonial agricultural policies.[30] Thus, the continued negligence of African producers especially in the high-producing areas such as Gusii resulted in the occurrence of the 1942-1943 famine. Thus, having been denied the right to grow inedible cash crops such as coffee, pyrethrum and tea, the Africans, especially the women, continued to produce food crops that were meant to supplement the war efforts but under changing gender relations.[31]

27 Lovett, M. (1989). Gender Relations, Class Formation and Colonial State in Africa. In J. L. Parpart, & K. Staudt, (Eds.), Women and the State in Africa. London: Lynne Publishers.

28 Robertson, C (1995). Women in the urban economy in Hay, J. M & Stichter, S. (eds) African women South of the Sahara. New York: Longman publishing.

29 Ibid

30 Zeleza, T. (1992). The colonial Labour system in Kenya. An Economic History of Kenya (eds.) Ochieng' W.R. and Maxon R M.

31 KNA/BV/1/31: 1943-44

From archival sources, it is evident that since the movement of people was restricted during the war, men labourers were forced to remain in their workstations for longer periods than was previously the case.[32] Men's absenteeism in the reserves meant that the bulk of the agricultural labour fell on women. Eventually, as much as more men migrated to urban centres in search of employment, women too took part in this mobility but in a smaller number compared to men. Thus, the importance of women's labour during the war is evident by the control of their movement.

Barnes[33] points out that controlling the women's movement was not just to prevent them from selling their produce but also due to other factors. Here, the main reason was rising social and economic demand where a significant number of the women who had gone out to work were not returning to their rural homes. This created a big gap in labour supply as well as the general agricultural production in the reserve.

Furthermore, the demand for food supplies during World War II also led to a greater demand for the supply of cattle and other agricultural produce. Due to the increased demand, the colonial state took to encouraging the Gusii to sell more cattle to meet the needs of the war. The state however realised that voluntary cattle sale was not meeting the needs of the war and it started forced auctioning of cattle. This led to the sale of large numbers of cattle so that by 1945, almost ten thousand heads of cattle had been involuntarily sold.[34] This particularly affected the Gusii gender relations as regards marriage and dowry payment as discussed later in this chapter.

Increased Demand for Agricultural Production and the War Efforts in Kisii

The World War II period saw the British interested more in the increase of cereal production, the sale of cattle and the acquisition of migrant labour both for civil works and military services. This was a result of the wartime need to feed allied forces in Ethiopia and Egypt. European settlers' agriculture during this period enjoyed relative prosperity as World War II provided market opportunities for the farmers to produce and sell more agricultural produce.

---

32 KNA/CS/1/2/21, 1952)
33 Selhausen, Felix Meier Zu; Weisdorf, Jacob (2016). "A colonial legacy of African gender inequality? Evidence from Christian Kampala, 1895–2011". *The Economic History Review*. 69 (1): 229–257.
34 Maxon R.M Going their Separate Ways.

Furthermore, the settlers were able to influence statutory boards and committees, which they were now part of and which controlled agricultural and marketing policy [35]

In 1942, the Production of Crops Ordinance was promulgated by the colonial government. The ordinance guaranteed European settlers minimum prices for scheduled crops, also minimum return per acre, and free government grants for bringing new land into crop production. The scheduled crops included wheat, maize, rye, flax, oats, rice, rubber, barley, potatoes, pyrethrum, and vegetable seeds.[36] Though, initially, indigenous African crops were not guaranteed minimum prices, this did not deter the African people from producing those crops.

The colonial state also ensured that it provided good prices for wartime agricultural produce, especially maize as a motivation for increased production. In December 1941, maize prices were increased from the previous 4.50 shillings to 8.50 per 200-pound bag. Later, the prices were revised to 9 shillings in 1942 and later to 13 shillings per bag.[37]

The colonial state agents, on their part, called for an increase of the acreage under food crops in the Kisii Reserve while calling for the intensified cultivation of food crops like sweet potatoes and *wimbi* as buffer crops against famine, Furthermore, the colonial state reached out to women in Kisii to increase maize production. If only the increased maize production would increase the chances of rescuing the emerging subsistence crisis in Kisii. However, the controlled market saw women shun formal marketing avenues. Oral interviews indicated that the women after realizing that they would sell their maize to their Luo and Kericho neighbours at better prices diverted most of their produce from the controlled market.

It should be noted that from 1941 onwards, the colonial state launched a maize expansion campaign in Gusii which resulted in increased land surface for cultivation that reduced other crops' surface area for cultivation.[38] The colonial state was faced with an urgent challenge of ensuring increased production forcing it to temporarily suspend the soil conservation campaign that had begun in the 1930s in the Kisii highlands. The soil conservation efforts were to utilize communal labour yet the labour base in Kisii was

35 R. M. Maxon , Agriculture , in William R. Ochieng: (Ed) 1990, *Themes in Kenyan History* Heinemann Kenya Limited,Naairobi.32
36 KNA/ DOA /AR, 1942:1.
37 Anderson and Throup, The Myth of the War as a Watershed, 335
38 Moses Ogega , 89, Masige Bobasi

depleted by the war conscriptions. The Department of Agriculture in 1943 urged for increased production in Kisii with a specific increase sought in maize production,[39] as it was indicated that the position in respect of foodstuff supplies was not satisfactory for the year that ended as the quantity produced and sold through the state recognized formal channels had declined.[40]

In February 1942, the colonial state issued a circular to the effect that all maize be mopped out of the African native reserves starting with the Kisii Reserve. The circular called upon the 'natives' (Gusii women in this case) to release the maximum amount of maize in their possession. With colonial state machinery directed towards getting more maize from the Kisii Reserve, the colonial state was determined to mop up the maize produced by the Gusii women and leave them with little or nothing. This is a confirmation that the colonial state was never interested in the well-being of Gusii women from the onset. The evidence is when the colonial state through the circular demanded that the women release all the maize in their possession and their families to consume alternative foods. This informed the response by the Gusii women to shift from maize farming to root crops such as sweet potatoes and cassava as they controlled the use of the land during the Second World War.

Furthermore, during this period, the Gusii were also experiencing good harvests and guaranteed prices for their maize and finger millet that they sold to their neighbours especially the Luo and the Kipsigis. They, therefore, had enough cash to pay taxes and make household purchases. Therefore, it can be stated that the colonial state was more interested in ensuring more food was produced to support the colonial office in the war efforts than soil conservation in the Kisii Reserve. Sir Robert Brook the colonial governor noted in his address to the nation at the break of the Second World War:

> ... the more reason then for all of us in Kenya to help Great Britain by every means in our power, ... that we continue to be self-sufficient in all essential foodstuffs and so far as we are able, we produce what Great Britain wants most.[41]

Sir Brook confirms that the interest of the colonial office in London overrode the interest of the African peasants in the African reserves, especially the women in the Kisii Reserve. In this case, the Gusii

39 KNA: PC/NZA/2/12/76
40 North Kavirondo Annual Agricultural Report, 1943
41 Harold Macmillan, The Blast of the War 1939-1945 (London, 1967). In Tiyambe Zeleza, "Kenya and the Second World War 1939-1950." In W.R. Ochieng', (eds), (1989), A Modern History of Kenya 1895-1980. Nairobi; Evans Brothers.

women were to bear the demands of the colonial state through food production as more land, according to Ochieng', was brought under cultivation in African areas like Kisii.

As well, new technologies were adopted to guarantee the food-sufficiency for the British in the war efforts[42] as ox-drawn ploughs were bought in the area.

In Gusii, the increase in land under agriculture was to the detriment of soil conservation and therefore, the 1943 famine in Kisii was a long-term manifestation of the massive pressure on the land by the Gusii women during the war which manifested itself in soil degradation and declining yields which in the long run resulted in the 1943 famine. Oral interviews indicated that Gusii women did not allow the land in the area to go unutilized to allow for soil restoration while their families were ravaged by hunger and famine.

State pressure to increase maize production continued being enhanced with the Nyanza Provincial Commissioner holding local meetings to encourage farmers to double or even triple their efforts in the cultivation of maize. The PC even coerced the colonial chiefs to push their subjects to plant more maize,[43] with limited results.

Because investment in increasing the productivity of family labour was only one of several investment opportunities open to men, they tended to try to maximize their family labour productivity with a minimum investment of their resources. Women, on the other hand, provided the bulk of the labour force for household reproduction, and were left with few economic opportunities beyond the limits of the household economy, and were thus almost completely reliant on that family sustenance sector. They therefore often demanded more investment in household agriculture than their husbands/fathers/brothers were willing to make.[44] This increased tension in many households, as members vied with each other for control of resources. Thus, to understand women's resource allocation in particular, we must analyze their insecurity relative to the market and relative to the men on whom they depended for essential capital and land resources.

The 1940s equally saw the Gusii wholly internalize the concept of individual ownership of property. The Gusii now started scrambling

---

42 Ochieng' William, 'Food Production in the Pre-Colonial Period,' in Themes in Kenyan History
43 KNA: PC/NZA/3/1/446
44 Sarah Nyanchama 85, Keumbu, Nyaribari Masaba,Nov 2019

for whatever land was remaining in the highlands.[45] There was a big rush in the individual ownership of land during this period though at that time the population density was not as high as in other parts of the country like Central and Western. Individuals started acquiring whatever land was remaining unoccupied just to increase their acreage for agricultural production.[46] Rose Ogega of Bobasi says that she saw her father, who was one of the prominent businessmen of the time, put boundaries to a hill that the community had left unoccupied as a source of herbal medicine and livestock grazing. Initially, he claimed that he was protecting it from any interference but eventually, he cleared the bushes and planted exotic trees that had been introduced by the whites. The land eventually became his private property.[47]

More significantly, women's access to subsistence and income was reduced through the emphasis on cash crop production and the increased male control over agricultural resources. In addition, the declining land base in Gusii compared to the 1930s resulted in small family holdings. Particularly, it was noted that farms owned by young families were getting smaller over time. Both subsistence and cash crop production had to be based on these small holdings. Further, agricultural studies in some areas of Gusii showed that, on average, one-third of the total acreage was taken up by cash crops such as coffee, tea, and pyrethrum.[48] Thus the decline in farm size made subsistence plots smaller and smaller, which affected women more than men since the latter did not contribute much to the children or household upkeep. Milkah moraa indicated that her mother who initially produced a lot of maize with surplus for sale could not get much for sale when their father took more of their family land to plant coffee.[49]

In initial situations where land was in abundance and the social organization of the society ensured that women held secure structural positions, women's right to access to land was secure. However, the war period saw increased land use and the transformed land tenure and agrarian changes that accompanied it. Women gradually lost the security and the utility power they had hitherto enjoyed. Their inability to get access other than through the status

45 Orvis: Agrarian Question, 219
46 R. M. Maxon: Going Their Separate Ways.251
47 Rose Kemunto Ogega, 94. January 2020
48   Kongstad, P. & Monsted, M. (1980). *Family Labour and Trade in Western Kenya.* Uppsala: Scandinavian Institute of African Studies.
49 Milkah Moraa Nyangweso. 84 Bobasi January 2020

of a wife, and the inability to inherit land, adversely affected their future land rights. The whittling away of women's land rights by the changes instituted by the subsequent periods was a direct result of the colonial imposition of land use policies that favoured men and women's disabilities arising from the customary rules of inheritance and the customary division of labour which had resulted in women not being able to acquire land for themselves. As noted by Whitehead & Tsikata:

> "Most rural African women play a substantial part in primary agricultural production, making the complex of local norms, customary practices, statutory instruments and laws that affect their access to and interests in a land very significant not only to them, their dependents and their male relatives, but also arguably to levels of agricultural production"[50]

The principles of obligation and responsibility under African land tenure guaranteed women's access to land and control over certain food crops. However, the colonial Second World War intrusion brought inherent conflict between the European-managed systems and the traditional economies.[51] Thus women's ownership, control and use of land got modified by a major intrusion of colonialism in the Second World War, accompanied by capitalist relations of production and reproduction. Colonial land reforms introduced male domination in income-generating agriculture with the introduction of cash crop farming in the 1930s.

According to Nasimiyu[52] since the production of cash crops and subsistence crops were directly linked to the access to land, women were confronted with a whole range of handicaps in fulfilling their role as primary producers. Lack of control over land and all that goes with it became a major cause of women's economic dependence and marginalization. Without land, women were reduced to a state of dependency with no security. As more land was reserved for cash crops, women became increasingly reliant on cash to buy food they could no longer produce and turned their labour to cash crop production the monetary benefits of which were reserved for men.

---

50 Whitehead, A & Tsikata, D. (2003). "Policy Discourses on Women's Land Rights in sub-Saharan Africa: The Implications of the Return to the Customary. Journal of Agrarian Studies, 3 (1-2), 67-112.
51 Munro, J. F. (1968). *The Machakos Akamba Under British Rule, 1889-1939: A Study of Colonial Impact*. Ph.D Thesis, University of Wisconsin.
52 Ruth, N. (1985). Women in the Colonial Economy of Bungoma: Role of Women in Agriculture, in Women and Development In Africa 56-73 (G.S. Were ed.)

Thus, colonialism in the word of Kossok[53] was not only a question of simple integration, assimilation, and accumulation but was a complex dialectic change in the relations of the mode of production and social political class struggle and existing gender relations. These colonial initiatives altered the existing indigenous land use mechanisms that allowed women access to land for cultivation. Furthermore, it is also evident that, in the absence of men, settlers had to depend on women to provide the necessary labour to work on the farms for crop production. In Nyanza for instance, Owen argues that in 1944 women would not take part in the war because of the workload they were carrying. He aptly indicates:

> Women in the reserves are not able to do what is generally counted as war work, because owing to the absence of so many men from this reserve, the fieldwork and the upkeep of Kraals, and even the care of cattle, increasingly devolves upon the woman. All millet which this reserve has produced, not to speak of other food such as eggs and chicken, could never have been attained the bulk it has without the hard work of thousands of women and girls.[54]

Institutional and Statutory Production Control Measure and Policy Pronouncement During the War in Kisii

The outbreak of the war gave settlers a chance to control the colonial state by establishing a Settlement and Production Board in 1939[55] which coincided with the onset of the Second World War as the colonial state concentrated on the war. The sole function of the board was to coordinate the economic activities in the colony. This put the settlers at an opportune position in the wartime economy leading to the compromising of the production in the Kisii Reserve. Ochieng' notes that, during the Second World War, settlers achieved great influence on the statutory boards and committees which controlled agriculture and marketing policies[56]. This negatively affected women's use of land in Kisii.

---

53 Kossok, M. (1973). *Common Aspects and Distinctive Features in Colonial Latin America*. In *Science and Society 46* (1), Spring.
54 Owens L. O. letter to D.C. October 13, 1942, KNA as quoted in Ndeda, 1991:191
55 Tiyambe Zeleza, *Kenya and the Second World War 1939-1950* in W. R. Ochieng', (eds), (1989), A Modern History of Kenya 1895-1980. Nairobi: Evans Brothers.
56 Ochieng' William, 'Food Production in the Pre-Colonial Period,' in Themes in Kenyan History

The Resident Labourers' Ordinance passed in 1937[57] had given the settlers in Kericho and neighbouring areas an upper hand to control the African (Gusii) squatters on the settler farm which saw an extension of the days the Gusii squatters were to work in the Kericho settler areas to 180 days per annum. Further, the children of the Gusii squatters in Kericho under the provisions of the Ordinance were perpetually squatters as the settlers had to determine what the squatters were to produce and had direct control over the marketing of the produce of the squatters.

In 1942, the Governor established the Civil Defence and Supply Council. The council was made up of eight members, six unofficial members, all of whom were settlers and two colonial state officials. This civil defence was a system of defensive measures designed to protect civilians and their property from enemy attack. In addition, it was to solicit war supplies. The domination of the Council by settlers consolidated their position for labour procurement for themselves. The settlers influenced the state to their advantage as both the colonial state and the colonial office concentrated on the war efforts than the internal wrangles within the colony.

The Emergency Power Act passed in 1939 by the British Government gave the settlers a leeway to appropriate the colonial state to themselves. The Act provided that all constitutional approaches were suspended with the outbreak of the war which was equally applicable to the colonies. The Emergency Powers Act of 1939 was an emergency legislation passed just before the outbreak of World War II by the Parliament of the United Kingdom to enable the British Government to take up emergency powers to prosecute the war effectively. It contained clauses giving the government wide powers to create Defense Regulations that regulated almost every aspect of everyday life in the country.

Furthermore, even though coffee growing of coffee was overshadowed as both the state and the Gusii farmers concentrated on food crop production, the coffee that was planted in the 1930s made production keep increasing, gradually, as the coffee plants were maturing. Moreover, the prices of coffee were so good that the Gusii farmers found themselves with a lot of returns from the sales. In addition, the local Native Council took over the sale of the coffee produce and the payment of the farmers was done through

<hr>

57 Tabitha Kanogo, (1987). Squatters and the Roots of Mau Mau. London: James Currey. See also Gavin Kitching, (1980). Class and Economic Change in Kenya. London:Yale University Press.

its official accounts that were managed by the Colonial Agricultural Officers. Equally, to improve efficiency in coffee production, in 1943, the DC forced the creation of a Coffee Board whose Chairman was the District Agricultural Officer for South Kavirondo. The board took over the management of coffee from the Local Native Council. The Board eventually developed into a Co-operative Society in 1946 with Senior Chief Musa Nyandusi as the Chairman and the District Agricultural Officer as the Patron. Initially, the majority of the coffee growers were chiefs as well as men with some form of education and religious exposure. Women, however, were left behind as they were never made chiefs nor did they have formal education.[58]

In 1942, the colonial state decreed that all maize produced in Kisii was to be sold to the Maize Control Board established on 1st July 1942.[59] The board was to fix the maize prices in advance for African maize from Gusii and other areas. As already shown, the colonial state policy to mop up maize from the African native reserves was partially responsible for the 1943 famine in Gusii and other areas. The colonial state issued a circular in February 1942, to the effect that all maize be mopped out of the African native Reserves starting with the Kisii reserve. The circular read:

> The government's most immediate and urgent problem is to ensure that sufficient rations are made available for native labour working in the towns, railways and in essential farming industries and for the troops. In all these cases the maintenance of essential services is dependent on the daily ration. Wherever, therefore, there is any surplus maize available most urgent steps should be taken to place it immediately at the disposal of the control and to impress upon the natives in the reserves the importance of using alternative foodstuffs and releasing the maximum amount of maize possible.[60]

Market and Price Incentives in Gusii War Production

For the Gusii, the 1940s were times of significant transformation in their agrarian economy. There was an increase in the sale of agricultural products as well as increased migrant labour. This was the result of the emphasis put in place by the colonial government on the production of more cereals for the war as well as the

---

58 Ibid
59 Ian Spencer. "settler Dominance, Agricultural Production and the Second World War in Kenya." In Journal of African History 21 (1980)
60 KNA:PC/NZA/3/2/8. Secretariat Circular Letter No. 16, confidencial, 16 February 1943. In Robert Maxon. (2003). Going Their Separate Ways: Agrarian Transformation in Kenya, 1930-1950. London: Associated University Press

solicitation of direct labour for the war. The increased demand for Gusii agricultural produce in the war period due to increased demand saw the Gusii becoming more responsive to the increased market availability.

The increased sale of cereal products, in turn, motivated the people to increase production and expand the acreage under the plough. Consequently, the 1940s saw the Gusii sell their maize produce at attractive prices. Consequently, market forces influenced the community to expand the acreage of maize production. However, as the prices kept fluctuating, the low price season made Gusii farmers shift to the growing of finger millet whose market was always locally available and fetched good prices.[61] However, the colonial government introduced the Maize and Finger Millet Control Policy that put in place restrictions on the marketing of finger millet while promoting the sale of maize. This led to increased demand for maize during the war. However, as much as the colonial government encouraged the production of maize, the crop remained in short supply between 1942 and 1943 as the war raged on.

It has been noted that the colonial state's maize expansion campaign of 1942 was responsible for the 1943 famine in Kisii.[62] The Department of Agriculture targeted to increase maize production in Kisii for the war needs. As Ndege writes, while the Gusii women were responsive to market opportunities[63] in the area, they reacted to the assured prices for their produce by enlarging the land under cultivation[64].

Gusii women also secretly sold their maize to the areas of Kericho and Luo Nyanza at higher prices than those set by the state.[65] These sales though on a small scale cushioned the women's source of income and helped boost their sources of livelihoods and gave them some form of independence in handling matters of food security and other household matters.

Therefore, the Gusii community's response to market forces engendered household structures that reflect what Makana refers to

61 South Kavirondo Agricultural officer's Report 1942: KNA/DC/KSI/3/66
62 Robert Maxon. (2003). Going Their Separate Ways: Agrarian Transformation in Kenya, 1930-1950. London: Associated University Press.
63 Robert Maxon, "Fantastic Prices" in the Midst of "An Acute Food Shortage:" Market, Environment, and the Colonial State in the 1943 Vihiga (Western Kenya) Famine. In African Economic History, No.28. (2000), African Studies Program. Madison: University of Wisconsin.
64 Group discussion with Nyansongo Women Nyaribari Chache. Dec 2019
65 Agricultural Officer South Kavirondo, to the DC South Kavirondo. 18th January 1943. KNA: DC/KSI/OP/13/3

as embryonic processes of social differentiation and class formation in the rural Western Kenya region[66]. The peasant households became increasingly stratified as they accessed the market for their agricultural products and received capital from off-farm income. This supported their effort to hire manpower and ox ploughs which promoted an increase in production and expansion of acreage under farming. Women were still disadvantaged in this stratification as they lacked direct access to the returns from the sales of cash crops especially coffee,

Consequently, in the World War II period, Gusii witnessed a near-complete transformation of the process of social reproduction from the pre-World War II system based on cattle, wives and grain to straddling system based on men's off-farm income and its re-investment in household agriculture and education. The peasant community and peasant households created during the 1920s were thus further estranged by market integration, especially in the World War II period. The communal institutions where elders had control over young men, controlled communal labour groups and had inalienable land rights and controlled bride wealth were all but buttressed, with only the latter continuing to have limited economic importance. In their place had arisen a straddling system, in which men's off-farm income was combined with education and the intensification of household agricultural production via increased labour input, principally from women.

The exportation of male labour from Gusii also affected gender relations and consequently agricultural production. However, a full understanding of smallholders' insecurity requires an analysis of how straddling re-defined the positions of men and women within Gusii rural households. In the pre-World War II era, as discussed in chapter three, men and women were both fully dependent upon household agriculture for short and long-term needs. Despite the very unequal sexual division of labour, men were required to provide essential investment in agriculture to ensure the survival of their households. Under straddling, men's access to off-farm income freed them from short-term reliance on household agriculture. They could choose to invest in household agriculture or non-agricultural endeavours, or they could simply consume their wages.

---

66 Makana, N.E; Transformation of the peasant sector: The missing link in African Economic development. International Journal of Sustainable Development, Volume 1 number2, 2008, 32

The demand to satisfy the war needs and to cope with the economy that was increasingly involving cash, made communities abandon food crop production meant for subsistence in favour of marketable crops. This meant that households began to gradually turn to the market to satisfy their subsistence supplies.[67] However, the war made the government intervene in African production through the encouragement and distribution of cereal seeds to the farmers. This intervention was made necessary by the failure of the maize harvest in 1942, which caused widespread famine. The African communities were forced to rely on root crops such as cassava, hence the Gusii labelled this episode as the 'cassava famine' *(enchara ya emiogo')*.[68] The famine made the government start focusing on the agricultural problems in the reserves.[69] However, despite the recognition of agricultural problems in the areas occupied by African natives, the government did not take specific measures to solve them.

In this regard, analyzing the centrality of marriage for household reproduction allows us to understand the importance of marital instability in creating insecurity in rural households in the World War II period in Gusii. Consequently, increased tensions in the "conjugal contract" under straddling arose as the positions of men and women in the rural Gusii household became re-defined. This socio-economic situation gave men greater freedom from short-term reliance on household agriculture and increased household competition over resource control and usage, with men producing more cash crops while women were for increased subsistence production, which often resulted in marital instability.

At the family level, the men were unable to pay the much-prized bridewealth and cohabitation eventually became the norm rather than the exception. This created a lot of insecurity for the women. They knew that their marriages were not secure because they could be sent back to their homes in case anything happened. In Gusii's cultural setting, it is after the payment of dowry that a marriage was sealed. Non-payment of dowry meant that the woman was not entitled to access to land which would ensure the security of inheritance for her sons.

---

67 Robertson, C (1995). Women in the urban economy in Hay, J. M & Stichter, S. (eds) African women South of the Sahara. New York: Longman publishing.
68 Group interview of women from Botondo, Nyaribari Masaba
69 Robertson, C (1995)

War Time Technical and Technological Support to Gusii Production

The colonial state on the other hand ensured the provision of quality farm seeds, provision of markets, improved road networks and provision of extension services. The increased production of maize eventually led to challenges in storage and transportation. The Kisii area had few seasonal roads that made it difficult for farmers to transport their produce to the market for sale. On the other hand, there were limited market centres where the maize could be sold. An example is the high production of maize that took place at Ramasha to the Southern part of Gusii near Maasai land in 1942, yet there was no good road to transport the farm produce for sale in the neighbouring areas until the then District Commissioner started a market centre in the area and constructed a seasonal road that connected Ramasha to Keroka to allow for the easy transportation of the surplus Maize.

Further, with the support of the Colonial Agricultural Officers, the colonial state set up thirty-eight farm produce buying centres in South Kavirondo between 1942 and 1945 which helped in the sale of more agricultural produce.[70] The poor road network and lack of sufficient market centres, that had limited the region's potential for agricultural production, were therefore improved.

By the mid-1940s a large number of Gusii men were out on migrant labour, leaving their wives with increased agricultural and household tasks.[71] On the other hand, despite their labour, colonial policies tended to marginalize women not only in cash crop production but also in formal education. Gusii women were, however, presented with new socio-economic opportunities and openings in terms of increased marketing of their food crops and the creation of legal institutions for the advancement of their interests, especially for the protection of their sexual rights.[72] To sell their produce in the face of the poor road network, women used donkeys for ferrying heavy loads of maize and finger millet at home and even to markets thus increasing their income.[73] The sale of the food crops gave women some level of financial independence as they would use the money they got for personal and family use.[74]

---

70 11 Robert M. Maxon,1984. Going their Separate Ways. 224
71 Omwoyo, S. (2008). Assessing the Impact of Coffee Production on Abagusii Women in Western Kenya: A Historical Analysis (1900-1963). In C. W. Kitetu (Ed.), Gender, Science and Technology: Perspectives from Africa (156-167). Senegal. African Books Collective
72 KNA DC/KSl/1/2, 1913-1919.
73 KNA DC/KSl/1/2, 1913-1919.
74 Livingstone Asiago 96, Machoge Oct 2019

At the end of the war, African reserves started experiencing socio-economic problems, which made the colonial government attempt the reconstruction of African agricultural practices. Communal farming and individual land ownership, which were perceived as the best ways of reconstructing African areas had not succeeded.[75] Also, to a limited extent, colonial reconstruction was tried among African communities through the improvement of agricultural practices. Men were provided with incentives such as quality seeds and ox ploughs. Such government action enabled the men to enter the money economy as the only producers of commercial agricultural commodities and aided in denying women similar status. Consequently, a pattern was established whereby cash crop production was supervised by men and, consequently, its proceeds were controlled by men. Furthermore, the growth of commercial agriculture in the reserves generated increased demands for land and shaped people's strategies to gain access to the land.[76]

The war period also saw a great increase in the demand for formal education. The Gusii had not developed a meaningful interest in formal education before the war. This attitude changed substantially following the conclusion of the war, majorly because of the exposure of the ex-World War II servicemen to what was happening in other parts of the country and beyond. The increased demand for education made the chiefs demand the expansion of schools in their areas. For instance, the Local Native Council with the support of the DC supported the building of schools, and by 1946, Kereri School was started as one of the pioneer educational centres in Gusii.[77] Once more, those who benefited from this education were majorly men. Milka Nyanchama observes that her twin brother was taken to Nyanchwa Elementary School together with the brothers of her age-mate girls. Their mothers worked so hard to supplement their fathers' school fees efforts because they believed that educating a son gave a mother security as the son would take care of them in old age.[78] For women, therefore, while they were losing access to and usage of the land, they turned to educating their sons for a sense of future security.

75 Wangari, M. (2010). Gender Relations And Food Crop Production: A Case Of Kiambu District   Kenya, 1920-1985.
76 Berry, S. (1989). No Condition is permanent: The Social Dynamics of Agrarian Change in Sub- Sahara Africa. University of Wisconsin Press.
77 Gavin Kitching, Class and Economic Change in Kenya pg 277-299
78 Milka Nyanchama Obonyo.89 Nyaribari Chache, January 2020

The demand for education and off-farm income became the main entry points to household reproduction as the importance of women's labour and therefore bridewealth declined. Many households and family heads, with increased unpaid brideprice and sons who owed potential brideprice, tied the receipt and/or payment of brideprice directly to the perceived more important usages of income including savings for education, land purchase and improved housing facilities. Some amount of bridewealth, however, would almost certainly be transferred in all permanent marriages to ensure the rights of the husband's household over the children and eventual burial rights of the wife which was an important cultural activity in the Gusii society.[79]

Significantly, patriarchal African tendencies combined with biased colonial influences whittled away and eroded women's legal rights. This was done through the incorporation of traditional laws, that favoured males, into the new body of laws drawn up by the colonial administration, the later result of which would be the emergence of a new form of sexist colonial law.[80]

In Western Kenya regions such as Gusii, men were pulled into cash crop production for export,[81] while women were pushed into subsistence production. Their confinement to subsistence agriculture did not generate any new rights for women; rather, it increased their labour burdens and obligations for family support. Given that they were mainly confined to the rural areas within a network of communal relationships, it further increased their economic dependence. For instance, as Ochieng' notes, through a government policy, Gusii women and children were evicted from towns to offer [rural] agricultural labour[82]. Newman summarizes the position of women as follows: thus, in the post-war period, women lagged behind men in numerous ways; they had far less experience with the cash economy, were less educated, and had less technical training in 'modern' agricultural methods, and had suffered a serious loss of their social status.

From the beginning of the war period, women's rights over land became even more constrained and the woman's role was mainly to

79 Livingstone Asiago
80 Jane, P. (1986). *Women's Rights and the Lagos Plan of Action*, 8 HUM. RTS Q. 180
81 Falk M, S. (1996). Changing African Land Tenure: Reflections on the incapacities of the State, The European Journal of Development Research, 10; 2: 33-49.
82 T Zeleza Kenya and the Second World War, 1939-1950 in W.R. Ochieng' A Modern History of Kenya

fend for and produce food for the family. Thus, women were restricted to using land only for food production and rarely independently grew cash crops and had ownership to land. Grassroots Organisations Operating Together in Sisterhood (GROOTS NGO) Kenya,[83] avers that from the colonial period, women became more unduly disadvantaged with respect to the use, access to and/or control over land and other valuable property, both as members of a household or as heads of households. Cultural traditions and practices concerning women's use, access and control of land complicated this situation.

Gusii Women's Response to the War Complexities of Land Access, Use and Control

The colonial state did not understand the complex indigenous subsistence situation in Gusii which occasioned the decline of output in the area. Interestingly, since subsistence production in Gusii was under the purview of the women folk, they were more concerned with their subsistence production at a time when their husbands were absent and not concerned with the output for war.[84] This was despite the colonial state's call to upscale the output of maize by all means.

In reality, the colonial state amplified what the women in Kisii had already done to avert an impending crop failure. As noted by the women in oral interviews, the women extensively engaged in the cultivation of sorghum, sweet potatoes and cassavas as well as *sim sim* and millet.

While the set market prices reflected an increase intended to attract the maize produced by the Gusii women, it failed to achieve the results intended. Gusii women shied away from the capitalized commercial markets and reverted to their traditional economy of affection.[85] This was informed by the reality that the available women's labour did not permit much engagement beyond subsistence. In any case, the labour was both limited quantitatively and gender-biased. This pushed the Gusii women to spread the subsistence security risk by diversifying their subsistence production base away from the colonial state-compelled maize production.

In spreading their subsistence risk security measures, the Gusii women in 1940 experiencing adverse climatic conditions decided

83 Grassroots Organisations Operating Together in Sisterhood (GROOTS) Kenya (2012).
84 Kemunto Nyamasege,86. Bomachoge. Nov 2019. Also group interview with Bonchari women
85 Group discussion with women of Tabaka in South Mogirango

to engage in early planting caused by early rains. With dry spells provoking their immediate subsistence response mechanisms, the Gusii women planted more expansively than [they had done] previously.[86] The women's efforts during this period bore fruits when maize was ready for consumption in April,[87] a result that forestalled a mid-war food crisis in 1940 and 1941.

This unique cycle produced a bumper harvest and the Gusii women were sensitive to their ethics. Instead of selling their maize produce to the Control Board, they withdrew from the market and withheld their produce as insurance against future crop failure. However, this marketing practice was later widespread and continued throughout the 1940s, with the largest export of maize realized in 1944.[88]

The year 1942 and early 1943 were tough times for Gusii women in the Kisii Reserve. The area saw widespread famine that affected the state and the Gusii women in their reserves. Although the famine was due to ecological conditions,[89](there was a prolonged drought), the environmental causes were not adequate to trigger the famine in Kisii. According to Maxon and the Annual Report of 1943, in the Kisii Reserve, many households had given up on the short rains and begun to break the land with hopes that the long rains might be early. While it is true that rain failure caused crop failure, crop failure substantially meant maize failure.[90] The maize failure in Kisii was a threat to the colonial state in its war supplies efforts and food insecurity for the Gusii women back in the Kisii Reserve as maize had become the stable food for Kisii households, but *mtama* and *wimbi* were also produced advantageously, and rescued Gusii homes, as these had proper co-ordination by women cultivators.[91]

When the Agricultural Officer reported that the Gusii women had given up on the short rains in the area and started breaking land in preparation for the long rains, oral interviews indicated that the Gusii women swiftly reacted after the breaking of the land by planting famine-resistant crops which would take a shorter time to mature and intervene in the situation supplementing small portions of maize.[92] The Agricultural Officer, however, did not report

---

86 Robert Maxon. (2003). Going Their Separate Ways: Agrarian Transformation in Kenya, 1930-1950. London: Associated University Press
87 Group discussion with Bobasi and Bomachoge women
88 South Kavirondo Administration Report. 1944 KNA:DC/KSI/1/6
89 Colony and Protectorate of Kenya, (1943) Food Shortage Commission of Inquiry Report, 1943. Nairobi: Government Printer.
90 Ibid.
91 Group interview of Kitutu Chache Women Nov 2019
92 Colony and Protectorate of Kenya, (1943) Food Shortage Commission of Inquiry

on the crops that were planted after the breaking of the land. This is attributable to the position that the Gusii women, during the war, shied away from maize to produce root crops and other indigenous cereals that were not foods that would contribute to the war efforts and therefore, not worth colonial state recognition.

Thus, notwithstanding the 1942 short rains failure, the Gusii women were active in the January 1943 breaking of the land and eventual planting[93] amid a dry spell. The little January and February rains of 1943 relieved the Gusii women's root crops but, the disappearance of the rains afterwards negatively affected the maize in the area.[94] The situation changed in May as the root crops were ready for harvesting and consumption.[95] Therefore, the Gusii women never alienated themselves from affirming their role in controlling and utilizing the land in the absence of their husbands and during a famine scare evidenced by the increased volumes of *wimbi* and *mtama* which quickly substituted for the staple maize.

As discussed, the Gusii women reacted by planting more root crops and less maize which doubled up as cover crops for the soil. This proactive reaction to the 1943 famine was a reflection of the Gusii women's land control and utility in ensuring subsistence security without necessarily caving into colonial state pressure to produce maize for the war.

The partial failure of rains and the invasion of locusts in the Kavirondo region threatened food security further making the Gusii women store whatever surplus food they had to be used during the times of need. Furthermore, unlike many parts of Kavirodo, Gusii was not badly affected by the locust invasion. The Gusii, therefore, sold large quantities of finger millet to the Luo and Maasai who had been more badly affected by the locusts.

In Gusii, in the 1940s the population had not reached a level that would lead to massive soil erosion and land degradation. Furthermore, the Gusii had evolved indigenous agricultural techniques that minimized soil erosion, especially in areas with steep slopes that are common in Gusii. The people established contour terraces with shrubs on the slopes to prevent erosion and movement of soil, especially during heavy rain seasons. In addition,

Report, 1943. Nairobi: Government Printer, This was also observed by Boncharo women in a group interview at Suneka,Nov 2019.

93 Robert Maxon. (2003). Going Their Separate Ways: Agrarian Transformation in Kenya, 1930-1950. London: Associated University Press.

94 Ibid.

95 Thomas Nyaanga 90, Bobasi Dec 2019.

the people planted their crops on shallowly cultivated land and kept slashing the undergrowth weeds until their food matured thus reducing exposure of the topsoil to soil erosion during the heavy rains,[96] In livestock grazing, the Colonial Agricultural Officer observed in 1945 that the Gusii grazed their animals on hilltops and valley bottoms leaving the sloppy areas for crop farming[97] The Gusii also constructed trash lines as they planted their crops. In 1941, when asked whether there was a need to move the Gusii to other parts of Southern Kavirondo for settlement, DC Thompson responded that there was still land to spare in most parts of the Gusii highland.[98]The government, therefore, found the promotion of soil conservation in Gusii relatively manageable as reported by the District Agricultural Officers from 1943 up to 1945.[99]

However, the continuous tilling and cultivation of the same plots for production by Gusii women led to soil degradation and eventual soil erosion in the Kisii highlands which inevitably culminated in the 1943 famine. With the onset of famine, the Gusii women prioritized subsistence crops more so root crops as they avoided growing maize[100] which they would have been forced to sell through the established board. The shift by the Gusii women from maize production defined the nature of the 1943 famine in Kisii as caused by the perceived fear of locust invasion from the neighbouring Sotik area. Conventionally in Kisii, the possibility of famine preceded locust invasion which made the Gusii women initiate locust containment measures by planting root crops as opposed to maize.[101]

The increase in the sale of maize and cattle as well as the money brought in through wage labour led to the availability of relatively greater amounts of cash in Gusii. There were, however, limited consumer goods to buy due to the effects of World War II.[102] Those men who had accumulated money started paying higher brideprice for the wives they married above what was the norm. This led to a general increase in dowry payments in the community. However, the high dowry required would only be afforded by a few men who had accumulated wealth. Thus, the majority of the young men who were of age to marry could not afford the stipulated dowry. Some young

96 DC SK TtoPC NP 3 November1937, KNA; p/nza/3/28/30
97 R. M. Maxon,Going Their Separate ways,256
98 SK Ag AR 1941, KNA; AK/2/33.
99 AAO SK, Safari Diary,12-13 Oct 1943 KNA AK/21/34 and AAO SK Safari Diary
      30 May-6 June 1945 KNA;AK/25/34
100 Ibid.
101 Group interview with Bonchari women , Oct 2019
102 SKAR 1945, KNA:DC/KSI/1.7

men opted for unorthodox means such as the forceful kidnapping of women for wives in what came to be famously referred to as *ogokurura*[103] (hijacking of women), a practice that had never existed before. Women, on the other hand, waited for their suitors to get dowry for such a long period until they eventually agreed to elope with the men to start families and get security to access and use land. More so the women were scared of the social stigma since no woman of marriageable age was allowed to continue staying in her parent's home.[104]

Conclusion

The chapter has analyzed gender relations in Gusii within the context of colonial agrarian and military policies dictated by the occurrence of the Second World War. It has emerged in the chapter that the Second World War saw the colonial government place emphasis on a cash economy forcing Africans either to produce commodities for sale or join wage labour. This led to increased production of maize as well as cash crops such as coffee, tea and pyrethrum. The pressure for increased production of these crops made the Gusii put the available land into more use, especially in the production of cash crops which led to a hunger for land, both for men and women, leading to strained relationships over the access, use and ownership of the land. Moreover, the improved tools of farming such as the plough which was now in good supply led to more land being put into crop farming. This also led to the strain on labour relations of production as household labour, which was largely a women's purview, was overstretched. Specifically, the women had to work harder to produce more to meet both the demands of the colonial government and for subsistence.

Further, we have shown in the chapter that women got some form of control over agricultural production when their husbands were away for wage-related work. They controlled the tilling of the land, and planting, harvesting and sale of their farm produce while the men were away. Being the managers of their homes gave women some independence to use the money they got from selling their harvests as they wished. Also, it was during the war period that continuous land use throughout the year began as available land for farming was getting limited. The use of land through all seasons would lead to land degradation and other related land problems

103   Group discussion with women of Nyaribari Chache. November 2019
104   Norah Mainga 85, Riokindo Bomachoge Dec 2019

that prompted the colonial state to put in place measures for land conservation. The war brought major social and economic changes that eventually affected both the social relations in Gusii households in particular and the rural economy in general. These effects would be felt way beyond 1945 into the 1950s and 60s as will be discussed in the next chapter.

Chapter Six

Post WWII Agrarian Reform Agenda and its Impact Upon Gender Relations in Kisii 1945-1960

Introduction

The period of World War II saw the Gusii transition into a more capitalistic economy, as detailed in the previous chapter. The colonial state's pressure to produce more agricultural products for the war resulted in more land being put under the plough in Gusii. It further led to the overuse of the land that would lead to land degradation compelling the colonial state to explore measures to boost soil conservation. Increased demand for production led to increased demand for labour supply which made more Africans and, specifically, Gusii men become migrant workers. The current chapter focuses on the post-World War II agrarian trajectory/reform and the impact it has on gender relations in Gisii. The chapter details the post-war agricultural reconstruction course, the Swynnerton Llan in the Kisii area having intensified agricultural production through increasing the land under cultivation of cash crops. In addition, it examines the increased attention given to maize production for the market and, in equal measure, evaluates the greater attention directed to agricultural training institutions like Siriba and how credit to farmers, through loans and rewards, was executed. Land kleptocracy in Kisii, as well as the gendered land relations in the area, is detailed. The chapter, further, examines how the pre-independence dynamics played out in Gusii with the futile attempts by colonial authorities to resolve the gendered Gusii problem among them being the scramble for land, land tenure complexities as well as land degradation. The chapter then analyzes how the agricultural and land dynamics impacted women's access, control and utilization of land in the period preceding Kenya's independence.

Post WW II Colonial Agrarian Reform and its Implications for Kisii, 1945-1960

The end of the Second World War left the British government with a debt of £600 million. After the war, Britain, like many other European nations, found her economy shattered. Billions worth of her imports and exports, machinery and even revenue had been sunk in the war effort. Almost £900 million in depreciation needed to be recovered. It was estimated that Britain needed to raise her exports to 175% of her pre-war levels to recover from the post-war economic mess.

After 1945, Britain's dominance in the capital export market was taken over by the USA, while a large number of British colonies were becoming a burden to sustain. As well, Britain had to find ways of making the colonies productive as sources of revenue. In the Kenya colony, a ten-year Development Plan in 1946 was formulated to speed up economic expansion as a comprehensive scheme was also started to investigate the problems of African areas like Kisii by establishing agricultural investigation centres[1].

Considering the size and the enormous contribution of the Kisii area to the agricultural output of Nyanza Province, and the conservatism and illiteracy of the inhabitants and the staff available, it was obvious that rapid improvement in farming methods through agricultural training[2] was a major approach for sustaining the production trend. While this highlights the imperative for agricultural training in Kisii, the study affirms that the increasing interest by the Gusii women in agricultural production, and the growing confidence between them and the district agricultural staff, as the provincial report observed, were the most encouraging signs[3] in agricultural progress in Kisii. In general terms, the Assistant Director of Agriculture reported that the Kisii area was in a very critical progressive stage and it was thus hoped that building up more agricultural training centres would be imperative for more catalytic and robust production in the area. With the establishment of a new agricultural training centre in Kisii, which opened in 1960, the tempo of agricultural development in Kisii in particular and the province at large increased. Mr. T. Hughes-Rice, the Assistant Director of Agriculture observed that this was due to the improved

1 R.J.M Swynnerton, (1955). A Plan to Intensify the Development of African Agriculture in Kenya. Nairobi, Government Printetrs.
2 KNA:PC/NZA/1/45 Nyanza Annual Provincial Report 1950
3 KNA:PC/NZA/1/54 Nyanza Annual Provincial Report 1958

spirit of Gusii women and their cooperation in agricultural training, and their determination to increase agricultural output, more so, of a subsistence nature. This was confirmed in 1959 when the annual report showed that good progress was being made by Gusii women in general farm management with an increasing desire on their part to produce more and of better quality[4]. The eminence of Gusii women in agriculture was therefore evidenced by their cooperation with the agricultural training initiative, which previously did not exist and now was becoming apparent. With the further establishment of the Siriba Diploma Agricultural Training College in 1961,[5] agricultural training in Kisii was on a firm footing and accounted for increased production by women in the area. At Siriba, training in sound patterns of Kisii farm layout became customary and the practice was first spreading in the area, courtesy of the trainees, the majority of who were women. The simply planned farm layouts provided useful examples to their neighbours which not only countered soil erosion but enhanced crop production in the area[6], in addition to farm planning and layout, farm-enclosure and general methods of farm husbandry, where planting had evolved with training to universal rows. Equally, manuring and better weeding were widely learned and acknowledged by the Gusii women as better and more productive farm practices. Due to this training, a record production of maize was recorded, principally due to the extra time the Gusii women invested in their farms as recommended in their training. Besides the extensive production of maize by Gusii women, the Kisii highlands continued to be the main coffee-producing area in Nyanza Province as evidenced by the continued increase in acreage under coffee. With these developments, the rural reserves, as exemplified by Kisii, were poised to remain an important factor in the economic recovery of Britain.[7]

Another key facet of Britain's post-WWII economic recovery strategy that would exercise a direct impact on Gusii was the policy geared towards the encouragement of multinational corporate capital. To this end, Britain allowed direct foreign investments in the Kenya colony through multilateral institutions. Consequently, multinational organizations like James Finlay were allowed to venture into industrial development in areas like Kisii with plantation agriculture and extractive industries meant to fill the void

4   KNA: PC/NZA/1/55 Annual Provincial Agricultural Report 1959.
5   KNA: PC/NZA/1/56 Annual Provincial Agricultural Report 1960.
6   KNA: PC/NZA/1/55 Annual Provincial Agricultural Report 1959.
7   W. R. Ochieng. Themes in Kenyan History, 126.

left by the collapse of the importation of processed foods. According to Fearn, the demand for imported goods was stimulated by the presence of the tea industry in Kericho and Kisii[8], which increased the purchasing power of the locals. As will be demonstrated in subsequent sections of this chapter, such encouragement of cash crop-oriented agricultural enterprise rendered land a prime resource and presaged greater contestation over it among the Gusii.

The period covered by this chapter also witnessed restive African nationalism in British colonies. In an attempt to placate Africans within their colonies, the British colonial office came up with development and welfare programmes like loans and grants to cater to the situation and permitted financial support for programmes developed in colonies as demonstrated by the Swynnerton plan.

It was envisaged that, through such programmes, the colonies would be empowered to help in the reconstruction of the British economy. In 1947, the colonial state in Kenya declared that there was a need to reduce expenditure, expand agricultural production and increase import substitution industrialization.[9] The post-World War II hunger for food and raw materials prompted the colonial state to tilt away from settler agriculture. For this reason, the 1950s saw the colonial state compel the Gusii to escalate production as was indeed the case in other parts of the colony. The state made efforts to promote food and cash crop production in the area.

As such, the period after WWII saw the colonial government embark on reforming African agriculture. The Worthington Plan, for instance, was drawn to run for 10 years from 1946.[10] It was funded by the African Land Development (ALDEV) Programme which targeted African agriculture, especially the restoration of soil fertility for specific reasons. According to the plan, the problem facing African areas like Gusii was not overpopulation but mismanagement of soil. Under the plan, ALDEV was to limit the number of stock kept and the growth of cash crops in the African reserves[11]. In the Kisii area, it was necessary to restore soil fertility to avoid a recurrence of food shortage as had been experienced during the war. Therefore, money was directed toward soil conservation projects such as terracing, manuring and systematic culling. Farming according to s good soil

8 H. Fearn, (1961). An African Economy: A Study of the Economic Development of the Nyanza Province of Kenya 1903-1953. London. Oxford University Press. 155.
9 Kenya Colony Annual Report, Government printer, Nairobi, 1947,4
10 P. T. Zeleza, Dependent Capitalism, 269-270
11 Van Zwanenberg, 1975

conservation practices did solve the problem of soil conservation,[12] though. The Gusii were encouraged to produce not only to meet their subsistence needs but also to have a surplus for export that would help the colonial state invest in the reconstruction effort at home.

The urgent necessity for the introduction of better farming practices throughout the African areas was never far from the minds of the officers chiefly concerned with the matter.[13] In Kisii, bench terracing was taken as the major way of reducing soil erosion where real stress on land was manifest. Leslie Brown and Colin Maher, officials in the agricultural department, advocated for broad-based terracing. This, according to two, although difficult to construct, would provide more permanent defences against soil erosion and reduce the burden of communal terracing.[14]

In Kisii, these officers sought to create a stratum of prosperous smallholders who practised mixed farming rotations and were allowed to grow high-value cash crops on permanent bench terraces, while domestic food crops were concentrated on the tops of ridges. The agricultural soil conservation campaigns in Kisii coincided with Gusii women's ambitions, [thus] offering them [opportunities] for higher living standards[15]. In practice, the campaign was dominated by bench terracing since all those to be considered progressive had to protect the soil on their slopes.

By 1947, thrash lines with guidance from agricultural department staff enhanced soil conservation efforts. The construction of these thrash lines soon became a pre-condition for permission to cultivate such high-value crops like coffee. Unlike in 1943, when the use of thrash lines was concentrated in North Mogirango, 1947 saw the thrash line use widely accepted and used in the entire Kisii for soil conservation. As acknowledged by the SAO, "work on thrash lines was proceeding well and there was progressive improvement in the work".[16] However, being a communal undertaking, both men and women were required to devote two mornings a week to the task. The work had no pay and absentees were liable to fines. The chiefs and headmen, as exemplified by senior chief Musa Nyandusi, were required to meet a specific target of workers which made them resort to coercion to achieve the targeted labour.

12 Prisca Tanui Differential Gender Access to Agricultural Resources in Kenya
13 KNA: PC NZA/1/46. 1951 Nyanza Provincial Annual Report.
14 Throup D. 1988 Economics & Social Origins of Mau Mau 1945-53
15 Mary Mong'ina, 85 years Bomachoge.
16 SAO NP, QR first quarter 1947 KNA:PC/NZA/3/2/89

In effect, this programme disrupted and disenfranchised the Gusii agricultural labour orientation. The impact of terracing was severely felt by persons who had small pieces of land, as a huge portion would be taken up by the terraces. For women, the whole exercise was backbreaking as a majority engaged in the exercise in the absence of the men. To avoid being enlisted, women used all sorts of excuses. Furthermore, a steady advance was made in the protection of the soil in the area by the use of grass contour strips at regular intervals in cultivated fields. This was achieved by laying thrash lines and constructing terraces. The greatest success was seen in the Kisii highlands with trash lines being very evident, and some lands now had achieved distinct terraces by soil banking up behind the trash lines[17].

The colonial state also channelled resources into colonial primary and industrial production as a measure to achieve its short- and long-term exit reconstruction strategy. The government invested in expatriate services by increasingly rewarding meritorious Gusii women farmers and in short-term loans to approved applicants[18]. Grants were availed to lead Gusii peasant farmers in an attempt to entrench and sustain Gusii peasant production. As noted by PC Nyanza Province, "the Local Government Authorities within the province functioned smoothly and gave mature consideration to the allocation of funds[19]" available to the locals to spur production. Besides the proven methods of achieving the desired goal of soil conservation through terracing and trash lining, large sums of money were spent on rewards and loans for better farmers. The African District Council in Kisii passed better farming by-laws. The Kisii area, therefore, witnessed an increase in rewards to meritorious farmers and short-term loans to approved applicants. In addition to these incentives, a large mechanical unit was promised by the soil conservation service. The Kisii local Native Council, on its part, included, in the Agricultural Betterment Fund Estimates, funds to purchase smaller mechanical soil conservation units, when the machinery became available[20] and distribute them to the meritorious farmers in the area.

Furthermore, the cultivation of cash crops, like coffee in Kisii, was used as an incentive and reward to the same farmers. As Throup notes, only those cultivators who had built cattle *bomas,*

17 KNA:PC/NZA/1/43Nyanza Province Annual Report, 1948
18 KNA:PC/NZA/1/48 Annual Report Nyanza Province 1952
19 KNA:PC/NZA/1/56. Nyanza Annual Agricultural Report 1960.
20 KNA:PC/NZA/1/43. Nyanza Province Annual Report 1948.

terraced their land and manured their crops were allowed to plant coffee[21]. Throup's position is echoed by the Agricultural Officer who maintained that only prosperous smallholders who practised mixed farming rotations were allowed to grow high-value cash crops.

With such support, the peasants gained the ability to purchase elementary farm inputs. This point was reinforced in the 1951 annual report which noted that, in addition, large sums of money were spent on rewards and loans for better farmers. In Kisii, the increased support saw women in search of increased access, control and use of land as reiterated by the group interview with the women of Kitutu-Chache.[22]

All these official policy interventions were made in the face of population pressure in the Kisii reserve and the attendant increased demand for agricultural production during and immediately after the Second World War, which led to intensive land utilization in the area. The resultant effect was that land became scarce, especially after 1945, as all available unoccupied land in the 1930s had now been occupied. The farmers, therefore, had to intensively utilize the land at hand to realize increased production as the demand and prices of their produce such as maize, coffee, tea and pyrethrum increased.[23] In the aftermath of the war, the call to increase agricultural production was accelerated by import substitution industrialization. Gusii women, on their part, intensified agricultural production after 1945 mainly because of their spontaneous response to the prevailing market dynamics coupled with the existence of a hungry population to feed within and outside Gusii, as well as hungry machinery around the region.

In 1946, through the Worthington Plan, the colonial state allocated over £5m to the African Land Development Programme mainly for soil conservation in areas like Kisii[24]. These funds translated into Kisii women's intensification of agriculture. As the P.C. indicated in the 1949 Nyanza Annual Report; "Generally, agricultural production in the African areas of Kisii continued to increase steadily. Economically, there was solid, if not spectacular, progress, in the area with maize crops".[25] Equally, cash crop production in African areas, particularly Kisii, increased during the year and the

21 Throup, D 1988. Economic & Social Origins of Mau Mau 1945-53.
22 Group discussion with woman at Kitutu Chache South.
23 Orvis, 127
24 Zeleza T. Kenya and the Second World War 1939-1950 in Ochieng' W.R (eds) A Modern History of Kenya
25 KNA:PC/NZA/1/56 Nyanza Province Annual Report

value rose[26], which is attributed to the resource investment into coffee by the ex-World War II soldiers as women shunned it due to limited returns to them from the cash crops. Gusii women's intensification of subsistence production was lauded in the 1948 Provincial Annual Report when the Provincial Agriculture Officer observed that the situation concerning food production in Kisii was excellent; in fact, the province produced a considerable surplus for export from the 1948 planting, mainly maize which will probably total nearly 700,000 bags.[27]

In 1950, the Annual report affirmed the efforts of the Gusii women in the intensification of agriculture. The report indicated that the harvest of cereals was estimated to create a new record and would touch the figure of 1.5 million bags for export from the province, after providing for its internal population of 1,820,000 African souls.[28] Although food shortages prevailed in certain areas of Nyanza Province, in Kisii, famine relief was not necessary as supplies of foodstuffs were readily obtainable though often at unauthorized prices from within.[29] Mary Moraa corroborated this when she observed that each household now utilized all its available land to produce both food and cash crops without allowing any time for the land to rest.[30]

By 1946, conscription of labour for war had come to an end. The number of men going out of the district for wages, however, continued to increase. Men sought wage labour because of the increased need for cash to purchase consumer goods for their households as well as the increased need for school fees for their sons.[31] By 1946, around 10,376 Gusii men constituted almost 32 % of able-bodied men who had joined wage labour.[32]

With the emphasis on cash crops, the land now became the most important commodity and competition for the same resulted in a new system of land tenure and social relations. As this competition for land increased, and land got scarce, individuals started developing ties to individual ownership and production, thus transiting from group rights to property ownership to private property ownership.[33]As the population increased, more and more

26 Ibid.
27 KNA:PC/NZA/1/43 Nyanza Province Annual Report 1948
28 KNA:PC/NZA/1/45 Nyanza Province Annual Report 1950
29 KNA:PC/NZA/1/48 Nyanza Province Annual Report 1952
30 Mary Moraa, 85, Kitutu Chache, Oct.2019
31 Maxon R. M. Conflicts and Accomodation. 123. 129
32 Kenya African Manpower at 31 Dec 1946, KNA: PC/NZA/3/13/13
33 Neigus; Conflicts over Land, 69

land came to be permanently cultivated and individually owned by households. Later, single-family farms got crowded and became multifamily farms where sons and grandsons grew up and needed separate plots for their wives to cultivate.

By the end of 1946, the Gusii veterans of World War II returned home. At the same time, men who had avoided the war by going for civilian employment returned home. The returnees came with a lot of money which they put into locally owned business ventures such as farming, wholesale and retail shops, transport and maize mills. This gave them an added advantage compared to women for they could be able to support their households without necessarily relying on family labour.[34]

Consequently, it became more appealing to get money and grow cash crops instead of food crops.[35] Particularly, money was needed not only for the purchase of goods and provision of services but also for tax payments. By 1948, the food crop growing had become increasingly a woman's affair; the capitalization on farming brought by the state reforms resulted in further marginalization of women both labour-wise in cash crop growing as more land was unilaterally allocated to cash crop production at the expense of food crops. The study notes that the major obligation and responsibility under traditional land ownership had guaranteed women user rights to land, and control over food crop production had been significantly eroded by the end of 1948.

Effectively, colonial land reforms and the emergent capitalist economy eroded traditional land ownership modes that guaranteed women user rights to land, and control over household food production by introducing male-dominated cash crop agriculture.[36] These colonial land reforms facilitated increased limitations to user rights as land previously used for food production became increasingly alienated for cash crop production. Therefore, women continued losing both the right to access, ownership, control and use of land than ever before. Most notable of these events was the near depletion of the Gusii food crop stock; the emphasis placed on maize production to replace *wimbi*, the demand for labour and

---

34 Orvis 1989, 127
35 Downs, R. E. (1988). The Kenya Land Tenure Reform: Misunderstandings in the Public Creation of Private Property, in *Land and Society in Contemporary Africa*, 98.
36 Okoth-Ogendo, H. W. O. (1975). *The Adjudication Process and the Special Rural Development Process*. Unpublished Occasional Paper no. 12, Institute of Development Studies, University of Nairobi.

the associated hut and poll taxes. Livestock herding was one sector of the Gusii economy that was badly affected by the imposition of colonial rule and her ally settler farming.

Changes in the land utilization system by 1950 had influenced the mechanism of decision-making in terms of the amount of land to be put under food production. The state of affairs unfolding in Kisii during this time is aptly captured by Davison[37] who maintains that the less land an individual had, the less it was devoted to food crops and the bigger the land one had, the less was devoted to food production. Davison's study concurs with Tanui's findings concerning the impact of differential gender access to resources in agricultural production in the Nandi District.[38]

Other studies by Njiru[39] also replicate the scenario observable in Kisii, that agricultural activities before the adoption of commercialized tea production in the area initiated social-economic differentiations among households. These differentiations became intensified by tea production in Meru just as the case was in Kisii where the prioritization of labour to livestock, food production and other household activities was in acute competition with that directed to cash production. Njiru establishes that, although tea production increased women's workload generally, like in Kisii cash production, it brought some advantages for some; most tea-producing households had relatively more income than before, better housing, clothing and other amenities in their houses.[40]

On the other hand, Njogu[41] points to the fact that most of the farmers in the tea-producing areas devoted most of their land to tea production at the expense of food, which corresponds with the case in Kisii concerning cash production after the Second World War. In this study done in Kirinyaga, she found that tea-producing households gave priority to food whenever they received their money. This, however, was not the case in Kisii as women were left to toil as an alternative to producing food for their families. These households did not get enough food through home production and

37 Davison, M. J. (1987). Without Land we are nothing. The Effect of Land Tenure Policies and Practices upon Rural Women in Kenya, *Rural Africana*, 27.
38 Tanui, P. Differential Gender Access to Agricultural Resources in Kenya: The Impact on Agricultural Production in Nandi District From 1954-2000.
39 Njiru, E. (1990). *Effects of Tea Production on Women's Work and Labour Allocation in Embu District*. M.A. Thesis, Nairobi University: Nairobi.
40 Johnson Ong'esa 85 years
41 Njogu, E. (2002). *Household Food Security and Nutritional Status of Children in Tea and Non-Tea Producing Households in Ndia Division Kirinyaga District*. Unpublished Thesis: Kenyatta University.

therefore, the Gusii women had to purchase from the market.[42] After gaining from commercial maize farming the Gusii could now embrace cash crop farming, and more farmers started growing coffee. By 1950, the acreage under coffee had increased from 91 acres in 1938 to 222 acres in 1948 and 271 by 1950.[43] The colonial state ensured a decrease in the size of plots of coffee growers to discourage the capitalistic big-man class that had started [coffee] growing.[44] However, by 1950, the size of the plots per grower had declined to a third of an acre from around an acre in 1938, implying that even small landholders were growing the crop. This meant that farmers were now allocating parts of their land used for subsistence to grow cash crops as shown in the table below.

Table 5.1: Land acreage committed to coffee growing in the Gusii Highlands, 1946-1950

Year	Acreage	%	Growers	Acreage Per Grower
1946	189.27	21.6	312	.606
1947	196.78	22.4	339	.580
1949	221.6	25.3	530	.418
1950	269.10	30.7	789	.341

Source: SK Arabica Coffee Fourth Quarterly Report 1946-1949, KNA: AK/11/60 and AR for Kisii Coffee Growers Co-operative Society Ltd. For the years 1949-1950, KNA: AK/11/58

It can be deduced from Table 5.1 that there was a consistent increase in acreage under coffee by 9.1% from 1946 to 1950. The study notes that the increasing acreage devoted to coffee after the Second World War was attributed both to the Ex-World War II soldiers and the return of Gusii men who had sought civilian employment. The intersection of the two groups in Kisii loaded with money prompted the competition among men to see who could grow a bigger acreage of coffee than the other. However, the shrinking acreage per grower by 13.6%, as shown in Table 5.1, is attributed to the tussle among men members of the households, each seeking their portion on which to grow coffee. This underlines the land crisis among brothers in Kisii which was escalated by primitive accumulation by the state officers. For instance, in 1945, an African Tribunal noted:

---

42 Ndege, P. the struggle at the market place,
43 Maxon R. M. 1884, Conflict and Accomodation,118-120
44 Ibid

> It is regrettable that chiefs and other influential men, including members of the Tribunals, are taking advantage of the present uncertainty to acquire large areas of land and are seeking to advance their position to become feudal landlords.[45]

The primitive accumulation orchestrated recurrent conflicts over land as evident in the land cases handled by the Tribunal Court in the late 1940s and early 1950s,[46] which took long before any conclusion was arrived at. Court cases were further prolonged because many persons did not accept a verdict of defeat. This is evidenced by the many appeals made.[47] The high fee charged in the African courts is a further confirmation of how important land ownership had become in Kisii in the aftermath of the Second World War. In 1949, for instance, a total of £13,000 was raised as court charges compared to £24,000 in 1951.[48]

Inter and intra-homestead land disputes became more intense as plots were further subdivided into smaller sizes. Families and individual quarrels over land escalated and the Gusii opted for litigation over boundary issues.[49] The Gusii became one of the most litigious people in Kenya by 1950. Levines note that almost every Gusii male had been involved in land-related court cases ten or more times.[50] This denoted a shift from the early 1940s, where court cases revolved around marriage and dowry, to land consolidation cases in the aftermath of the Second World War and the early 1950s. This is corroborated by Mayer's observation that, by the end of 1946, land cases in the courts were increasing. Disputes over boundaries and land litigation dominated the courts in the 1950s until the official registration of land began in the mid-1950s. According to the Kisii District Commissioner, in the Manga Court, the number of land cases grew steadily from 288 in 1949 to 982 in 1952 and after. It remained at 800 for the next three years and dropped to 539 in 1956[51]. The drop is attributed to land registration that began to take place after the Swynnerton Plan of 1954.

From 1956, kinship bonds began to dissolve as the individual acquisition of land was adopted and entrenched. The economic independence of individually owned land changed the attitude of

45 Sorrenson, 1964: 78
46 Orvis, 1989: 127
47 Mackenzie, F. (1990). Gender and Land Rights in Murang'a District, Kenya Journal of Peasant Studies, Vol. 17(4).
48 KNA: AK/11/58
49 P&I Mayer,1965,c, 67
50 LeVive,1966; 73
51 Kisii DC Report,1956

exchange within the community. Elements of measurement and calculation were introduced and by the beginning of the 1960s, *risaga* was virtually extinct. The land disputes within kinships intensified as kinsmen fought for individual access and ownership of land. This eventually led to high homicides within the Gusii community compared to other Kenyan communities as revealed below.

Table 5.2: Average annual homicide rates per 100,000 people (1955-1956)

Gusii	Kipsigis	Luo
5.5	4.8	4.5

Source: Neigus, D. L. Conflicts over land. 79

The high homicide cases in Kisii were validated according to the Nyaribari focus group discussions by the heightened intrafamily conflicts complemented by the rampant interfamily boundary conflicts as narrated by Moses Ong'esa of South Mogirango. Anyona of Bomachoge narrated how his father was butchered by his stepbrothers over the sharing of their late father's land. Being the only son of his mother, who was the third wife, the step brothers knew that, by eliminating him, they would take all the land. The intervention by the extended family ensured that Anyona's mother received a share of the land on which they currently reside.[52]

The Second World War had a significant impact on Africans' land and gender relations. Their involvement, both directly and indirectly, in the war efforts affected all aspects of their lives. As discussed in the previous chapter, Africans were encouraged to put maximum land under use during the Depression and the Second World War to offset the declining returns from the settler sector and provide food necessities for the war effort despite the looming soil erosion problem.[53] The soil erosion problem happened as a result of growing population congestion, over-grazing, and over-cultivation without allowing the necessary periods of fallow in the 1930s and 1940s.[54] Given that contour-terracing cut across the traditional pattern of Gusii landholding, running in narrow strips from the top to bottom of ridges, it had to be done communally.

---

52 Anyona Kibagendi, 79. Bomachoge Burabu
53 Throup, D. (1988). *Economic and Social Origins of Mau Mau, 1945–53.* (East African Studies.) Athens: Ohio University Press or James Currey, London. 1988. Pp. Xvi, 304.
54 Stichter, S. (1975-76). Women and Labour Force in Kenya, 1895-1964. In *Rural Africana* 29.

Maxon[55] notes that private land ownership was brought to Gusii in the early 20th Century, by the British colonial administration. It was a consequence of the colonial administration's unequal land policies, in which the settlers expropriated land by force, to the detriment of Africans. It was designed to facilitate European modes of production (for commercial purposes). Maxon postulates that the effect of this on Gusii women's economic status was to move them from a position of self-sufficiency to one of relative dependency, resulting in the loss of their socio-economic power. As more land was reserved for cash crops in Kisii, Gusii women became increasingly reliant on cash to procure food they could no longer produce and turned their labour to cash crop production, the monetary benefits of which were reserved for men.56

Throup[57] elaborates that the population explosion in Kisii resulted in increased land fragmentation. Before independence, in the late 1950s, a single household's (12 people) plot of land was less than 2 hectares (2 ha) and maize replaced finger millet as the main staple crop as demonstrated in the table below. The increasing popularity of cash crops contributed to the decline in food production to the extent that, by the end of the 1960s, land under food crops growing only accounted for 25% of cultivated land in Gusii.

Table 5.3: Produce in bags marketed in South Nyanza 1948/49 and 1949/50

Crop	1948/49	Percentage	1949/50	Percentage
Maize	205.533	89.92	442.924	93.57
Wimbi	13.425	5.88	21.362	4.50
Mtama	9.397	4.11	9.064	1.9
Total	**228.355**		**473.35**	

Source: SN Gazetteer, KNA DC/KSI/5/3

As indicated in Table 5.3, the preference for maize is evidenced by the increased production of maize compared to *wimbi*. Table 5.3 shows the increase proportion of maize production from 89.92% in the year 1948/49 to 93.57% in the year 1949/50, while *wimbi* production declined from 5.88% to 4.50% in the same period.

55 Maxon, R. (2003). *Going Their Separate Ways: Agrarian Transformation In Kenya, 1930-1950*. London: Associated University Presses.
56 Nasimiyu, R. (1985). Women in the Colonial Economy of Bungoma: Role of Women in Agriculture, in G.S. Were (ed.) *Women and Development in Africa*, 56-73.
57 Throup, D. (1987). The construction and destruction of the Kenyatta state, in *The Politcal Economy of Kenya*. Michael G. Schatzberg ed: Praeger.

Between 1948 and 1949, 89% of the bags produced were maize and by 1950, the percentage of maize had increased to 94%, while that of *wimbi* and *mtama* production remained minimal. This corroborates the view that the Gusii were embracing subsistence commercial production of maize. Oral interviews indicated that the Gusii loved white ugali for it was far sweeter compared to the wimbi one. They noted they could eat it without any accompaniment earning it the name *enchoro*. It should also be stated that maize production was less tedious and cumbersome compared to the growing of wimbi.

The Intervention of the Swynnerton Plan, 1954

In an attempt to resolve the multifaceted agricultural problems and increasing land issues that had led to increased calls for African emancipation, the colonial state came up with the Swynnerton Plan in 1954. It was aimed at reversing the colonial appetite and attitude toward the Africans' ability to maximize agricultural profits while maintaining soil fertility. Rodger Swynnerton prescribed that improved African agricultural and economic growth, as well as political stability, required developing an African agricultural sector comprised of 100,000 farms of approximately equal size, each achieving surplus marketed production at approximately £100 per year by 1959. This, he noted, could improve revenue for the colonial state and reduce the African hunger for land in European settlements. It was also to create a stable African middle class that would politically stabilize the country. This was to be done through the creation of a class of progressive farmers in African reserves like Kisii to support the colonial state operations. The plan endeavoured to intensify agricultural production through increased cultivation of cash crops, and food crops as well as improve dairy farming. This was to be done by establishing training institutes for farmers like the Kisii Agricultural Centre, increasing extension services in agricultural and veterinary departments,[58] funding farmers through credits and co-operatives as well as promoting land consolidation and enclosure.[59] The plan would also lead to the creation of a landless class that would work for the landed class, who would mostly be Gusii women and children in Kisii; and Swynnerton viewed this as a natural outcome of a developing economy.

Using the plan, the colonial state created a freehold land tenure system that would be based on an individual holding that would

58 KNA:DAR/KSI 1939-1946
59 SNAR 1959, KNA: DC/KSI/1/21

replace the dominant traditional communal tenure system already discussed in chapter two. It was argued that a secure freehold tenure system would motivate Africans to invest in their land for increased long-term productivity. The land tenure policies formulated by Swynnerton in 1954 included the views that the proponent of the plan advanced and supported the individualized land tenure in Kenya and particularly in Kisii to enhance agricultural production which the colonial state adopted and began to implement. The implementation of the Swynnerton plan marked the beginning of an evolution in Kenya's land tenure reform system with a major shift from the traditional Gusii land tenure system to individual ownership.

According to the proposal, communal land tenure in African reserves like Kisii was to be discouraged in favour of land consolidation for eventual registration as private property. At this point, the colonial state perceived African customary land access and usufruct as a major obstacle to the realization of greater agricultural production and proper land use practices in African reserves like Kisii. The state proposed its replacement with a Western-style system which is based on individual land access and usufruct rights. The plan formed the basis for the pre-independent and post-independence land policies in Kisii and Kenya at large. Moreover, the plan introduced absolute entitlement to land[60] by an individual. Consequently, this left the Gusii women in a precarious economic state as men were accorded absolute rights over land through land registration done in their names. On the whole, the proposed policy failed to acknowledge even the derivative rights of women to land.

The Practicality of the Swynnerton Recommendations on Gusii Agriculture

The most striking manifestation of the Swynnerton plan in Kisii, which turned out to be the most spectacular liberation step towards emancipating the Gusii woman, was made in the domain of land enclosure and eventual consolidation, especially of the planned land. The value of land enclosure, consolidation and planning came to be appreciated in Kisii when the new emerging proto-capitalist Gusii began affirming the interest in agricultural production. As is corroborated by the 1957 Annual Report, land enclosure, consolidation and planning were carried out under the auspices of the indigenous land authorities in Kisii and their efforts and

---

60 Ibid.

the response of the Gusii to them was most heartening.[61] This, in practicality, depicts the Gusii agency in shaping their agrarian trajectory especially where they adopted, adapted and customized the colonial state policies as exemplified by the Swynnerton plan to their advantage. These sentiments by the PC Nyanza were corroborated by Mr. T. Hughes-Rice, the Assistant Director of Agriculture when he observed that land consolidation and enclosure in Kisii was making steady progress voluntarily with organization and direction remaining in the hands of indigenous tribal authorities.[62] The voluntariness of the Gusii must be emphasized to lay bare the agency of the Gusii, which was instrumental in their agrarian transformation, especially among the agricultural agents who were the Gusii women. With this willingness, the Gusii witnessed a marked increase both in demand and in the number of farm layouts especially when bubbling with the methods of improved agricultural production from the Siriba agricultural training and demonstration centre. This was noted in the 1959 Annual Agricultural Report which indicated that the build-up of trained Gusii farmers was the most important development at the time and they guaranteed land enclosure and the sound patterns of farm layout which had fast spread in Kisii.

The annual report acknowledged the utility value of these by noting that the demonstration plots at Siriba provided by farm planning were beginning to pay dividends, in the long run, providing useful examples to their neighbours.[63] The Kisii area was lauded for its familiarity with farm planning over many years which went hand in hand with soil conservation. Land consolidation, planning and enclosure in Kisii began immediately after the coming into force of the Swynneryton plan as the 1954 provincial annual report for the year indicates. The report notes that in the Kisii District, one could observe the fencing of enclosures in many parts of the highlands; and there has been tremendous enthusiasm in Butende.[64] These enclosures further motivated the Gusii as the farmers who enclosed their farms decided to form several farmers' clubs all of whose farms were planned and successfully enclosed.[65]

The study affirms the cooperation between the agricultural staff and the Gusii as the latter carried out land consolidation, planning

---

61 KNA: PC/NZA/1/53 Annual Provincial Agricultural Report 1957.
62 Stephen Orvis: The Political Economy of Agriculture in Kisii, Kenya
63 KNA: PC/NZA/1/55 Annual Provincial Agricultural Report 1955.
64 KNA: PC/NZA/1/50 Annual Provincial Agricultural Report 1954
65 Ibid.

and enclosure with energy. As a way of motivating the progressive Gusii farmers and catalyzing the uptake of land consolidation, planning and enclosure, the colonial state, through the Department of Agriculture, devised a system of giving awards[66] for merit which opened up in 1954. The land consolidation, enclosure and planning paved the way for the eventual land registration[67] as was provided for in the Swynnertyon plan.

After 1954, maize production in Kisii continued increasing as the conditions of production in African reserves like Kisii improved. The increased pressure from the colonial state together with the increased prices which had risen from Ksh 11/95 in 1949 to Ksh 26 a bag in 1954 provided the impetus for the increased production.[68]

After the mid-1950s, the colonial state, through the Department of Agriculture staff, laid more emphasis on cash crops such as coffee and pyrethrum as they strove to replace maize with cash crops.[69] The colonial state was keen to increase coffee production among the Gusii to cover up for the diminished settler acreage under coffee. To encourage Gusii to do more production, a local coffee board was established for easy organization of financing farmers as well as the marketing of their produce in Kisii.

In summary, the Swynnerton plan in the Kisii area stressed an intensification of agriculture through increased cultivation of cash crops and mixed farming. It equally increased attention given to production for the market of such crops as maize, vegetables and fruits and provided greater attention to training institutes for farmers with credit to farmers as loans and rewards[70] as already discussed. Consequently, the Kisii highlands strongly felt the effects of the plan in all agricultural production domains.

The key aspect of land tenure reforms in Kisii was the initiation of private land ownership through the issuance of title deeds. These land reforms involved an adjudication of demarcated fragmented parcels of land to ascertain individual ownership. However, in Kisii, the adjudication of land was an entirely male affair without any representation of women.[71] Once the title deeds were issued, the

66 KNA: PC/NZA/1/54 Annual Provincial Agricultural Report 1958
67 KNA: PC/NZA/1/56 Annual Provincial Agricultural Report 1960.
68 South Nyanza Gazeteer, KNA: DC/KSI/5/3
69 SNAR 1959, KNA: DC/KSI/1/21
70 Maxon, R.M 1989. Conflict and Accommodation in Western Kenya. The Gusii and the British, 1907-1963. London; Associated University Press.
71 Downs, R.E. (1988). The Kenya Land Tenure Reform: Misunderstandings in the Public Creation of Private Property, in *Land and Society in Contemporary Africa*, 98.

Gusii men handled the land as personal property as they needed no consent from anybody, family included, to either use or even sell as they wished, according to oral interviews.

In particular, the issuance of individual title deeds in Kisii was premised on the patriarchal perspectives of the indigenous Gusii society where women were not allowed to directly own and/or inherit land.[72] Eventually, with the intensified cash crop farming in Kisii and the cash-based economy, land use activities and economic goals were transformed as the land itself was quickly transformed into a commercial commodity.

The land tenure reforms of the late 1950s in Kisii triggered a series of things including the sale of land, land disputes, and denial of land rights particularly for the vulnerable Gusii women, children, widows, and orphans. In this scheme, Gusii women had no formal claims to the household land as the title deed was in the name of the husband, the father, or the father-in-law. As such, they could not use the land as collateral for loans or even merely rent it out as their husbands or fathers controlled the crucial household resource. Widows' rights faced challenges from male relatives after the death of their spouses.[73]

Land Kleptocracy and Gendered Relations among the Gusii

The interplay between the system of land ownership and crop production cannot be well analyzed devoid of gender and labour relations in a given society. Since gender relations are the distinctive social relations between men and women, studies on gender relations during the colonial and post-colonial periods cannot be ignored in the present analysis. Stichter established that among the Gusii, it was women who were primarily responsible for food production, household management and the nurture of children[74].

Women in Kisii had user rights to their husband's land and occasionally, if they were unmarried with a child, they had user rights to their father's land.[75] Conventionally, land among the Gusii was needed for subsistence. It was neither sold nor exchanged. However, as land got scarce and money circulation in the area

72 Milka Bosibori, 78 years, Bobasi
73 Masese, R. E. (2006). Traditional Land Tenure.In Akama, J. S and Maxon, R. M, (Eds) *Ethnography of the Gusii of Western Kenya. A Vanishing Cultural Heritage,* Emp, New York, USA.
74 Ndeda (2019): The people of Western Kenya
75 Henrysson, E & Joireman, S. F. (2009). On the edge of the law: Women's property rights and dispute Resolution in Kisii, Kenya. *Law & Society Review,* *43*(1), 39-60.

improved, it became commoditized. The introduction of cash crops (maize and coffee) in Kisii made land one of the most sought-after commodities and competition for it resulted in a new system of land tenure and social relations. As competition for land increased, land got scarce, and individuals started developing ties to individual ownership and production, thus transiting from group rights to private ownership.[76] For instance, Charles Omwenga's father, who after coming back from service in the Second World War, bought pieces of land in the nearby village and moved with only his family to the new land. His father's efforts to persuade him to share the land with his brothers failed.[77]

The establishment of absolute male land ownership in Kisii was validated by the Registered Land Act (RLA), which destroyed a married Gusii woman's ability to claim and protect her interests and rights to matrimonial property.[78] While in communal land tenure systems, Gusii women had indirect access and rights to use communal resources through their roles as household managers, they were excluded when land tenure was individualized and invariably adjudicated and registered in the name of heads of households (men). Without legal and social/communal protection, Gusii women constantly faced the risk of suddenly becoming landless. The wars for independence were caused by the question of rights over land[79] which had been unjustly apportioned to the "White-Settlers" by the colonial regime. In Kisii for instance, the British did not take sufficient regard for customary land tenure and particular rights to land proprietorship meant for the Gusii population.

The reforms gradually and systematically destroyed the socio-cultural fabric on which Gusii women's socio-economic power and stability were anchored and maintained. Instead, they introduced a new system which neither maintained nor guaranteed any rights for women in return for what they had lost.[80]

In this regard, the land reforms did not take into consideration the strong social and cultural status and levels of power that were accorded to women in indigenous Gusii as regards land user rights.

76 Neigus 1971, Confllicts over Land, 69,
77 Charles Omwenga, 80. Bonchari, Nov 2019.
78 Okoth-Ogendo, H.W.O. (1989). Some Issues of Theory in the Study of Tenure Relations in African Agriculture, *59 Africa* 6.
79 Newsinger, J. (1981). Revolt and Repression in Kenya: The "Mau Mau" Rebellion, 1952-1960. *45 Science & Society* 159.
80 Maxon, R. (2003). *Going Their Separate Ways: Agrarian Transformation In Kenya, 1930- 1950.* London: Associated University Presses.

Thus, priority was given to individual ownership of land by the men without protecting the user rights of the Gusii women. This did not only obliterate the usage rights accorded to Gusii women under the Gusii indigenous tenure systems but, led to very few Gusii women (if any) being registered as individual land owners.

As the Gusii population grew, more land was put under the permanently cultivated individually-owned household status. Single-family farms soon became crowded multifamily farms as sons and grandsons grew up and demanded their shares of the existing family land for themselves to cultivate. The Gusii found themselves embroiled in what Orvis terms "land scramble."[81] This intensified inter and intra-homestead disputes as family land was further divided into even smaller sizes. As previously presented, the family and individual quarrels over land would lead the Gusii to opt for litigation over boundary issues,[82] rendering them the most litigious people as recurrent land disputes gave them more reason to visit the courts.

Land conflicts escalated in Kisii on the eve of independence as kinsmen fought for individual access, control and ownership of land which culminated in rampant homicides among the Gusii. John Nyandoro recounted that for the first time in the community, people were fighting and even killing each other within families and community elders could not stop the evil activity.[83] Nyandoro narrated how his father who had been a clan elder observed that they had never seen such a selfish spirit in the community.[84]

Moreover, the pre-existing kinship bonds gradually dissolved as individual acquisition and commoditization of land were adopted. The economic independence of individually owned land changed the attitude of exchange within the community as the elements of measurement and calculation were introduced. By 1960, the 'institution' of *risaga* was extinct since there was no virgin land to clear and land holdings were not large enough to require *risaga*, a practice that had sustained kinship ties in the Gusii community. Since the food products that were initially exchanged on reciprocal terms could now be sold for money, mutual sharing faded away, seriously hurting the Gusii kinship ties. Mokoro noted that he saw his uncles refuse to lend his father two heads of cattle for his

81 Orvis, Agrarian Question, 44
82 P. &I. Mayer, 1965.The Nature of Kinship Relations. Manchester University
    Press. 67
83 John Nyandoro, 89. Nyaribari Chache
84 John Nyandoro Oigo 85, Nyaribari Chache, Jan 2020

brother's bridewealth in 1956, even when they knew he would return when they needed it as had been happening before.[85] Mokoro's family epitomizes what became of the initial mutual cultural sharing as the Gusii community came to embrace capitalistic and individualistic practices at independence. Women suffered more in these new relations for they shared more in subsistence as land got scarce and food production steadily declined.

As land conflicts increased in Kisii, issues of witchcraft relating to land matters rose as the Gusii looked for alternative ways of solving land disputes amongst themselves. Accusations were often made against co-wives, brothers and close kin to try to push them away either as witches or as victims of witchcraft.[86] The scarce land became a major reason for an increase in issues of witchery among the Gusii. Onsongo Nyamwange of Ibacho revealed that his father was forced to look for some new land for his mother who was the younger wife in the family of two wives because she was always sick and the family believed it was the first wife who was bewitching her so that she moves out and leaves the land for her three sons.[87] Women, who felt that their access and usage of their husband's land for the good of their subsistence was threatened, could use unorthodox means to push away their co-wives. Accusations of witchery, in such cases, could be the excuse.

The late 1940s saw more men go for migrant labour. However, by 1960 the numbers had drastically dropped to almost 20% of the total men population in Kisii.[88] At this time, fewer men were going for migrant labour from North Kisii than from the South. In North Mogirango, for instance, the percentage of men who went for migrant labour dropped from 30% of their total male population in the area to only 8% in 1962.[89] This, the study attributes majorly to the men's private ownership of land and their increased role in cash crop cultivation where returns were high. For instance, by 1964, returns from coffee to the farmers in Kisii stood at over nine million shillings.[90] Pyrethrum was also introduced in 1952 and tea in 1957.[91] The men of Mogirango and Kitutu then gradually abandoned migrant labour as a means of earning cash for they

85 Richard Mokoro 79, Bobasi, Dec 2019
86 Levine,1963. Witchcraft and Sorcery in a Gusii Community. In Wtchcraft Aand Sorcery in East Africa, J. Middleton and E, Winter (Eds). New York, 240
87 Isaac Onsongo Nyamwange, 78, Ibacho, Nyaribari Masaba, Dec 2019
88 Neigus 1971,99-100
89 Maxon, R.M. Conflict and Accommodation , 136-137.
90 Ibid.
91 Ibid

could earn more from farming on their privately owned land. In all this, they took more land for cash crop production and left the Gusii women with less land for food production. As a result, this trend reduced food production and supply in the northern part of Kisii. On the other hand, the southern part of Kisii (Bobasi, Machoge, South Mogirango and parts of Nyaribari) concentrated on maize production and the sale of the surplus, some of which was sold to the Gusii women of north Kisii whose large parts of their farms were utilized for cash crop production.[92]

After the world war, the colonial administration turned its focus to ensuring that soil conservation was taken care of just like in other reserves. Although the Gusii farming methods had helped in soil conservation, increased demand for agricultural production and good prices for the products made the Gusii overutilize the land to produce as much as they could. The agricultural department staff guided the farmers, mostly men, to construct thrash lines across their land whose demarcation ran from the top of hills down to river valleys. Any planting that was done went hand in hand with the construction of these thrash lines. This form of soil conservation was so successful in Gusii that by 1959, the agricultural officers commended the "almost universal use of trash lines in Kisii highlands."[93]

The increased production of coffee after the Second World War saw the Gusii get good money from its sales. The Gusii received more money from the increased produce and sale of cereals, compulsory sale of cattle as well as wages accrued from the conscripted labour. This money was then directed to trade, most of the men ventured into setting up shops for cereals, transport services as well as increased production of coffee.[94] Oral interviews indicate that this gave men an opportunity to promote their economic well-being aside from household resources. Gusii men could now buy and sell goods as well as render transport services without necessarily needing family labour. At the same time, they were able to hire and pay for labour outside the household labour, giving them an advantage over Gusii women. The men as indicated in oral interviews now had fully reached the status of the "big man" as indicated by Maxon.[95]

---

92 Ibid 102, The women of Kitutu also affirm this in a group interview on how their mothers and at times themselves went to markets in Nyaribari and Bonchari to buy maize for their families because they produced less at home.
93 SKAgAR1949, KNA: AK/2/33
94 Maxon R. M. Conflict and Accomodation, 117
95 Ibid.

Wafula[96], examining the colonial land policy in North Kavirondo African Reserve, points out that this policy was mainly a metropolitan transplant designed to serve settler needs. He notes that the North Kavirondo reserve was created to ensure adequate labour supply to the neighbouring Uasin Gishu and Trans-Nzoia settler areas. In Kisii, however, increased land disputes were experienced resulting from individual rights being imposed on pre-existing Gusii system of multiple rights. The European-based tenure reforms that were introduced in Kisii in 1954 by the British created greater uncertainties and conflicts among men in Gusii who were the principal landholders and who thus assumed exclusive individual rights in a given parcel of land to the detriment of the Gusii women and children because their rights remained either secondary or usufructuary.[97]

Gusii women had user rights to their husband's land and, occasionally, if they were unmarried with a child, they enjoyed user rights to their father's land.[98] This was a continuation of the customary laws where Gusii women were often dispossessed off the land in traditional patriarchal family ties. In homes where they were born, Gusii women were considered strangers for they were expected to get married and belong to the husband's lineage. However, the introduction of the Swynnerton plan's registration of land gave a greater advantage to Gusii men who could now exercise full control of the land and use or dispose of it as they wished without any consent or input from their wives. This would eventually trigger intra-family conflicts over land as women and their sons were now completely alienated from their previous right of access and usage of the land.

There is no question that the years 1945 to 1960 schematically transformed the gendered land relations in Kisii. The resolution imposed by the state aimed at intensifying agriculture and affirming cash crops with emphasis on male-controlled agriculture became a primary determinant of the Gusii women's loss of status, access, control and power in land and agriculture. The result of state-created private enterprise in Kisii was the re-structuring and re-

---

96 Wafula, S. (1981) "Colonial land policy and the North Kavirondo African Reserve to 1940." M.A Dissertation, University of Nairobi.

97 Okuro, S. O. (2011). "Rethinking World Bank Driven Land Tenure Reforms". In OKuro, S.O and Punyana, Am. (Eds). *Strategies against Poverty Designs from the north and alternatives from the south.* Buenos Aires: Clasco.

98 Henrysson, E & Joireman, S. F. (2009). On the edge of the law: Women's property rights and dispute Resolution in Kisii, Kenya. *Law & Society Review, 43*(1), 39-60.

engineering of gender roles. The affirmation of cash crops for export in Kisii brought about greater gender segregation in labour tasks with Gusii men increasingly becoming agricultural managers. It is essential to understand that given the labour division, Gusii women were the backbone of rural agriculture before then.

Gutto posited that women had virtual control and monopoly of crop production which led to them having rights to land they controlled for the maintenance of their households[99]. Gusii women's status in their agricultural productive tasks was secure under the traditional land tenure system until the colonial land policies introduced legislative programmes designed to replace the traditional land tenure system. One may cautiously conclude, therefore, that land tenure systems in Kenya and particularly in Kisii cannot be blamed for the engendered land crisis. The unavailability of sufficient land on the eve of independence was one major factor that made both Gusii men and women renegotiate labour within and without the district.

The post-World War II population growth can undoubtedly be attributed, in part, to improved adult life expectancy. However, with time, increasing numbers of women desired to restrict child-bearing, reflecting a growing sense among young households of the severe constraints of land and demand for education expenses. This strong sentiment in favour of "no more" often represented the resistance of women to their husband's desire for the social status that still came with large families. Some women desiring to cease child-bearing reported their husband's disagreement with them. Interviews revealed that one out of the 60 women had secretly taken birth control measures, though several others threatened to do so. A Gusii woman's strategy in this situation was delicate, in the sense that her husband could marry a second wife (though polygyny was increasingly becoming rare) if the first ceased to bear children. In such eventuality, it would require the first wife to yield half of her land to her co-wife, much a worse option than simply having one or two more children.[100] The increase of land stress in Kisii forced Gusii women to become innovative, as Kiogoro Focus Group Discussion[101] explains:

---

99 Gutto, S. B. O. (1975). Gender, Land and property rights in modern constitutionalism: Experiences from Africa and possible lessons for South Africa.

100 Kiogoro Focus Group Discussion, Nyaribari; (30 December, 2019).

101 Ibid.

"In a house of three wives, the first wife had one son and one daughter, the second wife had 6 daughters, and the third wife had 3 sons and 4 daughters. The patriarch of the family, Francis Oira, was a councillor in the African Local Native Council. He bought land in two other places, Menyinka and Bonyama-Sicho where he settled his 1st and 3rd wives. The second wife (with 6 daughters) was left in the ancestral land. Because she only had daughters, she married a woman who bore her a [grand]son. The boy later died mysteriously. As well his mother and the old lady also had died earlier. The land now lacked somebody to inherit it. One of the daughters, a primary school teacher stayed there until she retired and left for her home [where she was married]. Then she died. The remaining daughters had agreed that they could not subdivide the land amongst themselves because of cultural restrictions. They agreed to sell the land and share the proceeds."

To a large extent, women were still responsible for all of the daily work in agriculture; they did the tilling, planting, weeding and harvesting as a part of their responsibility for feeding the family. They were also in charge of fetching firewood and water as well as all the other household chores.[102] For these tasks, Gusii women relied very much on their children's labour contribution. Significantly adding to the perceived importance of children among the Gusii is the havoc that illness caused to almost any household. Time lost to illness further enhanced Gusii women's desire for children. A sick or pregnant mother whose husband works off the farm can call on her daughters to fetch firewood, water and cook, and on both sons and daughters to replace her labour in the field. A household without children will suffer when such tasks are left undone.

Consequently, marriage and children remained crucial to household reproduction under straddling Gusii family labour. A significant part of insecurity is the instability households face via marital instability, health problems or the potential disaster of not having children for labour and old age security. The decline of pre-marital bridewealth transfer and the increased competition over resources within rural households threatened the dissolution of the household itself.

---

102 Kongstad, P. & M. Monsted (1980). *Family, Labour and Trade in Western Kenya*. Centre for Development Research (Copenhagen), Publications 3. Scandinavian Institute of African Studies, Uppsala.

Generally, the establishment of a colonial economy and political order in Kisii had the effect of destabilizing the position of Gusii women both socially and economically. Major sources of change included the individualization of land ownership in Gusii men's names, the recruitment of male labour to the settler economy, cash crop production and formal education. All the land in the household principally belonged to the father. Gusii women acquired usufructuary rights of the land because they cultivated it. Inheritance of rights in land, though common, was not a significant concept.

The sudden loss of labour, particularly a woman's labour, could severely constrain household agricultural production. Examples of this abounded and were a lesson for any households that were fortunate enough to have avoided such calamities. A major illness or problematic pregnancy could cause the loss of an entire season's subsistence production, not to mention the expenses of health care. Even more severe were cases of longer-term illnesses in which household resources had to be fundamentally reallocated to overcome the loss. Not every household faced such trauma, but those that did stood as examples on the importance of guarding against the worst effects of ill health.

Furthermore, women under straddling suffered a two-fold insecurity. Like men, they perceive market access to key resources as tenuous. Women's principal concern was access to key inputs into agriculture and their local small-scale businesses, rather than off-farm employment (though they were affected by the insecurity their husbands faced in the latter). Women were also directly dependent on their husbands for key resources for agriculture and children's education. Because they had a greater reliance than their husbands on household agriculture, they could not be certain of their husband's continuous contribution to that sector. Combined with market insecurity, the uncertainty of their husband's support caused women to diversify their productive activities and diffuse resources to an extent which was even greater than that of men. They diffused their most important resource, their labour power, over a variety of agricultural endeavours and local businesses in an attempt to minimize exposure and risk in subsistence agriculture.

The dissolution of pre-colonial institutions designed to ensure each household had minimal access to land, labour and food increased the dependence of women on the market and their husbands. Thus, the rise of the individual, household estate constituted the end of community control over land. With it went the community's ability to allocate unused land to households that were in need. Instead, households with inadequate land resources (a situation worsened by an increasing number of people causing population pressure on land) had to purchase or rent additional land. All land purchases and most land renting relied on men's off-farm income, making women vulnerable to abuses of their land rights from their male counterparts.

In periods of scarcity, women were similarly dependent on the market and their husbands for maize purchases[103]. Overall, access to grain to meet subsistence shortfalls was heavily dependent on market purchases, even in a year of unusually poor production due to drought. While women's business income was often adequate for some grain purchases, men's income was typically so much greater than an unusually large shortfall required men to purchase grain to compensate for the shortfall.

Omwoyo[104] analyzed the organization and transformation of agriculture among the Gusii of Western Kenya in the colonial period. He demonstrated that the dynamism and innovativeness of Gusii indigenous agriculture showed its efficiency and productiveness. He further demonstrated how colonial penetration modified and marginalized Gusii's indigenous agriculture. Nonetheless, he attributes this transformation to colonialism. Moreover, Omwoyo[105] points out that women in Gusii adopted several approaches to counter the impact of coffee production on labour relations as established in the oral interviews. First, they deliberately intensified their labour. As they were forced to undertake the duties of their absent husbands, offer their labour in coffee farms, and perform their domestic chores, women had no alternative other than to work a little more and longer than before. Second, they used the working parties more than before. The working parties went around soliciting for jobs to do in rich farmers' coffee holdings to be paid in cash.

---

103   Ndege, P. The Struggle at the Market Place
104   Omwoyo, S. M. (1992) "The Colonial Transformation of Gusii Agriculture" M.A.Thesis, Kenyatta University: Nairobi.
105 Omwoyo, S. M. (1997). 'Women and Agricultural Production among the Gusii c. 1875-1963, *The Eastern Africa Journal of Historical and Social Sciences Research*, Vol .2 No.1.

In addition, they sought employment locally in the rich men's coffee *shambas* as individuals. This meant working for their employer in the morning hours and working on their holding late in the afternoon. Another strategy employed by the women to cope with their continued marginalization from the cash crop economy was to increase the production of profitable crops within their reach like *wimbi* and maize. Such women established vegetable gardens and were often seen selling vegetables in marketplaces on appointed market days. Last, women formed small-scale cooperatives or merry-go-rounds to raise the required capital to be detailed in the next chapter.

Davison[106] argues that gender relations to land in Africa have been modified over time by internal conquest and power struggles and by major intrusions from abroad. Studying land registration in Mutira and Chwele divisions in former Central and Western Provinces respectively, Davison asserts that the implementation of the Swynnerton Plan from the mid-1950s affected food production and caused gendered tension, especially at the family level. This was because land registration negatively impacted food crop production, which was a woman's sphere. Further, the household was impacted as the unit of production specifically addressing land policies and how they affected women's usufruct rights.

Conclusion

The chapter set out to examine the post-World War II Gusii agriculture. It maintained that the Swynnerton plan was a turning point to not only agriculture in Kisii but to women's access, use and control of the land. It further affirms that the intensification of agriculture in Kisii was predominantly founded on Gusii women's initiatives compounded by market imperatives and subsistence needs. This chapter further evaluates the post-World War II gendered Kisii agrarian trajectory and land relations. The chapter evidenced the post-war agricultural reconstruction course as stimulated by the Swynnerton plan which orchestrated land kleptocracy in Kisii. The chapter contextualizes the pre-independence dynamics in Kisii intending to shape the independence legacy in Kisii. It concludes that land reforms in Kisii resulted in the issuance of individual land title deeds which legalized individual land ownership and legitimized Gusii men's ownership of land to the disenfranchisement of women.

---

106 Davison, M. J. (1987). Without Land we are nothing. The Effect of Land Tenure Policies and Practices upon Rural Women in Kenya, *Rural Africana*, 27.

This increased land conflicts for such arrangements ignored the traditional overlapping and multiple rights and uses of land, reduced land accessibility and rendered Gusii women "landless". The next chapter undertakes an examination of the period 1960-1970 to ascertain the extent to which these colonial agrarian policies continued to exercise an imprint on women's access, control and utilization of land among the Gusii in post-colonial Kenya.

Chapter Seven

Post-Colonial Land Ownership and Gender Rights, 1960-1970

Introduction

The pre-independence period saw the Gusii deeply entrenched in the capitalistic economy as will be documented in this chapter. The previous chapter evaluated the post-World War II gendered agrarian trajectory and land tenure relations in Kisii. It elucidated the post-war agricultural reconstruction course as stimulated by the Swynnerton Plan which orchestrated the emergence of land kleptocracy in Kisii. The chapter also contextualized changes in the dynamics of land ownership and the attendant gender relations within broader developments that occurred in the aftermath of WWII thereby shaping the evolution of land use as relates to gender in post-colonial Kenya. The chapter concluded that land reforms in Kisii resulted in the issuance of individual land title deeds, which legalized and legitimized the ownership of land by men to the disenfranchisement of Gusii women.

The current chapter focuses on the post-independence agrarian trajectory and the restructuring of the same on gender relations in Kisii. The chapter details the impact of the colonial legacy on the evolution of agrarian policy, and the role of the policies contained in Sessional Paper Number 10 of 1965 on the land question in Kisii, especially as pertains to gender relations. The chapter explores how the early independence dynamics played out in Gusii with the futile attempts by the state to settle the gender land question among the Gusii. Further, it analyzes how the agricultural land dynamics impacted Gusii women's access, control and utilization of land in the period immediately after independence. This chapter, therefore, concentrates on the post-independence period and the transition of land rights from the settler dispensation to African ownership. It thus examines whether there was continuity or change in gender land access, use and control in Gusii.

To plot such continuity and change in women's access, control and use of land in Kisii, an analysis of the ensuing labour policies and government initiatives to promote cash crop production to shape the pre-independence and post-independence periods is undertaken. Further, the chapter evaluates the expansion of economic space and the need for Gusii women to take advantage of the opportunities availed by the market to access the elements of continuity and change, predominant in the period covered by the chapter. This chapter thus serves to create linkages between the agrarian and land policies pursued during the colonial and post-colonial dispensations within the context of gender relations in Kisii.

The Colonial Legacy and the Evolution of Land Policy

The pre-independence land tenure and agricultural dynamics were guided by the delicate complexities of the state of emergency and the agitations for independence by African nationalists. The Lyttleton prescription[1] and the Swynnerton injection were the only ways out of the complex transitory situation in Kenya. On the political dimension, for purposes of continuity and transition, the Lyttleton proposal provided for the federal principles of transition but lacked the economic aspect that would solve the larger impending economic transition crisis which only the Swynnerton plan[2] sought to address through the Kenyanization of the economy.

The Kenyanization of the economy entailed the emergency of agricultural complexities in Kenya in general and Kisii in particular which were to be straightened and beaconed on the provisions of the Swynnerton plan. The plan advocated for land consolidation, enclosure, individuation and titling for the independence transition in the agricultural sector. These provisions were intended at addressing both the delicate situation of putting agriculture firmly in the hands of Kenyans while at the same time guaranteeing continuity and sustainability of the country's agricultural sector as the sum of the peasant production sections as exemplified by Kisii. For the broad Kenyanization, the Red Plan and the Green Plan were fundamentals of change and continuity in the country's agricultural sector in the transition period. Kenyanization was highly characterized by the educated Kenyan elites who had evolved during the colonial period and were taking over the land that was vacated at independence by departing white settlers in the high-potential areas. This left the vast majority of the population on

---

1   Reference is made here to Oliver Lyttelton's constitutional proposals of 1954 which sought to create more political space for Africans at the national level. see
2   Roger Swynnerton (1954) A Plan to Intensify African Agriculture. Government Printer

mostly limited land that had previously been designated as native reserves.[3]

During the period close to self-rule in Kenya, group interests in land and their approach to the land question caused socio-political divisions that spilled over to the political party formation processes. The main political parties were the Kenya African National Union (KANU), Kenya African Democratic Union (KADU), the New Party of Kenya (NPK) for the settlers, and several other smaller parties representing smaller groups and interests.[4] Divisions around the land issue, therefore, became the foundation for different political projects for national independence. On one hand, KANU preferred a unitary form of government and advocated for a stay on further land reforms until political independence. On the other hand, KADU, motivated by fear of state domination, preferred a federal system of government with regional assemblies whose most significant duty would be the administration and adjudication of land matters.

Internally, the African parties were also deeply divided over the land reforms. The radical faction of KANU, rooted in a nationalist position on the issue of land, championed the wholesale seizure of the expropriated land in the White Highlands to settle the landless and squatters. Opposed to the radical wing, liberal capitalists within the parties sought to encourage the emergence of a free market in land to promote more rapid economic growth and provide a basis and greater security for accumulation by the landed elite.[5]

In particular, the liberal group feared that any radical departure from what the colonial land reforms had achieved would jeopardize economic growth by antagonizing relations with foreign investors. Whereas KADU made it clear that they wanted a constitutional provision that guaranteed ethnic groups' fair compensation for land that had been effectively expropriated by the colonial government, they also emphasized that respect for property rights in the land should apply to both individuals as well as ethnic communities.

The emerging political conflict at the time of transition to independence and the eventual defeat of the radical group led

---

3   Maxon, R. (2003). *Going Their Separate Ways: Agrarian Transformation In Kenya, 1930- 1950.* London: Associated University Presses.

4   Kanyinga, K. (2000). *Re-Distribution from above. The Politics of Land Rights and Squatting in Coastal Kenya.* Nordic Africa Institute Programme; Research Paper No. 115.

5   Kanyinga, K. (2000). *Re-Distribution from above. The Politics of Land Rights and Squatting in Coastal Kenya.* Nordic Africa Institute Programme; Research Paper No. 115.

to an evolution of a constitutional framework that favoured the sanctity and inviolability of private property rights. This provided for the protection from deprivation of private property without any compensation. Second, it resulted in the adoption without alteration of the legal framework on which the colonial reform on land tenure was based.[6] This formed the basis for land administration and management in the post-colonial period.

As Kenya gained internal self-government in 1963, the independence administration was keen not to disturb the legal framework of development laid down by the colonial state. The administration was convinced that private property rights in land would lead to intensified agricultural productivity upon which the economy depended. As a result, the regime adopted without alterations, the legal and policy framework of the colonial land tenure.[7]

In this regard, the Kenyan independence elites inherited the British institutions alongside national liabilities. These elites opted for the retention of the colonial powers by whatever means possible to avert and eradicate perceived poverty. For example, the independence regime inherited the land framework from the colonial government and used various forms of coercion and intimidation to transfer large tracts of public lands to private use.[8]

As Okoth Ogendo puts it, in the 1950s, the colonial state embarked on the consolidation of the settlers through systematic diffusion of political nationalism and the incorporation of Africans into a colonial mode of production relations, where it was to create a social class within the African ranks with similar interests and ideals to those of the ruling economic elites.[9] This needed adjustment to the realities of giving Africans opportunities given the political situation where the Mau Mau war had sensitized Africans on issues related to land and equal farming opportunities.

In 1963, the Registered Land Act was passed to resettle Africans on the land that was being left by the Europeans, as the independent government mooted two major strategies. First, was the transfer of over a million acres of land belonging to the departing settlers

6   Kanyinga, K. (2000). *Re-Distribution from above. The Politics of Land Rights and Squatting in Coastal Kenya.* Nordic Africa Institute Programme; Research Paper No. 115.
7   Ibid.
8   Matthews, K. and Coogan, W. H. (2008). Kenya and the Rule of Law: The Perspective of Two Volunteers. 60 *Maine Law Review* 561.
9   Okoth Ogendo: 139

after independence. These acres of land were purchased for the resettlement of Africans in small to medium size holdings. The second strategy was to transfer large European estates to private individuals, Co-operations and partnerships.[10] This new system that came to be known as the Africanization of the economy of the white highland laid the foundation for straddling as far as land holding in independent Kenya is concerned.[11]

A Land Development and Settlement Board was established to handle resettlement schemes for all races whose main activities were to stabilize prices of European-owned farmland and offer credit to Africans who wished to purchase farmland in scheduled areas. The board managed to settle Africans on a European post-World War II modelled schemes where over 700 farmers were settled in high-density holdings with total financing from the United Kingdom, World Bank and Colonial Development Corporation.[12] Many radical Africans such as Oginga Odinga, Bildad Kagia and Achieng' Oneko opposed this arrangement, referring to it as "political leverage of the settlers", at a time when it was clear that European rule was over.

The departure of colonial settlers left many squatters who had lived on their land for many years, some who never had homes to go back to, thus finding themselves landless. This emotive situation, now confronting the independence government, needed an immediate solution. In 1962, The Million Acre Plan was inaugurated, modelled to settle peasant and on small holdings. Schemes of this kind were expanded to accommodate the large numbers of landless and unemployed Kenyans. The financial and technical requirements for these settlement groups were either scaled down or done away with altogether to allow for quick settlement of people. By 1971, when the Million Acre Plan wound up, nearly 35,000 families had been settled on around 470,000 hectares of land at £30 million[13]

With the independence-era government agreeing that land had to be paid for, those who qualified to get the land had to demonstrate the capacity to repay the loan given by the government to purchase the land. Eventually, the majority of those who got the land in the settlement schemes ended up not being the absolute landless that these schemes were meant for. In reality, the land ended up in the hands of those who had accumulated cash from farming, business

10 Republic of Kenya, National Development Plan 1964-1970, Nairobi, Government printer
11 Okoth Ogendo, Tenants of the crown. 156
12 Ibid
13 Ibid, 158

and wage employment.[14] This arrangement, in effect, signified the continuity of social stratification that had begun with the Swynnerton Plan. As the relatively rich landowners settled down in the schemes, it turned out that almost 99% of them were men because they were economically better placed to be able to secure the land.

The pre-independence and the independence-era state, therefore, succeeded in perpetuating European land policies to the independent dispensation. Gusii was not an exception to this state of affairs as will be subsequently demonstrated. During this period of transition, as Gibson Kuria contends,[15] individualization of tenure was aimed at defeating Kenyan nationalism as the landed class of conservative people was to be created through the replacement of customary land tenure with one that permitted a few individuals to own land[16] as discussed in chapter five.

Implications for the Specific Case of Kisii

At independence, the Kisii leaders including politicians such as John Kebaso, Lawrence Sagini Ndemo and James Nyamweya as well as senior chiefs such as Musa Nyandusi, Motaroki Mobegi of North Mogirango and Matayo of Bobasi put a strong case to the KANU government that the region around Sotik Highlands was part of the Kisii frontier land and that the Gusii had settled at the western end of Sotik before the onset of colonial settlement.[17] The Kenyatta government allowed for the curving out of the scheme to the west of Sotik and Bomet for the settlement of the Gusii farmers drawn from all parts of Gusii. In particular, the KANU government appointed a Tripartite committee to redraw boundaries between the Gusii, Kipsigis and the Luo. Eventually, land to the west of sotik which was allocated to the Gusii came to be named as Borabu Settlement Scheme.

As per the National policy, the land was meant for the settlement of the landless and poor people with small pieces of land. Accordingly, chiefs were given the task of enlisting people who qualified from the locations. Again, true to the prevailing patriarchal practice, it was majorly men as heads of the families who were chosen for land allocation.[18] Furthermore, the chiefs took advantage of the

---

14 Stephen Orvis; The Agrarian Question. See also Group interview at Masongo, Nyaribari Chache
15 H.W.O Okoth-Ogenda: Tenants of Crown
16 W. R. Ochieng: Themes in Kenyan History, 237
17 Araka Matundura 80 and Samuel Bosire 75
18 Bramwel Nyangeso 89, Kitutu Chache South, Dec 2019

power they possessed and allocated themselves large pieces of land running into hundreds of acres. The pioneer politicians and elites who formed the petite bourgeoisie of the time also took advantage of their position to acquire large tracts of prime land in what came to be called Borabu Location.

The process of registration of land within the parameters established by the former colonial masters, while ignoring the African traditional practices on land use and ownership by the independence-era government, further marginalized Gusii women's access and ownership of land. Bruce and Migot-Adholla[19] as well as Shipton and Goheen[20] detail the shifting nature of land rights, including women's right to land. They indicate that the right to use land does not confer the right to control or dispose of land. Thus, land may be owned by one person and used by another, and there may be certain other rights enjoyed by third parties to the land, who may neither own nor use it. Thus, rights of use may be either shared or exclusive.

Research[21] to a large extent confirms that, in Kenya, land determines the economic well-being, social status and political power of individuals in a society. The Kenyan Government has over the years pursued programmes to transform customary land tenure into statutory freehold tenure through land adjudication, consolidation and registration (privatization). But the problem was (and remains so to a large extent today) that the land titles were being transferred almost exclusively to individual men, thereby leaving no provision on how women's land access rights were to be defined and how women would realize the goals of privatization once the lands were registered in the name of individual males. In this case, land titling not only increased men's control over land ownership and distribution but also increased women's dependency on men.

In addition, the central perspective in the understanding of gender relations is the need to focus on the ways that development, the market, the state, culture, global forces and multiple regimes of property rights affect land use practice and access.[22] Furthermore,

19Bruce, J. and Migot-Adholla, S. (1994). *Searching for Land Tenure Security in Africa.* Dubuque, Iowa: Kenadall/Hunt Publishing Co.

20 Shipton, P. & Mitzi, G. (1992). Understanding African Land-Holding: Power, Wealth and Meaning. *Africa* 62/3: 307-425.

21 Nzioki, A. (2009). *The Effect of land tenure on women's access and control of land in Kenya.*

22Carney, J. (1996). Converting the Wetlands, Engendering The Environment: The Intersection of Gender within Agrarian Change in Gambia. In *Liberation*

the weakness of women's property rights in Kenya, in general, and in Gusii in particular, has been noted in the past as a problem rooted in both statute and customary law. The post-colonial agrarian and land policies did not only disproportionately empower men economically as land owners they also accentuated this process through programmes aimed at the promotion of cash crops.

Further Initiatives to Promote Cash Crops in Kisii

Agriculture remained the major source of government revenue as the country transitioned to independence. According to the National Economic Survey of 1960, agriculture represented, in the aggregate of monetary and non-monetary activities, some 40 percent of the gross domestic product. But on this note, cash crop production represented 16 percent of the gross domestic product.[23] For Kisii, higher incomes derived from the sale of cereals resulted in the Gusii women, having higher purchasing power and had an encouraging effect on their engagement and intensification of production in the area. Compared to the 1950s, the largest acreage in Kisii was given over to cereals, scheduled crops and cash crop production in the early 1960s accounting for 90 percent of the total land under crops in 1961.[24] The land occupied by cash crops in Kisii rose steadily as demonstrated by the increasing cultivation of coffee from 472 acres in 1952 to 2,996 acres in 1958. According to Orvis, and backed by oral evidence, the number of coffee growers in Kisii, for instance, increased from 36,149 in 1954 to 54,000 by 1963. In addition, tea growers in the same period rose from 2,362 to 39,612.[25]

The intensification of cash crop production in Kisii in the immediate pre-independence period compared to the post-Second World War II period was echoed in the 1961 Economic Survey which noted a remarkable increase in coffee and tea cultivation. Coffee planting, according to the survey, grew rapidly as the major cash crop under the Swynnerton Plan, and the acreage increased to 26,000 acres.[26] The production increased from 1,000 tons in 1955 to 6,000 tons in 1959. With land consolidation on the rise in South Nyanza, the acreage planted to pyrethrum was also on the increase and was expected to remain so for the foreseeable future.[27]

Ecologies: Environment, Development and Social Movements, Peet, R. and Watts, M. (Editors), London and New York: Routledge.
23 Republic of Kenya, National Economic Survey,1960. Government Printer.
24 Ibid.
25 Orvis, S.T (1989). The Political Economy of Agriculture in Kisii, Kenya.
26 Republic of Kenya, National Economic Survey,1961. Government Printer
27 Republic of Kenya, National Economic Survey,1967. Government Printer

On its part, although maize was largely perceived as a food crop, it doubled up as a cash crop in Kisii, more so at independence compared to the pre-independence period. The efforts of Gusii women in the production of maize, as both a cash and subsistence crop, were noticeable in the 1963 Economic Survey which observed that the most noticeable changes in the year were the continued decline in the acreage of cereals such as millet and wheat and a further expansion in the area under maize cultivation, Meanwhile, according to the report, the pyrethrum acreage rose from 9,000 to 48,500 acres.[28] This was even motivational to the women's efforts in the production of maize as its revenue rose despite the fall in the deliveries by farmers (the Gusii women) since they did not have to pay any export cess since 1961.[29] This was foregrounded in coffee production where it was reported that the production of clean coffee of 7,300 tons in 1960/61 had more than trebled since 1958.[30]

The acreage under coffee growing continued to expand as the second generation of farmers began to plant the cash crop. As in education, the gender disparity in off-farm income resulted in a concomitant disparity in the coffee acreage. Furthermore, women's businesses began to expand rapidly, as sons' wives began to engage in these activities in follower households and adopted the practices initiated by their pioneer and follower neighbours. In some cases, daughters-in-law in pioneer households also entered off-farm labour, working as well-paid nurses and teachers, further enhancing pioneer women's levels of wealth.

The fore detailed increase in cash crop production was made possible by deliberate policies and initiatives by the government. According to the Development Plan 1964-1970, the government undertook to ensure farm inputs were not only readily obtainable but were also reasonably priced. The prices of farm inputs such as phosphatic and nitrogenous fertilizers were subsidized[31]. The Plan, further notes that in comparison to the pre-independence period, the prices of these important inputs would continue to be subsidized in future as changing circumstances required. Besides the subsidies to the crucial farm inputs, the government equally subsidized the prices paid to the farmers in the early independence years compared to the pre-independence period. In particular, the prices of maize and wheat were heavily subsidized as indicated in the

28 Economic Survey,1963. Government Printer.
29 Economic Survey, 1963. Government Printers
30 Ibid.
31 Development Plan, 1964-1970. Government Printer

1964-1970 Development Plan[32] to further promote the production of these crops.

These subsidies made it possible to produce maize profitably in the face of price challenges in the 1960s.[33] Besides the input subsidies, cash crop yields were steadily rising, courtesy of the government policy of introducing better production methods as exemplified by the use of hybrid varieties of maize[34] that Gusii women were largely receptive to. The deliberate efforts by the government to increase farm mechanization research[35] also enabled the identification of more efficient methods of using a wide range of farm equipment in Kisii which offered alternative cultivation techniques hence permitting cheaper methods of cultivation and improved soil conservation measures.

In addition, the provision of agricultural credit was increased. The independence-era government, through Agricultural Development Corporation (ADC) and Agricultural Finance Corporation (AFC), provided financial credit to farmers[36] in Kisii intending to intensify cash crop production. For example, from 1964 to 1970, the National Development Plan devoted K£4.7 million of development funds to agricultural credit programmes. In addition, the AFC availed K£2.4 million from its resources for agricultural credit projects[37]. The credit facilities were complemented and supplemented by the government intensification of communication in the country generally and in Kisii specifically.

Furthermore, the government invested K£43 million in the construction of a country-wide road network. In Kisii, the improved and newly constructed roads directly benefitted women's agricultural production more compared to the pre-independence times. Now, women would deliver their agricultural produce to various markets efficiently and effectively. For example, in the tea-growing areas of Kisii and Kericho, K£1.7 million was spent on the road development programme. Consequently, as per the 1969-74 Road Development Plan, the Kisii region had achieved 52 trunk roads, 145 major secondary roads and 8 minor roads totalling 205 kilometres of a

---

32 Republic of Kenya, National Development Plan, 1964 - 1970. Government Printer

33 Economic Survey, 1964. Government Printer

34 Development Plan 1964-1970. Government Printer.

35 Ibid.

36 Economic Survey, 1967. Government Printer. & Development Plan 1964-1970. Government Printer

37 Ibid.

road network to facilitate communication with the various market centres in the area.

Marketing of agricultural produce was another initiative that contributed to increased cash crop production. In Kisii, for instance, the government directly ensured the involvement of statutory boards in agricultural marketing. For instance, measures were taken to decontrol maize marketing which reduced the share of the final price that was absorbed by the marketing system in Kisii.[38]

Further Expansion of Economic Space & the Need to Maximise on Market Opportunities

The place of markets in engendering Gusii agricultural continuity and change was well illustrated on the eve of and after independence. According to the 1964 economic survey, the principal cause of the buoyant domestic product was the high cash earnings of the agricultural industry.[39] For instance, the value of marketed production in 1963 rose by 9 percent to a new high level. This was despite a fall in the average price received for coffee in 1962/63 from £342 per ton to £280 per ton. In these circumstances, coffee, a Gusii-produced crop held its place as the most valuable produce in the country. The recovery in coffee prices was resounding in 1964 with an additional £2 million from the crop,[40] On the opposite side, the failure of the market for pyrethrum to expand in 1964 was attributed to the rapid accumulation of expensive stocks of pyrethrum extract occasioned by drastic cuts in farmers' quotas.

The marketing dynamics and measures to enhance agricultural production, as impelled by changes from the colonial system to the independence system of government, were best laid out in the 1964-1970 Development Plan. A major impact on the market dynamics was the introduction of marketing boards and cooperatives which were not just responsible for identifying all possible markets for agricultural produce,[41] in areas like Kisii, but decontrolled the markets themselves. In Kisii, for example, market conditions permitted a moderate increase in the production of coffee through the Coffee Board of Kenya. The marketing boards and cooperatives took up issues afflicting the economic dynamics of agriculture. Further, the cooperatives and marketing boards undertook research and provided agricultural extension services on farm management

38 Development Plan 1964-1970. Government Printer.
39 Economic Survey 1964. Government Printer
40 Ibid.
41 Development Plan 1964-1970. Government printer

and marketing. They expanded to farm management training programmes exemplified by Kenya Agricultural Research Institute and the Coffee Research Farm which enabled farmers in Kisii to take up agricultural production on a business and technical side[42] as compared to the part-time basis that characterized the pre-independent period.

Numerous market centres provided opportunities for trading services in rural Kisii which, according to the 1964-70 Development Plan, had the highest number of trading centres among them; Kisii was the main urban centre while Keroka, Manga, Nyambunwa, Ogembo and Kebirigo served as rural centres. On the other hand, Nyamache, Nyamira, Kenyenya-Majoge, Keumbu, Nyamarambe, Nyamaiya, Rangenyo, Riosiri, Gesima, Ikonge, Nyangusu, Tinga and Nyansiongo fed rural centres as market centres. The market centres were largely supplemented by local centres which were dominated by Gusii women as the main players in the local agricultural trading industry in centres like Mogonga, Gesusu, Igare, Riochanda, Birongo, Obwari, Nyanturago, Magombo, Kiamokama, Masimba, Mosocho, Etago, Riana, Ikoba, Borabu, Itumbe, Maroo[43] among others.

As the 1967 Economic Survey points out, in the period 1964-67 as a whole, the growth rate of monetary agriculture was substantial and the survey indicates that1966 was the year that witnessed the most improvement in agricultural harvests and, in consequence, the most vibrant period[44] on the local marketing centres with all forms of agricultural produce being traded and exchanged by women. This was reinforced by the 1961 Economic Survey which noted that the average producer returns for all agricultural products showed improvement over the years.[45] Even the average returns received from coffee were comparatively high compared to 1958 and 1959. This, in essence, underlines the commitment of the independence-era government not only to increase production but to better market prices and returns compared to the pre-independence one. The improvement in agricultural production meant that more and more land in Kisii was brought under the plough hence the need to analyze continuity and change in land issues in the area at independence.

42 Ibid.
43 Development Plan 1964-1970. Government Printer
44 Economic Survey 1967. Government printers
45 Economic Survey 1961. Government Printer

Continuity & Change in Land Regime and Legal Framework at Independence

The relationship between land and labour was critical, especially in terms of women's ability to keep the proceeds of their labour at independence time. In Kenya, there are certain commodities, such as coffee and tea, where payment was awarded to the title deed owner (the Gusii man), rather than the cultivator (the Gusii woman)[46]. This created critical problems around the keeping of the proceeds of women's labour. Even in a situation where women had invested their labour in producing coffee and tea, it was their husbands, as legal title owners under statutory law who gained access to the proceeds of women's labour.[47]

In theory, under statutory law, women had the right to own land. However, in the formal legal sphere, women faced many obstacles in owning land. First of all, the cost of legal procedures prevented many women from using the courts to uphold their land rights. Furthermore, women were subjected to violence if they attempted to take land disputes to court, as male members of the family considered land issues a "family matter," instead of a state one. Thus, although women had land rights under formal law at independence, quite often, they lacked the means to enforce these rights, meaning that only a few wealthy women would own land. This state of affairs was detrimental to land ownership, access and control at independence as it meant that women could not fully participate in social and economic development, even though they made up half of the population.

In this regard, Kenya is undoubtedly a stellar example of the negative effects of formal land registration and titling. The ideology of exclusive rights over land, set forth by European settlers, was followed after independence as the government continued the policy of consolidating land under individual ownership. According to Davison,[48] these policies gave "precedence to individual ownership invested in male heads of households and, in turn, marginalized the usufruct rights of women formerly guaranteed under customary lineage tenure."

---

46 Group Discussion with women from Kitutu Chache north

47 Verma, R. (2001). *Gender, Land and Livelihoods in East Africa: Through Farmers Eyes*. Ottawa: International Development Research Centre.

48 Davison, Jean, (1988). "Who Owns What? Land Registration and Tensions in Gender Relations of Production in Kenya." In Jean Davison, ed., *Agriculture, Women and Land: The African Experience*. Boulder: Westview Press, 157-76, at 165.

The issues afore discussed made women's property rights highly vulnerable. Women who lost their land or whose land was encroached upon by neighbours appear to have had a choice in terms of which type of adjudicatory structure to pursue their complaint, the formal court system (which incorporated some customary elements) or the informal use of clan elders and chiefs, which was the forum of choice for dispute resolution of conflicts over "family" or customary land.[49]

In 1963, The Colonial Land Tenure Reform continued in independent Kenya as a matter of policy. For instance, the Development Plan (1970-1974) pointed out that, the land tenure system in Kenya should be changed so that farmers could be issued with title deeds to their lands and that fragments of land be consolidated into one bigger holding (Development Plan, 1970-1974). Thus, in the post-colonial period, the process of tenure reform involved three distinct stages: adjudication, consolidation and registration.

In the context of post-colonial land reform, consolidation was a measure designed to remedy the division of rural property into undersized units unfit for rational exploitation and the excessive dispersion of parcels forming parts of one farm. The process was also contained in The Land Consolidation Act (1968) CAP 283 of the Laws of Kenya. The Land Consolidation Act, which was based on recommendations of Swynnerton's Plan was complemented, in certain areas, by the Land Adjudication Act (1968).[50]

According to the International Women's Human Rights Clinic (IWHRC), land adjudication and consolidation were enacted to determine existing customary rights to land and convert them to single, registered freehold parcels of land. Because customary law prescribes that men control land and property but women do not, the bodies that determined these land rights did not recognize women's claims. The organization further argues that these Acts were bound to exclude most women from acquiring titles to land.

Registration of titles was the final step after land adjudication and consolidation. The Lands Registrar prepared registers under the laws of Kenya, the Registered Land Act 1963, CAP 300. The impact of this was to transform the land owners as contained in the Land Adjudication Act into the proprietors of the Registered Land Act.

When these circumstances combined with the traditional Gusii

49Kiagayu, N. N. (1979). *Property Ownership Structure among the Kikuyus: Its Impact on the Status of Women*. MA Thesis. Nairobi: University of Nairobi.
50 H.W.O Okoth-Ogendo Tenants of the Crown.

attachment to the land, it became clear why there were many land disputes in Kisii.[51] Private land ownership was the foundation of the colonial economy and administration, and it subsequently became part of the Land Law in independent Kenya. This was done without regard to the existing cultural concepts of land ownership and use, and so there remained tension, particularly in densely populated areas like Gusii, between the traditional concept of land and the imposed law of private property ownership.

Private land ownership was justified on the basis that it was necessary for efficient sale and transfer; that it would establish and maintain well-defined, legally enforceable rights to land; that it would be used as collateral for agricultural loans; that it would enhance land management and conservation; and that it would allow for mechanization of agriculture.[52] Unfortunately, none of the foregoing justifications considered the gendered socio-cultural aspects of land, and so the land became just another commodity to be transferred on a "willing seller-willing buyer" basis.

Reference to the 1964-1970 National Development Plan shows that changes and continuity in land policy were inevitable. In the period, the Land Use Committee was established with the primary objective of advising the Government on the best use of land where conflicting interests existed.[53] In Kisii for instance, the Land Use Committee struck a stable gender balance between male-dominated agriculture, especially of coffee and pyrethrum, and female-straddled production with maize taking the lead. Besides the advice on use, the land change and continuity policy prioritized land adjudication and registration programme in Kisii which was a pre-condition for the gendered rapid agricultural development in the area. For instance, the Land Adjudication Act of 1965 notes that by 1965, a total of 1,845,809 acres had been registered in 15 districts, including Kisii,[54] In Kisii, in particular, the 1966 Economic Survey indicates that between 1956 and 1963 no adjudication had been declared in the area. But, between 1964 and 1966, 7,000 acres in Kisii had been registered and declared for adjudication.[55] This registration and declaration designated the engendered change in the land registration in Kisii while at the same time, it showed continuity of policy in the land usufruct among Gusii women. Land

---

51 Group Discussion with men of Bonchari Jan 20120
52 Swynnerton Plan.1954
53 Development Plan 1964-1970. Government Printer
54 Economic Survey, 1966. Government Printer
55 Ibid.

registration had steadily spread from Central Province to every other province, including Nyanza which Kisii was part of. In addition, the land was speedily registered and adjudicated for transition purposes from the colonial to the independence regime[56]. With the increased registration and adjudication in Kisii, women were the major beneficiaries.

The 1969 Economic Survey observed that the most noticeable change was the continued decline in the acreage of coffee (a male-dominated crop) due to the coffee disease in favour of maize, a women-dominated crop.[57] This was unlike the pre-independence time when the gender question was cultured. Neigus reiterates this when he noted that the 1960s saw Africans engage more in cash crop farming than waged labour. In the northern areas of Kisii, farmers were encouraged to grow cash crops because the crops did well there. Further, he notes that the men from Kitutu, North Mogirango and parts of Nyaribari abandoned labour migration after independence and embarked on cash crop farming in their plots[58] after registration and adjudication, where they got more money than labour wages could match.

With the enthusiasm to engage in more production of cash crops and the quick shrinking of the land under occupation in Kisii, the Gusii agitated and advocated for more land inclusion under their territory after independence. Led by Washington Ondicho a member of the ADC, the Gusii petitioned the government to affix the Kisii boundaries to bring Sotik under them to allow the Gusii to benefit from the Sotik Settlement Scheme.[59] The petition, in part, read as follows:

> We Kisii people claim that a large portion of our land was included in the Kericho reserve ... if we are joined to them, the dangerous feeling would wash away. If there is [no] boundary between Kisii and Kipsigis, it will mean endless troubles ... it will increase tribal war ...[60]

While the petition from the outlook appeared to be a genuine case of peace and tranquillity, however, the covert motive by many Gusii men was the hunger for a more expansive portion of land to be registered under their name for cash crop production as the Gusii

---

56 Neigus, 1971. Conflict over Land
57 Economic Survey, 1969. Government Printer
58 Neigus 1971. Conmflict over Land

59 Ibid.
60 R. M. Maxon: British Rule in Gusii Land, 1907 – 1963.

women were increasingly after independence securing land for maize production as compared to the former years.

A study on women's land rights in sub-Saharan Africa observed that local-level land- management fora "... make moral and material evaluations of inputs and behaviour between male and female household members over a very wide spectrum when adjudicating land claims".[61]

In the1960s, the former reserves, including Kisii, were densely populated. According to the 1962 Kenya census, Kisii district had a total population count of 519,148 of which approximately 518,000 were Gusii.[62] This population density resulted in an unsustainable subdivision and use of land, causing land degradation, soil erosion, and eventually, increased poverty as shown in Table 6.1 below:

Table 6.1: Gusii population Density per square mile

Location	1948	1962
Bubaasi[Bobasi]	231	505
Kitutu	349	864
Machoge	302	651
Wanjare	302	480
North Mugirango	314	808
Nyaribari	368	632
South Mugirango	262	502

Source: R. M. Maxon (1989). Conflict and Accommodation in Western Kenya: The Gusii and the British 1907 – 1963.

As Table 6.1 illustrates, the population in all locations in Kisii more than doubled in a decade. This evidenced the excess pressure mounted not only on the population to produce more to feed themselves and the market but also the strain on the limited land available for gendered production in Kisii. This justified the fore-discussed Gusii guest for more land resources in the Sotik area.

When these circumstances combined with the traditional Gusii attachment to land, it became clear why there were many land disputes in Kisii. Private land ownership was the foundation of the colonial economy and administration, and it subsequently became part of the Land Law in independent Kenya. This was done without

61Whitehead, A & Tsikata, D. (2003). Policy Discourses on Women's Land Rights in Sub-Saharan Africa: The Implications of the Re-turn to the Customary. 3 *J. of Agrarian Change,* 67- 112.
62 Morgan, W.T & Shaffer Manfred N, 1966. Population of Kenya: Density and Distribution. Nairobi; Government Printer.

regard to the existing cultural concepts of land ownership and use, and so there remained tension, particularly in densely populated areas like Gusii, between the traditional concept of land and the imposed law of private property ownership.

The Impact of Kenya's Post-Colonial Land Policies on Gender Relations in Kisii

All over Africa and Kenya in particular, powerful groups and people were in control of expansive land, while large powerless sections of the peasantry were still marginalized and excluded from getting access to land[63] at independence. Essentially, at independence, the nature of the land tenure system in most parts of Africa was still male-dominated and existing social organizations and institutions were designed to meet that goal. Accordingly, Gusii rural women were one of the disadvantaged sections of the peasantry when one looks at their ownership, control and use of land.[64]

In the 1960s, therefore, women comparatively gained their influence and power when patriarchy and colonial continuity changed gender relations. Men dominated the transfer of the former white farms at independence as the economy became more and more dependent on cash crops for exports especially coffee, pyrethrum and tea[65] in Kisii while maize was dominated by Gusii women. This further peripherally mainstreamed Gusii women where they were forced into the informal economy with women trading their maize through informal market channels. This was illustrated in the 1966 Economic Survey which noted women's response to the stringent policies of the Maize Marketing Board. The survey noted that the actual sales of maize were larger than deliveries to the Maize Marketing Board and large quantities were exported illegally to Tanzania or sold in the internal black market at prices well above those paid by the Maize Marketing Board[66]. While these reveal Gusii women's active role in their economic life, it shows the continuity for them from the subsistence production and marketing in the pre-independence days to the affirmative change and their firm grip on cash crop maize production in the independence period.

The customary land-tenure systems that once provided women with access, ownership and use of the land were substituted for

63Cotula, L. (2007). (ed.) *Changes in "Customary" Land Tenure Systems in Africa.* Great Britain: IIED·

64 Ibid

65 Development Plan 1970-1974. Government Printer.

66 Economic Survey, 1966. Government Printer

land commercialization which favoured those with access to wealth earned from the sale of cash crops. Moreover, the access to European-type education at independence widened the gendered gap in favour of boys over girls.[67] It is important to state that title deeds just like identity cards rarely came into the hands of women, thus alienating them from control over land. Thus, land titles were invariably in the name of men, and a woman's limited access, control and use of land was only through her relation to men. With land titling, the customary rights of men gained legal force and market value over women ones. When the land was registered, the registered person was conferred with absolute rights and could, therefore, evict any occupier at his discretion. This according to Mzee Samson Nyandusi[68] saw women's security of tenure in the land that they occupied or had accessed and utilized threatened by these independence adjudications.

Gusii women in the mid and late 1960s gallantly faced the market forces as a redemption strategy and tact out of the Gusii socio-cultural complexities of the 1950s. The dissolution of the communal land tenure system hinged on the Swynnerton charter of 1954 that was polished out in the 1964-1970 Development Plan. The latter partially liberated Gusii women's dependence on male-dominated market production forces of cash crops. The 1967 Economic Survey[69] plots this redemption graph as it noted that sales to the maize and produce board and minor crops increased between 1965 and 1966 with all this increased production derived from the traditional small-farming areas[70] like Kisii which at the time was dominated by women compared to the male-dominated production of the cash crops in the pre-independence period. This made the Gusii women increase their production for the market, unlike the former period when they largely produced for subsistence. Therefore, independence for the Gusii women came with the accentuating continuity in their economic and land liberation struggles. This was evidenced in the 1968 economic survey[71] which indicated that the predominance of small-holders (Gusii women) in maize production had already been mentioned. In Kisii in particular, women had been highly responsive to the exhortation of the market[72] incentives to grow more maize for

67 Group Discussion with Bonchari men and women
68 Samson Nyandusi, 81 years. Nyaribari Chache
69 Economic Survey 1967. Government Printer
70 Ibid.
71 Economic Survey 1968. Government Printer
72 Ibid.

the market than for food as was the case in the 1940s and 50s as already discussed.

Gusii household's ability to respond to market opportunities or independence-era agricultural policy initiatives in a given agricultural enterprise was expansive because of the availability of resources spread across numerous sectors by the independence-era government. The 1964-70 Development Plan, corroborates these by explicitly revealing government commitment to support the agricultural hardware and software when it asserted that, a high proportion of agricultural development funds was to be used for programmes intended to help a large proportion of farmers[73] including Gusii women to increase production. For example, the 1964 economic survey noted that surpluses for most food crops were higher which meant that greater quantities were available for the markets. For the software aspect, the plan went further to devote K£2.2 million for agricultural education and extension while K£3.2 million was invested in agricultural research.[74] The economic surveys of 1962 and 1970 affirmed this by indicating the development and introduction of drought-resistant varieties of maize.[75] Moreover, K£4.7 million was designated as credit for farmers like Gusii women in small-scale farming for them not only to intensify their production efforts but to economically liberate themselves compared to the 1940s and 50s when they were economically chained to their men or husbands. Concerning the hardware, the AFC sunk K£2.4 million worth of agricultural credit besides the government's K£4.7 million. To ensure Gusii women benefited more from their production liberation efforts after independence as compared to the pre-independence period, the government through the Department of Physical Planning expanded urban centres, market and rural centres in Kisii. To facilitate women's effective and efficient access to the markets to sell their crops, the government invested in the roads network worth K£1.7 million in addition to the K£1.6 million already committed for the same.[76]

Increased agricultural production became intimately intertwined with independence. The independence decade, on the whole, witnessed increased agricultural production largely attributed to small-holder production characterized by women like in Kisii and the transfer of former settler farms to Kenyans. As the 1962 economic

73 Development Plan 1964-1970. Government Printer.
74 Ibid.
75 Economic Survey,1962. Government Printer.& Economic Survey, 1970. Government Printer.
76 Development Plan, 1964-1970. Government Printer.

survey noted, African (Kenyan) farmers commenced farming in the scheduled areas[77], in Kisii and particularly regarding Sotik, the Gusii received allocations of land through the land development and settlement board.[78] In Kisii, people who received land from the Land Development and Settlement Board were the political elites who were exclusively male[79]. According to Robert Maxon and backed by oral interviews, the political elites were exemplified by James Nyamweya, Lawrence Sagini, Zephania Anyeni, and Thomas Mong'are Masaki among others.[80] In essence, this represented the continuity from the colonial days of male grip on the land. However, the Gusii men's struggle for land in Sotik also permitted the Gusii women an opportunity to access the conventional Gusii land and control it for maize production, an element that was elusive in the colonial period, especially with the rolling out of land registration in 1954 as envisaged by the Swynnerton plan where land was registered in men's name.

With the Gusii women able to access and control land as their men and husbands tussled for more in the Sotik area, as Samson Omwenga, a member of the ADC had indicated in the petition to the government,[81] Gusii women devoted their time, energy and labour on the production of the crops under their domain as denoted by maize hence the increased production was inevitable. The 1962 economic survey opened the graph of sustained increased production in Kisii by singling out the expansion in the area under maize production and that of pyrethrum.[82]

In the independence year 1963, despite the heightened political temperatures in the country, the Gusii women were more determined to maximize gains from the market by producing more. The economic survey for the year affirmed a notable expansion in the year in the acreage under coffee and tea.[83] The increased production was motivated in part by the anticipated higher cash earnings from cash crops as exemplified by the 9 percent rise in the maize prices of 1964.[84] This was not exclusive to the women-controlled maize but covered coffee, tea and pyrethrum. This signifies Gusii women's amplified agency in the struggle to access, control and utilize land

77 Economic Survey 1962. Government Printer.
78 Development plan 1964-1970. Government Printer.
79 Women Discussion Group of Kitutu Chache
80 Maxon R.M British Rule in Gusii, 1907-1963.
81 Orvis 1989. Political economy of agriculture.
82 Economic Survey 1962. Government Printer.
83 Economic Survey 1963. Government Printer
84 Economic Survey 1964. Government Printer

which was minimal in the 1950s before independence. The women's efforts were recognized in 1965 with the increased production which indicated that the upward movement of marketed production during the last 2 years of independence was encouraging and its magnitude in small-scale production areas[85] like Kisii is relatively steady, something that could not be mentioned in the area before independence.

Gusii Women's Agentive Response to Constricted Economic Space.

As the independence government settled the many Kenyan citizens in the former settler farms, it became clear to the Gusii women that the colonial land policy would still be practiced in independent Kenya. Because it was clear that all land registration would be individual and that the whole purchasing exercise would be a men's affair, a few hard-working women acquired land for themselves using their husband's names, while widows used the names of their brothers-in-law for registration.

Gusii traditional brewed beer and processed sugarcane liquor were common women enterprises in the independence years. The 1960s witnessed Gusii women's agency in the form of increased commercial beer brewing as an alternate means to make money as it mainly required subsistence farm inputs and could be done at home.[86] The 1964 economic survey confirmed this by affirming that most of the agricultural production in the small farm Gusii women sector was retained on the farm for home consumption[87] and entered the monetary economy in a different form. The different form referenced here was through the Gusii women's enterprising agency. A good example is beer brewing where the same farm produce was harnessed for raw materials for brewing. Men with cash income were already frequenting local bars owned largely by non-Gusii traders in urban centres and other townships in the Gusii region. Women's entrance into this venture allowed them to increase their share of men's income. Even if a woman was receiving very little of her husband's off-farm wages, she could receive a share of other men's wages by selling them the local beer at a profit,[88] In effect, this reduced her dependence on her husband for key investments and house needs and therefore lessened her economic insecurity.

85 Economic Survey 1965. Government Printer
86 Group discussion with women from Kitutu Chache, Dec, 2019
87 Economic Survey, 1964. Government Printer
88 Norah Kemuma, 75, Bomachoge

This was followed especially in the independence era, by an explosion of these forms of businesses and an expansion on the part of businesswomen into other types of endeavours involving both breweries and other forms of trade. Initially, commercialized beer brewing began as a farm-supplied enterprise, requiring only maize, finger millet, and a large clay pot which served as a container for the beer.[89] This not only confirmed the women enterprise agency among Gusii women, but reveals their active and dynamic perception of maize production, both for delivery to the maize boards and for the informal domestic market in the area. In this respect, Gusii women's local breweries were reputed to be most interesting as narrated by Norah Kemuma.[90]

Accordingly, Gusii women maintained their brewing businesses because their husbands occasionally provided needed cash to cushion occasional losses or emergency household needs without consuming their working capital. The Machoge women's group discussion hinted at the fact that husbands would occasionally give their wives money, especially when they were drunk and in some cases when they found out that the brewing was not at its best.[91] Gusii women, as revealed in the discussions, invested such monies in pressing needs such as education, and illness, or used it to upset losses due to low harvest. Cash demands for these could easily destroy the working capital of a brewery if their husbands could not or would not meet unexpected expenses. Women in such circumstances entered brewing and other trades more often than did their wealthier neighbours, but they frequently could not sustain such participation in the face of other crucial and unmet household needs.

Several Gusii women began profitable businesses such as daily fruit and vegetable retailing in the central market of Kisii town and other townships. The 1964 economic survey paints this clear picture by documenting that surpluses for most food crops were higher and this translated to greater quantities being available on the markets.[92] The 1968 economic survey echoed the same noting that as far as food production was concerned, assured satisfactory supplies as the good harvests sufficiently fed the population both directly at home and through commercial enterprise at the markets.[93] Moraa

---

89 Ibid.
90 Ibid.
91 Machoge women group discussion.
92 Economic Survey, 1964. Government printers
93 Economic Survey,1968. Government printers

Onyangore indicated the same in oral interactions.[94] The beer enterprise was equally reflexive in the local evening porridge sales at the expansive market centres in Kisii.

Given the return to most women enterprises, they continued to pursue it more strongly after independence. The centrality of the Gusii women's agency in motivating their economic behaviour was responsible for the persistence and sustainability of their business enterprises. As indicated by the Bonchari women group, the enterprise unlike in the pre-independence period ensured that women accessed and controlled money and land in part.[95]

Besides the women's business enterprise, the Gusii women's agency was revealed through self-help groups. According to Moraa,[96] in this financial scheme, each member contributed every week and the total contribution was given to each woman in turns. This allowed a woman to receive extra earning which was immediately placed in secure savings, such as purchasing livestock that she could later utilize in the acquisition of household goods that were not purchased by the husband. In this regard, many women achieved extra earnings than what was necessary for basic subsistence needs, that their husbands expected them to provide.

Thus, Gusii women's beer brewing and other small-scale businesses represented attempts to increase their share of off-farm income and to meet their household subsistence requirements. In most instances, these activities did allow them to overcome their dependence on men partially through investment in education and agriculture for the long term. As such, these business activities did fundamentally alter the colonial entrenched existing gendered power relationships within Kisii and reduced the insecurity Gusii women faced vis-a-vis the market and access, control and utilization of land.

In addition to business and self-help groups, Gusii women's agentive response to independence was quickly reorganized in labour form. Many families invested in both hired labour and land ownership to be used across the agricultural spectrum in Kisii to enhance income generation and to minimize exposure to price fluctuations that tended to happen in a single agricultural produce. The 1968 economic survey acknowledged this, noting that the present price

94 Moraa Onyangore, 78 years. Nyaribari. A renown businesswoman in Kisii town in the 1960s
95 Bonchari women group discussion
96 Moraa Onyansi 85 Bonchari

structure not only led to large losses on exports but because the consumer price was so high, it encouraged black-market dealings outside the official channels[97]. As a result, Gusii women engaged in broader mixed farming activities that were small-scale in nature, but with cash crops especially maize, unlike the pre-independence times. By 1969, most Gusii women grew substantial amounts of maize, while Gusii men grew coffee, tea, pyrethrum and sugarcane. In this regard, the Bobasi women group observed that no household relied exclusively on one cash crop or subsistence crops such as maize[98].

Gusii women also diversified investment of their resources by allocating principally their labour power in both agricultural and non-agricultural endeavours. All women combined labour and land investment in staple and cash crops. In the cash crop sector, women's labour allocation varied with the returns they directly obtained from the crop, which in turn depended on their relations with their husbands. Thus, tea, coffee, pyrethrum and cooperatively marketed milk were sold via official marketing agencies/boards, payment from which was made only occasionally and almost exclusively to the Gusii men. This made the Gusii women invest more of their labour time at independence to maize production and other off-farm ventures which they directly received the payment and controlled their production, as the Bomachoge women group revealed.

Due to the prevailing circumstances at the coming of independence, women's networks met emergency needs for food. Men's loans could vary from small amounts for school fees to very substantial amounts needed for medical and other demanding expenses. While it is impossible to ascertain the exact amount of such transactions, it is clear that they were significant for assisting in an emergency, but did not fundamentally alter the distribution of wealth and resources created by economic transitions. Women's networks served different purposes, involved different people and were maintained in different ways than men's. Most importantly, women's networks principally involved connections within a woman's original native clan, not her husband's. A woman would rarely turn to her neighbour (the wife of her husband's brother or cousin) if she could gain assistance from her sister or cousin from her original home clan. According to the Bomachoge women discussion group,[99] women married into a

---

97 Economic Survey, 1968. Government printers
98 Bobasi women group discussion.
99 Bomachoge group discussion Dec, 2019.

given clan, and particularly wives of brothers, were said to distrust one another because they competed over the resources of their husbands who were brothers and cousins. Networks developed among sisters and cousins who were dispersed throughout Kisii, since women married into various clans. This gave women networks greater geographical spread, complexity and diversity than those of men. A woman may well have obtained emergency assistance to cover hospital bills or a young girl to care for her sick child from her mother's brother's granddaughter, involving a 'path' of connections covering four clans and four distinct locations. Most commonly, women's networks were used to provide child care, food assistance, and health assistance, and served to locate land and labour for hire in distant locations.

Additionally, at independence, Gusii women's networks assisted women to lessen women's dependence on men. While women's businesses did not wholly alter their dependence on men/husbands, they did provide limited independent income that was highly valued by virtually all Gusii women. A wife starting a new business could sometimes acquire her initial capital from her women's folk network if her husband could not provide it. Also, if for instance, sickness destroyed the fragile juvenile businesses, the woman according to Machoge women group discussion re-engineered her business anew via assistance from the network established from her enterprises or from the networks established at the elementary training institutions[100] they had begun attending at the time of independence. Because of this slight Gusii women's liberalism at independence, many Gusii men/husbands quietly attempted to limit the degree to which women could use such networks. Thus, while valuing the ability of women to obtain emergency subsistence through such networks, some men attempted to limit women's visits to their businesses and "school" associates. Yet, their membership was fluid because of alternative demands for women's labour, illness, disagreements among members, and husbands' opposition to them as organizations in which women "gossip" about their ill-treatment at home. According to Richard Ong'esa[101], this was more than just a 'traditional' desire to limit a woman's agency; it was often an attempt to limit economic independence that might threaten the conjugal contract as the man/husband had been able to negotiate it.

---

100 Bomachoge women group discussion.
101 Richard Ong'esa, 78 years.

Unlike men's networks, the maintenance of women's networks required some degree of reciprocity. Women attempted to maintain close contacts with their native families and clan members who may have been willing to help when needed. In this regard, simple reciprocity was all that was needed to maintain these networks because women constituted a dependent and vulnerable group due to their structural position in the economic hierarchy. Consequently, a woman's network consisted of those she had known and trusted for a lifetime who were in the same position she was in concerning their husbands and the market, and did not compete with her for resources. Reciprocity alone would maintain a network in this situation, doing little to alter fundamentally the structurally dependent and insecure position in which women found themselves, but helping to reduce the consequences such insecurity might entail.

Consequently, between 1960 and 1970, Gusii women attempted to use *ebisangio* to expand their total agricultural labour time (as *amasaga* did in the days of old) by having them work in the evening (customarily *ebisangio* normally functioned in the morning hours, when virtually all agricultural labour took place). These evening efforts came to be made by women who were members of a new type of morning labour group, the "self-help" group, or *ekeombe* (pl. *ebiombe*). The *ebiombe* were initially intended to be multi-purpose grassroots development organizations at independence in Kisii. They combined communal labour efforts with community investment in a wide variety of self-help development projects.[102] An example of this is one particular *ekeombe* which was started by a female primary school teacher, with assistance from women from other households, and had 50 members at its peak. In addition to working on each member's field in turns, like in *ebisangio*, this group pooled community resources to build a nursery school. After the 1960s, nursery school attendance had become an almost essential prerequisite to primary school entrance and therefore was extremely important. In addition to the provision of labour and community investment functions, these particular *ebiombe* and others that developed later hired themselves out *en masse* to any farmer who would pay their price (usually approximately the current market rate). The earnings were either invested in a community project or, more commonly, divided among members at the end of the year.

102 Holmquist, F. (1975). *Peasant Organization. Clientelism and Dependency: A Case Study of An Agricultural Producer Cooperative in Kenya.* Ph.D. Dissertation, Indiana University.

Nonetheless, disputes between the educated and those not educated members became commonplace in *ebiombe*. Problems usually involved battles between leadership and members over the use of funds in investment projects. Coincidentally, in all groups, leaders were educated, because they had to be able to work with the Ministry of Cooperatives to receive government assistance in the investment efforts. Due to these forms of ritually and leadership wrangles several other *ebiombe*, consisting largely or totally of women, rose and fell within short time frames in the first independence decade. They failed for the same reasons *ebisangio* did – alternative demands on labour time, husbands' opposition to them, and disputes over fair division of labour time – and because they could not be used to pick tea, coffee and pyrethrum in the independence decade.

Similar to *ebisangio*, *ebiombe* did not represent a quantum increase in labour-power. They were a precise, egalitarian exchange of labour among members. Why, then, did they remain popular, especially among women at independence? First, like *ebisangio*, they slightly increased productivity and absolute labour time in agriculture, as the economic surveys of the 1960s. More importantly, they included a savings scheme through which women could physically remove money from their homestead and other family members, and manage it for their own needs. Each *ekiombe* required that a member paid a nominal fee each time the group worked on her fields. At the end of the year, this money and any earned from hiring themselves out was divided among the members.

In place of community socioeconomic support mechanisms that were destroyed by colonialism, women at independence relied on market mechanisms to obtain essential resources. For those without an abundance of market power (relatively high and secure off-farm income), this entailed significant risks of losing access to land and financial resources. Only the comparatively stable women with secure and consistent off-farm incomes provided the power that mitigated the insecurity majority of the Gusii women faced before independence.

Researchers who have examined the social milieu of rural Africa, dispute the utility of the standardized conceptualization of households as the chief units of the rural political economy. Guyer[103] for instance, has questioned the utility of the term, arguing that

103 Guyer, J. I. (1984). *Family and Farm in Southern Cameroon.* Boston: Boston University African Studies Centre.

its use often hides crucial relationships of conflict or cooperation between elders and juniors, men and women, women social groups, self-help groups, business partners and among other domestic groups in situations of extensive differentiation.[104]

Increasing land stress in Kisii at independence meant that even widows were no longer safe from encroachment. Interview with Getenga group discussion[105] relates: Widows could get title deeds of their husbands' land according to the law. But men still felt entitled to the land. They sometimes forced themselves on the land and others forced women out of their homes. On the other hand, widows were abandoned by greedy brothers-in-law, which prompted women to land purchasing in the 1960s. This was exemplified by Kerebi Marita, a widow who purchased land in the Borabu settlement scheme and registered it under her brother-in-law's name. The brother-in-law later turned against her and chased her away, forcing her to go back to her marital home where land was already scarce[106] and where tradition held that she was entitled to her father's land as a married woman. Such cases made the Land tribunals that used to solve land disputes more active in the independence period. They used both legal and traditional alternative ways of settling land disputes in the Kisii area. As already mentioned, it is women who always faced land injustices as they were not represented. Indeed, land disputes became an unending feature of life in Kisii. Land-related murders commonly occurred during investigations into land disputes that often took more than ten years, during which the litigant was killed. A Kisii High Court judge pointed out that murder of the litigants in land conflicts was common in Gusii.[107] Murder threats also contributed to injustice as litigants often lost hope and dropped land conflict cases.[108] Land feuds in rural Gusii commonly occurred between neighbours who were often close relatives and between brothers, cousins, uncles, in-laws, parents and their children.

The increased popularity and expansion of education in the 1960s saw girls start joining schools, though in limited numbers. Some parents, especially those who had gone to school, purposed to educate both daughters and sons. The women who got the

104 Guyer, J. I. (1981). Household and community studies in African studies. *African Studies Review* 24:(2/3):87.138.
105 Ibid
106 Kerebi Marita, 86 years
107 https://www.standardmedia.co.ke/article/2000024669/anxiety-as-murders-rise-in-kisii-over-land-disputes.
108 Nyaribari Chache group discussion.

opportunity to get educated and get employed are among the very few who could purchase land for themselves. Some women, who had been widowed, saw education for their daughters as the only way they could empower their daughters. Christine Omanga is a good example of a daughter educated by her mother from the sale of *chang'aa*. She eventually went to Eregi TTC and became a primary school teacher and eventually trained further to become a teacher of secondary school and even became a headmistress. The other pioneers of that period include Wilkister Ongubo and Nyarinda Moikobu.

In reaction to the system that disenfranchised them, women entrepreneurs that were able to access off-farm cash now started purchasing land for themselves and utilizing it as they wished

Conclusion

The chapter set out to detail how the agrarian policies pursued by the independent Kenya state between 1960 and 1970 represented elements of continuity and change from those initiated during the colonial era. It is demonstrated in the chapter that the independence government continued with the policy on land consolidation, registration and titling, and agricultural extension support and introduced the provision of credit to small-scale farmers like the Gusii women while supporting the expansion of cash crops by the small-scale Gusii women farmers. Gendered labour was the key resource limiting improved husbandry as family labour was generally strained because it was diffused over a wide variety of activities.

In a few wealthier families, where the agricultural potential and early government development efforts were greater, the transition to capitalism worked. Within this context, most women diversified their labour allocation into local market activities, which were relatively poorly paid in terms of real hourly wage. Their households did not successfully attain a balance between capitalism and subsistence where men's investment and women's labour combined to create relatively highly profitable agricultural and non-agricultural enterprises. In lower-income households, where overall income was lower and the development of the agrarian revolution less advanced, Gusii women diversified their labour more widely, as a result of existing market forces.

Historically, Gusii women "straddling" shows how the agrarian revolution developed so quickly, largely self-financed by peasants. Market integration in Gusii introduced rural women to market dynamics. In particular, straddling left Gusii women in positions of relative security and independence. This, combined with straddling's emphasis on education and off-farm income, expanded the degree to which Gusii women were willing to become specialized commodity producers.

The result is the rather counter-intuitive discovery that in Gusii, the most densely populated region in Kenya, rural women were the most significant resource in increasing agricultural productivity. The absolute amount of potential labour power was adequate, but the diverse seasonal agricultural demands under the resource diffusion characteristic of straddling left Gusii women in particular with little labour available to respond to market or policy changes. But, the necessity of off-farm income in straddling meant all men would continue to expend time and resources trying to obtain off-farm employment or business opportunities.

Chapter Eight

Conclusion

The need to improve access to land and strengthen women's land rights in Africa provided the main rationale for undertaking this research, with specific reference to the Gusii of Kenya, the effects of gendered land ownership, access, control and use. Gender relations and land tenure issues have been of concern during the pre-colonial, colonial and post-colonial periods globally. The book mainly deals with three intertwined issues: gender relations, colonial and post-colonial land policies on property rights, and ownership. It examines the changing Gusii women's responses, over time, on land access, ownership, control and usage. It contextualizes the extent to which differentiated access, control and ownership of land has impacted women in Kisii. The research examined existing historical patterns and the evolution of gendered relations and how they affected the utilization of land in Kisii between 1895 and 1970. It analyzed the relationship between indigenous land tenure systems and gendered relations; the effects of colonial land policies on gendered relations, and examined gender rights in relation to land access and ownership in the post-colonial period in Kisii.

The general objective of this research was to establish the impact of colonial and post-colonial land policies on gendered relations, property rights and ownership in Kisii. Specifically, we analyzed the relationship between pre-colonial land tenure systems and gender relations in Kisii, established the effects of colonial land policies on gender relations and examined gendered responses in relation to land ownership. The study was guided by the following questions: (a) What was the relationship between pre-colonial land tenure systems and gender relations in Kisii? (b) What were the effects of colonial land policies on gender relations in Gusii? (c) How did Gusii women respond to gendered land rights and ownership in the study period?

The analysis was undertaken within the framework of property rights and agency theories. Property rights and agency theories historicized the examination of the gendered land issues during pre-colonial, colonial and post-colonial periods among the Gusii.

The study affirms that property rights are 'the rights of individuals to the use of resources supported by the force of etiquette, social custom, ostracism, and formal legally enacted laws. The 'classical' form of the property rights theory focuses on the historical and institutional context that shapes and changes property rights. It is further established in the study that rights in land include more than the right of ownership, but also the right to its utilization. Within this study, therefore, property rights theory was considered the basic economic incentive system that shapes resource allocation.

Different specifications of property rights arose in Kisii in response to the economic problem of allocating the scarce resource, land. The theory was employed to analyze the relationship between Gusii indigenous land tenure systems and gender relations. Further, it establishes the effects of colonial land policies on gender relations among the Gusii; and gender rights in relation to land right and ownership in the post-colonial period in Kisii.

Agency theory was employed to analyze problem-solving that occurred in Kisii in the relationship between principals (land owners/government and men) and the women as self-agents. Agency theory, therefore, was used to examine Gusii women's responses to gender, land ownership, use and control under the indigenous land tenure systems. Using the theory, we further explored Gusii women's responses to the effects of colonial and post-colonial policies pertaining to gender-land relations.

The historical research design generated qualitative and quantitative data with verbatim submissions straddled with archival materials. The qualitative approach helped in capturing informants' exclusive experiences in a given historical perspective to facilitate cross-checking of data and increase the reliability of the research and findings. The research solicited views, opinions and comments relating to gender in ownership and control of land in Kisii. The study consolidated relevant primary and secondary data to generate adequate information. The primary data was synthesized and synchronized with the extant secondary data. Data collection was done through open-ended questionnaires and verbatim informal/ unstructured oral interviews. Data analysis was done thematically and periodically through descriptive accounts and was presented in the form of chronological historicized narratives organized sequentially in chapters

Chapter Two discussed indigenous land tenure and gendered relations in Gusii and the impact of initial colonial land policies on gendered land utilization and resource appropriation in Kisii. The chapter details the various aspects of indigenous land tenure systems, the interaction between traditional land tenure and how they shaped land reforms among the Gusii. The chapter further examines the concept of land among the Gusii, modes of land acquisition as well as the customary land tenure systems in relation to gendered relations of production. It maintains that the indigenous land tenure system, among the Gusii, was flexible and dynamic providing for relatively egalitarian access to land by both men and women during the pre-colonial period.[1] The indigenous land tenure system was anchored on the principle that land was owned communally and was handed down from the ancestors to the present and future generations. Therefore, although men remained the custodians of the land, there existed laid down customary laws and norms that guided how the land was handed down to the next generations. Rules, regulations and communal etiquette guided the community on the question of women's access to land thus ensuring that women were able to utilize the land to feed their families. Further, the chapter contends that customary land tenure systems and norms provided avenues for resolving critical land use issues. For instance, childless women or those without sons were not disinherited from family land for there existed arrangements that allowed them to access and use the land. Land issues were resolved through the Council of Elders either at the village or clan level.[2] It is argued, in the chapter, that the onset of colonialism destabilized and distorted the traditional marital system of access, ownership and use of the land with women in polygamous marriages resorting to alternative measures such as women-to-women marriages, witchcraft and in extreme cases homicide[3] to guarantee their safety in family land access control and use. The chapter lay down the historical foundation against whose backdrop the analysis of the effects of colonial land policies on land access, control and ownership in Kisii was undertaken.

Chapter Three analyzes the effects of nascent colonial policies and the question of land access, control and ownership in Kisii. It emerges that colonial policies between 1920 and 1939 had the net effect of constricting women's access, control, ownership and

1   Akama J.S & Maxon R.M (2006) The Ethnography of the Gusii
2   Nigus D.L (1971) Conflicts over Land
3   Ibid.

utilization of land as ownership became more competitive and contested. Key colonial land policies were informed by the post-World War I economic meltdown that compelled the enunciation of the dual policy of 1922.[4] The chapter interrogates the impact of these policies on women's access, control, and utilization of land in Kisii. Further, the chapter details the tormenting effects of the Great Depression on overall colonial agrarian policy and the resultant impact on Gusii women's access, control and utilization of land. The chapter addresses alterations and contradictions exhibited in colonial agrarian policy in the wake of Gusii's response to the measures instituted to stem the negative consequences engendered by the Great Depression on the colonial economy. It measures the impact of these "control strategies" on Gusii women as pertains to land access, control and utilization. The interwar period exerted pressure on Gusii women which resulted in their agentive response to property rights, especially the land usufructs.[5] With a majority of the Gusii men providing labour in the adjacent white highlands the resultant wages coupled with gendered education commoditized and individualized both land and marriage (dowry payment) which further narrowed down Gusii women's access, ownership and use of land. The introduction and entrenchment of coffee in the Kisii region in the pre-World War II period provoked Gusii women's agentive subsistence response to Post-World War II economic environment as women accorded pride of place to crops which came directly under their control such as maize and groceries. The traditional patterns of collegial labour organization, *amasaga*, demonstrated this agentive response as Gusii women sort to cope with emerging changes impinging on questions of land access, ownership and use.

The chapter concludes that in the aftermath of the First World War, the agricultural policies that were introduced favoured and assisted men in Kisii to produce more for the market than for consumption, while Gusii women were seen and treated essentially as a source of cheap labour. However, in an attempt to stem its negative economic repercussions, the Great Depression of 1929-1933 forced the colonial state to direct more attention toward the Kisii native reserve than hitherto. The consequence was that more land was put under the hoe or/and plough to the detriment of soil fertility and conservation as land use became contested between genders thus further straining gender relations in Kisii. Land degradation in

4   Maxon R.M (2003) Going their Separate ways
5   Maxon R.M (1989) Conflict and Accommodation in Western Kenya

the Post-Great Depression period ushered in new land use policies aimed at promoting agricultural production and soil conservation. Men left the women working on the land as they sought migrant labour employment in the European settlements. The increasingly common absence of Gusii men from their rural homes began to affect Gusii women adversely; now, women were required to take on a substantially increased share of agricultural labour coupled with other household activities, although with curtailed usufructs. This colonial impact on gender relations presented Gusii women with minimal potential opportunities for the enhancement of their roles in land ownership and usage. The importance of land in agricultural production in Kisii and the resultant gender-related issues became more manifest as the colonial state navigated the challenges posed by the Second World War, which chapter four interrogated.

The onset of World War II forced the emphasis of official policy on increased agricultural productivity with little regard for soil damage. This was required to provide supplies to military forces and generate more resources needed for war initiatives The war saw unprecedented mobilization of human (men) resources to serve the purposes of the war either as soldiers or as carriers.[6] As these policies were applied to the Gusii, they had a detrimental effect on women's access, control and use of land. As demonstrated in chapter four, the drive for increased agricultural production triggered more intense land use among the Gusii thereby exacerbating competition and contestation over this resource. The chapter maintains that this scenario exercised a profound impact on gender relations by further constricting control and access of women to land as a key factor of production. It concludes that this particular aspect of the war had the cumulative effect of increasing the agricultural workload for the Gusii women without bestowing any land ownership rights or any other benefit on them.

Chapter Four argues that the emphasis on cash economy privilege during World War II had the effect of forcing Africans either to produce commodities for sale or join wage labour. This led to increased production of maize, coffee, tea and pyrethrum. The pressure for increased production of these crops inclined the Gusii to put the available land to more use. This presseged a scenario characterized by hunger for land both for men and women leading to strained gender relationships over questions of access, use and ownership of this key resource. Improvements in farm technology occasioned by

6   Ochieng' W. R. (1985) A History of Kenya.

the use of the plough, which was now in good supply, led to more land being put into crop farming. Specifically, Gusii women had to work harder to produce more to meet the demands of the colonial government and for subsistence.[7] However, Gusii women got some form of control over agricultural production when their husbands were away for work. They controlled the planting, harvesting and sale of their farm produce while the men were away for war and labour. These gave the women some level of independence to use the money they got from selling their harvests. During the war period, continuous land use throughout the year began as land was getting limited. The use of land in all seasons would lead to land degradation and other related land problems that prompted the colonial state to put in place measures of land preservation. The chapter concludes that the war brought major social and economic changes that eventually affected both the social relations in Gusii households in particular and the rural economy in general. These effects were felt beyond 1945 into the 1950s and 1960s.

Chapter Five focuses on Post World War II agrarian trajectory/ reform and the impact of the same on gendered relations in Kisii. It detailed the post-war agricultural reconstruction course, the Swynnerton plan and land kleptocracy[8] in Kisii, as well as the gendered land relations in the area. The chapter examines how the pre-independence dynamics played out in Kisii with the futile attempts by colonial authorities to resolve the gendered Gusii land problem among them being the scramble for land, land tenure complexities as well as land degradation. Moreover, it analyzes the impact of agricultural and land dynamics on Gusii women's access, control and utilization of land in the pre-independence period. It emerges that the pre-independence dynamics in Kisii shaped the evolution of land policy pertaining to. The chapter demonstrates how land reforms in access, use and ownership among the Gusii as Kenya attained independence resulted in the issuance of individual land title deeds which legalized and legitimized individual ownership of land Gusii men to the disenfranchisement of Gusii women. This increased land conflicts for such arrangements ignored the traditional overlapping and multiple rights and uses of land, reduced land accessibility and rendered Gusii women "landless". In response to these economic changes, Gusii women's agency became

7   Orvis S.W (1989) A Political Economy of Agriculture in Kisii.
8   Odhiambo-Ndege P (2012) Inaugral Lecture: From the Accumulation of Women and Children to "Land Grabbing": Agrarian Kleptocracy and the Land Quesition in Kenya.

witnessed through such strategies as resorting to education and channelling produce via the black markets where prices were higher compared to those obtainable through official channels.

The independence period saw the Gusii deeply entrenched into the capitalistic economy as chapter six detailed. It emerged that at independence, the Gusii agrarian trajectory had a restructuring effect on gender relations in Kisii. The effects of the colonial legacy, the Sessional Paper Number 10 of 1965,[9] gendered kleptocracy in Kisii and the gendered land relations in the area spurred the Gusii women agency in the independence decade. The chapter explores how the early independence dynamics played out in Kisii with the futile attempts by the state to settle the gender land question among the Gusii. It emerged that in the independence period, the transfer of land rights to Africans (Gusii) failed to fundamentally alter long-standing impediments to land access use and ownership by women in Kisii.

Chapter Six concludes that households in the independence decade engaged in agricultural expansion, purchasing or hiring of land, and labour, and investing in capital inputs to increase their production. This gave Gusii women an opportunity for simple reproduction, permitting them a greater share of off-farm income to be used for investments in expanded reproduction. Within this context, Gusii women diversified their labour allocation into local market activities. However, these initiatives were relatively poorly paid in terms of real hourly wages. As a consequence, their households did not successfully attain a balance between capitalism and subsistence where men's investment and women's labour combined to create relatively highly profitable agricultural and non-agricultural enterprises.[10] In lower-income households, where overall income was lower and the development of the agrarian revolution less advanced, Gusii women diversified their labour more widely, as a result of existing market forces. The chapter affirms that Gusii women "straddling" showed how the agrarian revolution developed so quickly, largely self-financed by peasants. However, market integration in Gusii introduced rural women to market insecurities. In particular, straddling left Gusii women in positions of extreme insecurity. This, combined with straddling's emphasis on education and off-farm income (which the independence decade

---

9   GoK (1965) Sessional Paper No. 10 1965: African Socialism and its Application to Planning in Kenya.

10 Orvis S.W (1989) A Political Economy of Agriculture in Kisii

cash crops never overcame), limited the degree to which Gusii women were willing to become specialized commodity producers. The result was the rather counter-intuitive discovery that in Gusii, the most densely populated region in Kenya, labour was the most severe constraint on increasing agricultural productivity. The absolute amount of potential labour power was not inadequate, but the diverse seasonal agricultural demands under the resource diffusion characteristic of straddling left Gusii women in particular with little labour available to respond to market or policy changes. But, the necessity of off-farm income in straddling meant that Gusii women would continue to expend time and resources trying to obtain off-farm employment or business opportunities for family sustenance

Bibliography

A. **Archival Materials**

Colony and Protectorate of Kenya, (1943) Food Shortage Commission of Inquiry Report, 1943. Nairobi: Government Printer.

Colony and Protectorate of Kenya, *Forestry Department Annual Report 1930*(Nairobi: GP,1931), 17 *Committee on Economic, Social and Cultural Rights, 57t^h Session.*

Department of Agriculture Annual Report 1929, 651

Development Plan 1964-1970. Government Printer,

Development Plan 1970-1974. Government Printer.

Economic Survey 1961. Government Printer

Economic Survey 1962. Government Printer

Economic Survey 1963. Government Printer

Economic Survey 1964. Government Printer

Economic Survey 1965. Government Printer

Economic Survey 1967. Government printers

Economic Survey 1968. Government Printer

Economic Survey, 1966. Government Printer

Economic Survey, 1969. Government Printer

Economic Survey, 1970. Government Printer.

Government of Kenya, (1984). *Kisii Development Plan.* Nairobi: Government Printer.

Government of Kenya, (2002). *Report of the Commission of Inquiry into the Land*

Government of Kenya. (1999). *Report of the Judicial Commission Appointed to* Grassroots Organisations Operating Together in Sisterhood (GROOTS) Kenya (2012).

Great Britain (1934) Kenya Land Commission Evidence and Memoranda vol 3

Great Britain (1934) *Kenya Land Commission Report*

Kenya Land Commission Report (1933) Government Printer. Nairobi.

KNA/ DOA /AR, 1942:1.

KNA/DC/KSI/1/1-3 South Kavirondo District Administration Report 1924-32,167

KNA: Coast 40/922 Senior Commissioners report to police in Kisumu, 23 March 1921,

KNA: DC/KSI/2 SKAR 1914-1915,

KNA: PC NZA/1/46. 1951 Nyanza Provincial Annual Report.

KNA: SKAR DC Report 1939-1945, 14a

KNA: DAR/KSI 1939-1946

KNA DC/NN/10/ I, Political Association, 1926-1940.

Norman, H (1944) The Liguru and the Land: Sociological Aspects of some Agricultural Problems of North Kavirondo. Government Printer. Nairobi, Kenya

North Kavirondo Annual Agricultural Report, 1939. Native Affairs Report, 1939

North Kavirondo Annual Agricultural Report, 1940

North Kavirondo Annual Agricultural Report, 1943

KNA: PC/NZA/3/2/106: Department of Agriculture circular.22-31 October 1932.

KNA: PC/NZA/2/1/130. The Special Agricultural Officer writing to the Director of Agriculture

KNA: PC/NZA/3/1/446

East African Standard, 25 January 1908, 11.

KNA: PC/NZA/3/65/47" DC Spencer, 23 September 1914.

KNA: AK/2/33 SKAgAR1949,

KNA; AK/2/33 SK Ag AR 1941

KNA; PC/NZA/3/28/30: DC SK to PC NP 3 November1937,

KNA: PC/NZA/1/43 Nyanza Province Annual Report 1948

KNA: PC/NZA/1/43. Nyanza Province Annual Report 1948

KNA: PC/NZA/1/43Nyanza Province Annual Report, 1948

KNA: PC/NZA/3/13/13 Registrar of Natives to DC South Kavirondo 3rd June 1943.

KNA; AK/25/34: AAOSK, Safari Diary,12-13 Oct 1943

KNA AK/21/34 and AAO SK Safari Diary 30 May-6 June 1945

KNA: PC/NZA/1/45 Nyanza Annual Provincial Report 1950

KNA: PC/NZA/1/45 Nyanza Province Annual Report 1950

Kenya Colony Annual Report, Government Printer, Nairobi, 1947,4

KNA: PC/NZA/1/48 Annual Report Nyanza Province 1952

KNA: PC/NZA/1/48 Nyanza Province Annual Report 1952

KNA: PC/NZA/1/50 Annual Provincial Agricultural Report 1954

KNA: PC/NZA/1/53 Annual Provincial Agricultural Report 1957.

KNA: PC/NZA/1/54 Annual Provincial Agricultural Report 1958

KNA: PC/NZA/1/54 Nyanza Annual Provincial Report 1958

KNA: PC/NZA/1/55 Annual Provincial Agricultural Report 1955.

KNA: PC/NZA/1/55 Annual Provincial Agricultural Report 1959.

KNA: PC/NZA/1/55 Annual Provincial Agricultural Report 1959.

KNA: PC/NZA/1/56 Annual Provincial Agricultural Report 1960.

KNA: PC/NZA/1/56 Annual Provincial Agricultural Report 1960.

KNA: PC/NZA/1/56 Nyanza Province Annual Report

KNA: PC/NZA/1/56. Nyanza Annual Agricultural Report 1960

KNA/DC/KSI/3/66 South Kavirondo Agricultural Officer's Report 1942:

KNA: PC/NZA/2/12/76

KNA: PC/NZA/3/2/89 SAO NP, QR first quarter 1947

KNA: PC/NZA.4/5/7 SKMIR April 1931,

KNA: PC/NZA/3/2/8. Secretariat Circular Letter No. 16, confidential, 16 February 1943.

KNA: PC/NZA.4/5/8 SKMIR October 1936,

KNA: PC/NZA/3/13/13 Kenya African Manpower at 31 Dec 1946,

KNA: DC/KSI/1/1 South Kavirondo Annual Report1912-1913,

KNA: DC/KSI/1/21 SNAR 1959,

KNA: DC/KSI/1/21 SNAR 1959,

KNA: DC/KSI/1/2 South Kavirondo Annual District Report, May 1919

KNA: DC/KSI/1/2 South Kavirondo District Annual Report, 1914

KNA: DC/KSl/ 1/2 South Kavirondo District Annual Reports I 913JI 923

KNA: DC/KSl/1/2, 1913-1919.

KNA: DC/KSl/1/2, 1913-1919.

KNA: CS/1/2/21, 1952)

KNA: DC/KSI/1/2 SKAR 1918-1919, 1919-1920, 19201921, 1922,

KNA: DC/KSI/1/2 SKAR 1923,

KNA: DC/KSI/1/2. SKAR 1920,

KNA: DC/KSI/1/2 KNA: DC/KSI/1/2 South Kavirondo Administration Report 1913-1914,

KNA: DC/KSI/1/3 SKAR1932,

KNA: DC/KSI/1/3 South Kavirondo Administration Report, 1928,

KNA: DC/KSI/1/3 South Kavirondo Administration Report, 1929,

KNA: DC/KSI/1/3. South Kavirondo Administration report 1926,

KNA: DC/KSI/5/3 South Nyanza Gazeteer

KNA: DC/KSI/OP/13/3: Agricultural Officer South Kavirondo, to the DC south Kavirondo. 18th January 1943.

KNA: DC/KSl/1/4 1933-1938

KNA: DC/KSl/1/4 1933-1938 South Kavirondo Administration Report,

KNA: DC/KSI/1/4. South Kavirondo Administration Report 1942.

KNA: DC/KSl/1/6, South Kavirondo District Annual Reports, 1944

KNA: DC/KSI/1/6 South Kavirondo Administration Report. 1944

KNA: PC/NZA/A/5/8 SKMIR July 1937,

KNA: DC/KSI/1.7 SKAR 1945,

KNA: PC /NZA/2/1/22 Minutes of Kisii Bakoria LNC meeting, may 26 and 271932

KNA: PC/NZA/2/1/22, Minutes of KisiiBakoria LNC Meeting,26-27 Mau 1932

Oliver Lyttelton's constitutional proposals of 1954 sought to create more political space for Africans at the national level.

Swynnerton, R. J. M. (1955). *A Plan to Intensify the Development of African Agriculture in Kenya*. Nairobi, Kenya: Government Printer.

B. **Oral Respondents**

Anyona Kibagendi, 79

Araka Matundura 80

Asiago Nyang'aya 95

Bitutu Moronya 85

Bobasi women group discussion.

Bomachoge group discussion

Bonchari women group discusiion

Bramwel Nyangeso 89

Charles Omwenga, 80

Chief Chuma Agwata;85

ChumaNyachoti 83

David Omandi 55

Elders Group discussion Bobasi

Elkana Ongesa 60

Ernerst Monyenye 67

Ernest Ombogo 75

Gesare Bitengo Gotichaki 99

Group discussion Abanchari elders

Group Discussion at Bonchari

Group discussion Bobasi

Group discussion Bomachoge women

Group Discussion men of Bonchari

Group discussion Nyansongo Women Nyaribari Chache

Group discussion Nyaribari

Group interviews Masongo Nyaribari

Ibacho, Nyaribari Masaba 76

Japheth Monyenye, 80

John Nyandoro Oigo 85

John Nyandoro, 89

Johnson Ong'esa 85

Joseph Orang'o 85

Joshua Maobe 70

Kemunto Nyamasege 86

Kepha Omandi 62

Kerebi Marita 86

Kerubo Ondabu 71

Mary Mong'ina 85

Mary Moraa 85

Milka Bosibori 78

Milka Nyanchama Obonyo 89
Milkah Moraa Nyangweso 84
Miriam Nyanchama 89
Mokare Mandere 75
Mokeira Omari 94
Moraa Nyakundi 90
Moraa Onyangore, 78
Moraa Onyansi 85
Moronya Omaore 85
Mose Nyandusi 93
Moses Ogega, 89
Moseti Omandi 79
Motari Nteng'a 85
Musa Ayako 85
Musa Ondiba 85
Musa Onyango 79
Musa Orang'o 90
Norah Kemuma, 75
Norah Mainga 85
Norah Mong'ina, 90
Nyachae Ombongi 89
Nyanchoka Omare 64
Okioma Nyabaro 57
Omaore Moronya 89
Ombuchi Omayo 62
Ondieki Nyamari 76
Onteri Kemuma, 71
Onyambu Moruga 95
Onyambu Onyambu 92
Orina Nyakwara 90
Peter Maangi Omaore 84
Peter Orang'o 97
Richard Mokoro 79
Richard Nyatangi 57

Richard Ong'esa 78

Samson Nyandusi 81

Samuel Bosire 75

Samwel Bosire 75

Sarah Nyanchama 85

Stephen Omosa 89

Thomas Nyaanga 90

Thomas Onyangore 59

Women Group discussion Kitutu Chache

Women Group Discussion Kitutu Chache north

Women Group discussion Kitutu Chache South

Women Group discussion Nyaura, Nyaribari Chache

Women Group discussion Tabaka in South Mogirango

Women Group interview Botondo, Nyaribari Masaba

Zablon Nyakwara 85

Zachary Onyango 70

C. **Articles**

Abbott, S. (1980). Power among Kikuyu Women: Domestic and Extra-Domestic Resources and Strategies. In *Anthropological Papers in Honor of Earl H. Swanson, Jr.* L. Harten, C. Africa. *World Development, 25*(8).

Adamo, A. (2005). *Globalization, Gender and Land Tenure in the South: A Literature Review.* IDRC: Ottawa.

Agarwal, B. (1997). Bargaining and gender relations: within and beyond the household. *Feminist Economics.* 3(1).

Agarwal, B. (2003). Gender and land rights revisited: Exploring new prospects via the state, family and market. *Journal of Change, 3*(1).

Allendorf, K. (2007). Do women's land rights promote empowerment and child health in Nepal?" *World Development,* 35(11).

Anderson, M, D. (2000). Master and Servant in Colonial Kenya. *The Journal of African History,* 41(3).

Ayesha, M. I. (1997). *Engendering African Social Sciences: An Introductory Essay in Engendering African Social Science* (ed.) Ayesha M.I., Amina M, Fatou S. (Codesria Book Series).

Baden, S, Green, C, Otoo-Oyortey, N. & Peasgood, T. (1994). Background paper on gender issues in Ghana. Report prepared for the West and North Africa Department, Department for Overseas Development (DFID), UK. Bridge Development-Gender, Report No. 19. Retrieved June 24, 2018, from www.fig.net

Bentsi-Enchill, K. (1966). *Do African Systems of Land Tenure require a Special Terminology? J. AFR. L.* (9).

Bryant, R. L. (1998). Power, knowledge and political ecology in the third world: a review. *Progress in Physical Geography 22*(1).

Carney, J. & Watts, M. (1990). *Manufacturing Dissent: Work, Gender and the Politics of Meaning in a Peasant Society,* in Africa, 60(2).

Carney, J. (1996). *Converting the Wetlands, Engendering the Environment: The Intersection of Gender within Agrarian Change in Gambia,* in Liberation Ecologies: Environment, Development and Social Movements, Peet, R. and Watts, M. (Editors), London and New York: Routledge.

Cagatay, C. (2001). *Trade, Gender and Poverty, United Nations Development Programme.* Washington DC: UNDP Project. Cultural Heritage. New York: The Edwin Mellen Press.

Chigbu, U. E. (2019). Masculinity, Men and Patriarchal Issues Aside: How do Women's Actions Impede Women's Access to Land? Matters Arising from a Peri-rural community in Nigeria. *Land Use Policy,* 81.

Croppenstedt, A, Goldstein, M, & Rosas, N. (2013). "Gender and Agriculture: Inefficiencies Segregation, and Low Productivity Traps." *The World Bank Research Observer.* 28(1).

Daley, E & Englert, B. (2010). Securing Land Rights for Women. *Eastern African Studies,* 4(1).

Doss, C. (2005). The Effects of Intra-household Property Ownership on Expenditure Patterns in Ghana. *Journal of African Economies,* 15(1).

Eisenhardt, K. M. (1989). Building theories from case study research. *Academy of Management Review 14*(4).

Elin, H., & Sandra F. J. (2009). On the Edge of the Law: Women's Property Rights and Dispute Resolution in Kisii, Kenya. *Law & Society Review* 43(1).

Ezer, T. (2006). Inheritance Law in Tanzania: the impoverishment of widows and daughters. *The Georgetown Journal of Gender and the Law*, 8.

Feder, G., & Noronha, R. (1987). Land Rights Systems and Agricultural Development in Sub-Saharan Africa. *The World Bank Research Observer*, 2(2).

Goldstein, M. and Udry, C. (2008). The Profits of Power: Land Rights and Agricultural Investment in Ghana. *Journal of Political Economy* 116 (6).

Hakansson, T. (1986). *Landless Gusii Women: A Result of Customary Land Law and Modern Marriage Patterns*. Working Papers in African Studies Programs, Department of Anthropology, University of Uppsala.

Henrysson, E. & Joireman, S. F. (2009). On the Edge of the Law: Women's Property Rights and Dispute Resolution in Kisii, Kenya. *Law & Society Review*, 43: (1).

Jensen, M. C., & Meckling W. H. (1976). Theory of the firm: Managerial behaviour, agency costs and ownership structure. *Journal of Financial Economics* 3(4).

Knopp, L. (1992). Sexuality and the Spatial Dynamics of Capitalism: Environment and Planning. *Society and Space*, 10.

Lastarria-Cornhiel, S. (1995). Impact of Privatization on Gender and Property Rights In Africa. *World Development*, 25(8).

Leach, M. (1991). *Locating Gendered Experience: An Anthropologist's View from a Sierra Leonean Village*, in IDS Bulletin, 22(1).

Lasterria-Cornhiel, S. & Garcia, F. (2009). *Gender and land rights: Findings and Lessons from Country Studies*. FAO, Italy.

Mackenzie, F. (1995). *Selective Silence: A Feminist Encounter with Environmental Discourse in Colonial Africa*, in The Power of Development, Crush, J.(Editor), London and New York: Routledge.

Mackenzie, F. (1990). Gender and Land Rights in Murang'a District, *Kenya Journal of Peasant Studies*, Vol. 17(4).

Makana, E.N (2012) "Reinterrogating the interface between settler and peasant sectors of Kenya's colonial economy 1901-1929". A paper presented in a workshop on new frontiers in African Economic History, Geneva.

Makana, N.E; (2008) Transformation of the peasant sector: The missing link in African Economic development. International Journal of Sustainable Development, Volume 1 number 2, 32

Makura-Paradza, G. (2010). *Single Women, Land and Livelihood Vulnerability*;

Marshall, A. (1890/1956). *Principles of Economics*. 8th ed. London: Macmillan.

Mamdani, M. (2001). Beyond Settler and Native as Political Identities: Overcoming the Political Legacy of Colonialism. In *Comparative Studies in Society and History 43*(4).

Manji, A. (2003). Capital, Labour and Land Relations in Africa: A Gender Analysis of the World Bank's Policy Research Report on Land Institutions and Land Policy, *Third World Quarterly*, 24(1).

Matthews, K. and Coogan, W.H. (2008). Kenya and the Rule of Law: The Perspective of Two Volunteers. *60 Maine Law Review*.

Robert Maxon (2000) "Fantastic Prices" in the Midst of "An Acute Food Shortage": Market, Environment, and the Colonial State in the 1943 Vihiga (Western Kenya) Famine. In African Economic History, No. 28. African Studies Program, Madison; University of Wisconsin.

Nasimiyu, R. (1985). Women in the Colonial Economy of Bungoma: Role of Women in Agriculture, in G. S. Were (ed.) *Women and Development in Africa*.

Ndege O.P. (2006). Colonialism and its Legacies in Kenya. Lecture delivered during Fulbright-Hays Group project abroad program: July 5th to August 6th, 2009 at the Moi University Main Campus.

Newsinger, J. (1981). Revolt and Repression in Kenya: The "Mau Mau" Rebellion, 1952-1960. *45 Science & Society*.

Ntege, H. (1993). Women and Urban Housing Crisis: Impact of Public Policies and Practices in Uganda. *Economic and Political Weekly*, 28(44).

Nzioki, A. (2009). *The Effect of land tenure on women's access and control of land in Kenya.*

Nzioki, E. (2003). *Why Women's Right To Land?* Ad-Hoc Expert meeting on Land Tenure System and Sustainable Development. Lusaka, Zambia.

Okoth-Ogendo, H. W. O. (1989). Some Issues of Theory in the Study of Tenure Relations in African Agriculture, *59 Africa* 6.

Omwoyo, S. M. (1997). 'Women and Agricultural Production among the Gusii. 1875-1963 in The Eastern Africa Journal of Historical and Social Sciences Research, 2 (1).

Omosa, M. (1998). *Re-conceptualization Food Security: Interlocking Strategies, Unfolding Choices and Rural Livelihood in Kisii District.* The Hague: Service Centrum Vans Gils BV. Payne

Rocheleau, D. E. (2008). Political ecology in the key of policy: from chains of explanation to webs of relations. *Geoforum* 39.

Rose, L. L. (2002). Women's Strategies for Customary Land Access in Swaziland and Malawi: A Comparative Study. *49 Africa Today.*

Southall, R. (2005). The Ndungu Report: Land & Graft in Kenya. *32 Review of African Political Economy.*

Stiglitz, J. E. (1974). Incentives and Risk Sharing in Sharecropping. *Review of Economic Studies*, 41.

Schroeder, R., (1995). *Gone to Their Second Husbands: Marital Metaphors and Conjugal Contracts in The Gambia's Female Garden Sector*, in Canadian *Journal of African Studies*, 30 (1). *Science.* London, New York: Routledge.

Selhausen, Felix Meier Zu; Weisdorf, Jacob (2016). "A colonial legacy of African gender inequality? Evidence from Christian Kampala, 1895–2011". *The Economic History Review.* 69 (1).

Shipton, P., & Mitzi, G. (1992). Understanding African Land-Holding: Power, Wealth and Meaning. *Africa* 62/3.

Ndege, P. The struggle for the market: The Political Economy of Commodity Production and Trade in Western Kenya 1929-1939.

Trickland, R. (2004). 'To Have and To Hold: Women's Property and Inheritance Study Based on Fifteen Sites; *African Development Review*, 14(1).

Wangari, M. (2010). Gender Relations And Food Crop Production: A Case of Kiambu District Kenya, 1920-1985.

Wangari, M. (1996). Asian Versus Africans in Kenyans; Post-Colonial Economy in the Eastern *African Journal of History and Social Sciences Research.*

Whitehead, A & Tsikata, D. (2003). "Policy Discourses on Women's Land Rights in Sub-Saharan Africa: The Implications of the Return to the Customary. Journal of Agrarian Studies, 3 (1-2).

D. **Books**

Agarwal, B. (1994). *A Field of One's Own: Gender and Land Rights in South Asia.* Cambridge, Cambridge University Press.

Akama J.S., & R. Maxon (2006). *Ethnography of the Gusii of Western Kenya: A Vanishing Cultural Heritage.* Lewiston, NY: Edwin Mellen Press.

Akama, J. S. (2017). *The Gusii of Kenya: Social, Economic, Cultural, Political and Judicial Perspectives.* Canada: Nsemia Publishers.

Akama, J. S. (2018). The Untold Stories: Gusii Survival Techniques and Resistance to the Establishment of British Colonial Rule. Kisii University Press.

Anseeuw, W. L. Alden W, Cotula, L & Taylor, M. (2012). *Land Rights and the Rush*

Berry, S. (1989). No Condition is Permanent: The Social Dynamics of Agrarian Change in Sub-Sahara Africa. The University of Wisconsin Press.

Blaikie, P. M. (1985). *The political economy of soil erosion in developing countries.* London: Longman.

Bukh, J. (1979). *The Village Woman in Ghana.* Uppsala: Scandinavian Institute of African Studies.

Carney, J. (1996). Converting the Wetlands, Engendering The Environment: The Intersection of Gender within Agrarian Change in Gambia. In *Liberation Ecologies: Environment, Development and Social Movements*, Peet, R. and Watts, M. (Editors), London and New York: Routledge.

Caroline, E. (2005). *Imperial Reckoning: The Untold Story of Britain's Gulag in*

Castree, N. & Braun B. (eds.) (2001). *Social Nature: Theory, Practice and Politics.* Oxford and New York: Blackwell.

Clayton & Savage. (1974). Government and Labour in Kenya, 1895-1963. London.

Coontz, S. (1957). *Population Theories and Economic Interpretation.* London: Routledge

Cotula, L. (2007). (ed.) *Changes in "Customary" Land Tenure Systems in Africa.* Great Britain: IIED.

David Anderson and David Throup "Africa and Agricultural Production in Colonial Kenya; The myth of the war as a watershed" A Journal of African History 26 (1985)

Davison, J. (1988). *Land and Women's Agricultural Production: The Context* in Davison, Jean, (1988). "Who Owns What? Land Registration and Tensions in Gender Relations of Production in Kenya." In Jean Davison, ed. *Agriculture, Women and Land: The African Experience.* Boulder: Westview Press, 157-76, at 165.

Davison, M. J. (1987). Without Land we are nothing. The Effect of Land Tenure Policies and Practices upon Rural Women in Kenya, *Rural Africana.*

Downs, R. E. (1988). The Kenya Land Tenure Reform: Misunderstandings in the Public Creation of Private Property, in *Land and Society in Contemporary Africa,* 98.

Eniola, B., & Akinola A. O. (2019). "Women rights and land reform in Africa: Nigeria and South Africa in comparison," in *THE TRAJECTORY OF LAND REFORM IN POST-COLONIAL AFRICAN STATES: THE QUEST FOR SUSTAINABLE DEVELOPMENT AND UTILIZATION* eds Akinola A. O., Wissink H., editors, Cham: Springer International Publishing

Falk M, S. (1996). Changing African Land Tenure: Reflections on the incapacities of the State, The European Journal of Development Research, 10; 2.

Fanon, F. (1967). *Black skin, white masks.* London: Pluto.

Fearn, H. (1961). An African Economy: A Study of the Economic Development of the Nyanza Province of Kenya 1903-1953. London. Oxford University Press.

Flueret, A. (1988). Some Consequences of Tenure and Agrarian Reform in Taita, Kenya, in R.E. Downs & S.P. Reyna (eds.). *Land and Society in Contemporary Africa.* Fortmann, L. and Riddell, J. (1985). *Trees and Tenure: An Annotated Bibliography. For Land: Findings of the Global Commercial Pressures on Land Research Project.* ILC, Rome.

Forsyth, T. J. (2003). *Critical political ecology: The Politics of Environmental*

Fryer, R. G. (2010). The importance of segregation, discrimination, peer dynamics and

Fulbright-Hays Group project abroad program: July 5-6, 2009 at the Moi University Main Campus, Kenya.

Gavin Kitching (1980) *The Making of an African Petite Bourgeoisie*, Yale University Press, London

Gender: Challenges and Approaches for Strengthening Women's Land Tenure Ghana Publishing Company.

Giovarelli, R. (2006). "Overcoming Gender Biases in Established and Transitional

Giovarelli, R., Wamalwa, B & Hannay, L. (2013). Land Tenure, Property Rights and

Gutto, S. B. O. (1975). Gender, Land and property rights in modern constitutionalism: Experiences from Africa and possible lessons for South Africa.

Guyer, J. I. (1981). Household and community studies in African studies. *African Studies Review* 24:(2/3):87.138.

Guyer, J. I. (1984). *Family and Farm in Southern Cameroon*. Boston: Boston University African Studies Center.

Gyekye, K. (1998). *African Cultural Values: An Introduction*, Accra, Sankofa

Hakansson, T. (1988). *Bridewealth, Women and Land: Social Change among the Gusii of Kenya*. Uppsala Studies in Cultural Anthropology No. 10. Uppsala: Amquiest and Wilsell International.

Hakijamii, GI-ESCR & FIDA, (2016). *Joint Shadow Report to the United Nations*

Hanna, S. and Jentoft, S. (1996). Human Use of the Natural Environment: An Overview of Social and Economic Dimensions. In Susan S. Hanna, Carl Folke and Karl-Goran Maler (eds.): *Rights to Nature: Ecological, Economic, Cultural, and Political Principles of Institutions for the Environment*. Washington D.C. Island Press.

Harold Macmillan, The Blast of the War 1939-1945 (London, 1967). In Tiyambe Zeleza, "Kenya and the Second World War 1939-1950." In W.R. Ochieng', (eds), (1989), A Modern History of Kenya 1895-1980. Nairobi; Evans Brothers.

Henrysson, E & Joireman, S. F. (2009). On the edge of the law: Women's property rights and dispute Resolution in Kisii, Kenya. *Law & Society Review, 43*(1).

Hrold Macmillan,(1967). The Blast of War 1939-1945. London

Hugh Fearn, (1961). An African Economy: A study of the economic development of the Nyanza Province of Kenya 1903-1953. London; Oxford University Press.

Hugh Fearn, (1961). An African Economy: A Study of the Economic Development of the Nyanza Province of Kenya, 1903-1953. London; Oxford University Press.

Hyden, G. (1980). *BEYOND UJAMAA IN TANZANIA: UNDERDEVELOPMENT AND AN*

IFAD. (2001). *Rural Poverty Report: The challenge of ending rural poverty.* London: Oxford University Press.

Ikdahl, I. (2005). Human Rights, Formalization and Women's Land Rights in Southern and Eastern. Africa. In *Studies in Women's Law.* Oslo: Institute of Women's Law, University of Oslo.

Jane, P. (1986). *Women's Rights and the Lagos Plan of Action,* 8 HUM. RTS Q. 180 Johannesburg: Witswatersrand University Press.

Joireman, S. F. (2007). Enforcing New Property Rights in Sub-Saharan Africa: The Ugandan Constitution and the 1998 Land Act. *39 Comparative Politics.*

Jonathan Barker, (1989). Rural Communities Under Stress: Peasant Farmers and the State in Africa. Cambridge: Cambridge University Press.

Judith Heyer, 'Achievements, Problems and Prospects in the Agricultural Sector,' in Heyer Judith (et al), (ed), (1976), Agricultural Development in Kenya. Nairobi: Oxford University Press.

Kanogo Tabitha, (1987). Squatters and the Roots of Mau Mau. London: James Currey

Kanyinga, K. (2000). *Re-Distribution from above. The Politics of Land Rights and Squatting in Coastal Kenya.* Nordic Africa Institute Programme; Research Paper No. 115.

Kebede, B. (2002). Land Tenure and Common Pool Resources in Rural Ethiopia: A *Kenya,* Owl Books.

Kiagayu, N. N. (1979). *Property Ownership Structure among the Kikuyus: Its Impact on the Status of Women*. MA Thesis. Nairobi: University of Nairobi.

Kieyah, M, Joseph, P & Nyaga, L. (2009). Land Reform and Poverty in Kenya. GDN

Killian, B. (2011). The Women's Land Right Movements, Customary Law and Religion in Tanzania. *Religion and Development Working paper 57.*

Kitching, G. (1980). *Class and Economic Change in Kenya: the making of an African Petite Bourgeoisie*. New Haven and London: Yale University Press.

Kitetu, C. W. (Ed.) (2008) Gender, Science and Technology: Perspectives from Africa. Senegal: African Books Collective.

Kongstad, P. & M. Monsted (1980). *Family, Labour and Trade in Western Kenya*. Centre for Development Research (Copenhagen), Publications 3. Scandinavian Institute of African Studies, Uppsala.

Kossok, M. (1973). Common Aspects and Distinctive Features in Colonial Latin America. *Science and Society 46*(1), Spring.

Krishan M. Maini. (1967). *Land Law in East Africa*. Nairobi: Heinemann.

Lamba, D. (2006). *An African Story, Land Grabbing in Kenya*. Habitat Debate, December 2003.

Land Tenure, K. Kibwana in William R. Ochieng (ed) (1990). Themes in Kenyan History: Heineman Kenya Limited.

Lastarria-Cornhiel, S. (1995). Impact of Privatization on Gender and property rights in the *Law System of Kenya on Principles of a National Land Policy Framework, Constitutional Position of Land and New Institutional Framework for Land Administration.* Government Press, Nairobi, Kenya.

Levin, R. (1997). *When the sleeping grass awakens: Land and power in Swaziland.*

Levine (1963). Witchcraft and Sorcery in East Africa, J. Middleton and E, Winter (Eds). New York.

LeVine R, & LeVine. B. B. (1966). *Nyansongo: A Gusii Community.* New York.

LeVine, S. (1979). *Mothers and Wives: Gusii Women of East Africa.* Chicago: Chicago University Press.

Lonsdale, J. and Berman, B. (1979). 'Coping with the contradictions: The Development of the Colonial State in Kenya, 1894-1914,' Journal of African History 20.

Loury, M. (2002). *The Anatomy of Racial Inequality.* Cambridge: Harvard University

Lovett, M. (1989). Gender Relations, Class Formation and Colonial State in Africa. In J. L. Parpart, & K. Staudt, (Eds.), Women and the State in Africa. London: Lynne Publishers.

Mathew AB and Jackson O (eds) Handbook of Social Economics. Amsterdam:

Matthews, K. and Coogan, W. H. (2008). Kenya and the Rule of Law: The Perspective of Two Volunteers. 60 *Maine Law Review.*

Maxon R.M The years of revolutionary advance 1920-1929 in W. R. Ochieng, Ed, 1989) *A Modern History of Kenya 1895-1980*; Evans Brothers, Nairobi, 74

Maxon, R. (2003). *Going Their Separate Ways: Agrarian Transformation In Kenya, 1930-1950.* London: Associated University Presses.

Maxon, R.M (1989). Conflict and Accommodation in Western Kenya. The Gusii and the British, 1907-1963. London; Associated University Press.

Mayer, 1.(1975). The Patriarchal Image: Routine Dissociation in Gusii Families. *African Studies* 34.

Mayer, P. (1950). *Gusii Bridewealth, Law and Custom.* Rhodes Livingston Papers Number 18. London.

Mayer, P. quoted in Lucy Mair, *African Marriage and Social Change* (London, 1969), 52.

McGregor-Ross, W. (1968), Kenya From Within. London: Frank Cass.

Moore, D. (1993). Contesting Terrain in Zimbabwe's Eastern Highlands: Political Ecology, Ethnography and Peasant Resource Struggles, in *Economic Geography* 69.

Moore, D. (1996). Marxism, Culture and Political Ecology: Environmental Struggles

Morgan, W.T., & Shaffer Manfred N, (1966). Population of Kenya: Density and Distribution. Nairobi; Government printer

Nasimiyu, R. (1985). Women in the Colonial Economy of Bungoma: Role of Women in Agriculture, in G. S. Were (ed.) *Women and Development in Africa*, nature. In A. Biersack and J.B. Greenberg (eds.) *Reimagining political ecology.* Durham: Duke University Press.

Newberry, D. M. G & Stiglitz, J. E. (1979). Sharecropping, Risk Sharing and the Importance of Imperfect Information. In *Risk, Uncertainty, and Agricultural Development*, ed. J. A. Roumasset. New York: Agricultural Development Council.

Newsinger, J. (1981). Revolt and Repression in Kenya: The "Mau Mau" Rebellion, *45 Science & Society* 159.

Nussbaum, M. (2000). *Women and human development. The Capabilities Approach.* Cambridge: Cambridge University Press.

Nyamwaya, D. and Buruchara, R. (1986). Property and land Tenure, in G.S. Were and D. Nyamweya (Eds.). *Kisii District Socio-cultural Profile.* Nairobi: Government Printer.

Oberschall, A. (1978). *Theories of Social Conflict.* Nashville, Tennessee: Department of Sociology and Anthropology, Vanderbilt University.

Ochieng, W. R. (1974). *A Pre-colonial History of the Gusii of Western Kenya, c. 1500-1914.* Nairobi: East African Literature Bureau.

Ochieng, W. R. (1985). *A History of Kenya.* Macmillan Press Ltd.

Ochieng, W. R. (1986). *Kenya's People: Peoples of the South West Highlands, Gusii.* Nairobi: Evans Brothers.

Ochieng' W. (Eds) (1990) Themes in Kenyan History. Nairobi: Heinemann

Ojienda, T. (2008). *Conveyancing; Principles and Practice.* Nairobi, Kenya: Law Africa (K) Publishing Ltd.

Okoth-Ogendo, H. W. O. (1975). *The Adjudication Process and the Special Rural Development Process.* Unpublished Occasional Paper no. 12, Institute of Development Studies, University of Nairobi.

Okoth-Ogendo, H.W.O. (1989). Some Issues of Theory in the Study of Tenure Relations in African Agriculture, *59 Africa* 6.

OKuro, S. O. and Punyana A. M. (2011) (Eds). *Strategies against Poverty Designs from the North and Alternatives from the South.* Buenos Aires: Clasco.

Ongaro, W. A. (1988). *Adoption of New Farming Technology: A Case Study of Maize Production in Western Kenya.* Ekonomiska Studier 22. Department of Economics. Gothenburg School of Economics, Gothenburg.

P. & I. Mayer, (1965). The Nature of Kinship Relations. Manchester University Press. 67

Payne, G. K. (1997). *Urban land tenure and property rights in developing countries.* Intermediate technology publications.

Peterman, A, Quisumbing, A, Behrman, J & Nkonya, E. (2010). Understanding Gender Differences in Agricultural Productivity in Uganda and Nigeria.

Reeves, H. & Baden, S. (2000). *Gender and Development: Concepts and Definitions Bridge development-gender.* Brighton: University of Sussex, Institute of Development Studies. Regional Security in the Age of Globalisation. Nairobi: Heinrich Boll Foundation. Review, Intermediate Technology Publications, London.

Rhoda, H. (1984). Women's Rights in English Speaking Sub-Saharan Africa, in Human Rights and Development in Africa,

Robbins, P. (2004). *Political Ecology: A Critical Introduction.* Oxford: Blackwell.

Robertson, C (1995). Women in the urban economy in Hay, J. M & Stichter, S. (eds) African women South of the Sahara. New York: Longman Publishing.

Rocheleau, D.B. Thomas-Slayter, and E. Wangari (1996) (eds.) *Feminist political ecology: global issues and local experiences.* London: Routledge.

Ruth, N. (1985). Women in the Colonial Economy of Bungoma: Role of Women in Agriculture, in Women and Development in Africa 56-73 (G.S. Were ed.)

Sarpong, P. (1974). *Ghana in Retrospect: Some aspects of Ghanaian culture.* Accra: Ghana Publishing Company.

Shiroya, O, J. E. (1985). Kenya and World War II: African soldiers in the European war Nairobi: Kenya Literature Bureau.

Smith, L.T. (1999). Decolonizing Methodologies: Research and Indigenous Peoples. Bookstore and UB.

Sorrenson M.Y.K. (1968). Origins of European Settlement in Kenya, Oxford University Press. Nairobi.

Spencer, I. (1980) "Settler Dominance, Agricultural Production and the Second World War in Kenya." In Journal of African History 21

Spencer, I.R.D. (1981). The First World War and the Origins of the Dual Policy in Kenya,1914-1922, *World Development* 9.

Stephen Orvis. (1997). The Agrarian Quesition in Kenya. Gainesville: University of Florida Press.

Stichter, S. (1975-76). Women and Labour Force in Kenya, 1895-1964. In *Rural Africana*.

Talbot, I. D. (1974), The Kenyan Flax Boom, *Kenya Historical Review* 2.

Tambiah, S. (1989). Bridewealth and Dowry Revisited. *Current Anthropology 30*(4).

Thomas Hakansson; 1991, Grain Cattle and power: Social Processes of Intensive cultivation and Exchange in Precolonial Western Kenya, Journal of Anthropological Research vol. 50 No. 3. University of New Mexico

Thorp L. (1997). 'Access to Land: a rural perspective on tradition and resources, in S. Meer (ed.) Women, Land and Authority, Cape Town: David Phillip.

Throup, D. (1987). The construction and destruction of the Kenyatta state, in *The Political Economy of Kenya*. Michael G. Schatzberg ed: Praeger.

Throup, D. (1988). *Economic and Social Origins of Mau Mau, 1945–53*. (East African Studies.) Athens: Ohio University Press or James Currey, London. 1988..

Vayda, A.P. & Walters, B. B. (1999). Against Political Ecology. *Human Ecology 27*(1): 167-179.

Wanyeki, L. M. (2003). ed., *Women and Land in Africa: Culture, Religion and Realizing Women s Land Rights*. New York: Zed Books Ltd.

Warren, and D. Touhy, (eds.), Boise: Special Publications of the Idaho Museum of Natural History.

E. **International Organizations**

FAO. (2011). Gender differences in assets. *ESA Working Paper* No. 11-12.

FAO. (2010). *Gender and Land Rights Database*. Rome: FAO

FAO. (2002). *Land Tenure and Rural Development*; FAO Land Tenure Studies No.3; Rome.

FAO. (2011). "Gender differences in assets". ESA Working Paper No. 11-12.

FAO, (2002). *Land Tenure and Rural Development; FAO Land Tenure Studies,* FAO, Rome.

UN, (2015). *Transforming Our World: The 2030 Agenda for Sustainable Development*. New York.

USAID. (2010). Country Profile Property Rights and Resources Governance-Malawi Post-Conflict Situations and During Reconstruction: A Global Overview.

World Bank, (2001). *Gender Equality and the Millennium Development Goals*.

Gender & Development Group. Retrieved March 30, 2018, from www.siteresources.worldbank.org

World Bank, (2004). *Gender Country Profiles* Retrieved April 21, 2019, from www.worldbank.org/afr/gender/countryprofile.

https://www.standardmedia.co.ke/article/2000024669/anxiety-as-murders-rise-in-kisii-over-land-disputes

Rights in the Context of HIV/AIDS in Sub-Saharan Africa'. Washington, DC: Rights in the Context of HIV/AIDS in Sub-Saharan Africa'. Washington, DC: International Center for Research on Women.

Tengey W.2008. 'Gender relations, rural women and land tenure in Ghana: A communication nightmare', in FAO, Land access in rural Africa: Strategies to fight gender inequality. Proceedings of FAO-Dimitra Workshop: 'Information and communication strategies to fight gender inequality as regards land access and its consequences for rural populations in Africa', 22-26 September. Brussels: FAO.

Verma, R. (2001). *Gender, Land and Livelihoods in East Africa: Through Farmers Eyes*. Ottawa: International Development Research Centre.

F. **Theses**

1. Hay, M. J. (1972). *Economic Change in Luoland: Kowe, 1890-1945*. Ph.D. diss., University of Wisconsin Madison.

2. Holmquist, F. (1975). *Peasant Organization. Clientelism and Dependency: A Case Study of An Agricultural Producer Cooperative in Kenya*. Ph.D. Dissertation, Indiana University.

Lundika, R, W. (2010). Land Rental Markets, Investment And Productivity Under Customary Land Tenure Systems In Malawi; Ph.D. Thesis, Norwegian University of Life Sciences.

Monyenyere, S. (1977). The Indigenous Education of the Abagusii People. MA. Thesis. Nairobi: University of Nairobi.

Munro, J. F. (1968). *The Machakos Akamba Under British Rule, 1889-1939: A Study of Colonial Impact*. Ph.D. Thesis, University of Wisconsin.

Musalia, M. (2010). Gender Relations and Food Production: A case of Kiambu District 1920-1985. Ph.D. Thesis Kenyatta University.

Ndeda, J.M., (1993) The Impact of Male Migration on Rural Women: A Case Study of Siaya District c. 1894-1963. Ph.D. Thesis, Kenyatta University

Ndege, P. (1994)The struggle for the market: The Political Economy of Commodity Production and Trade in Western Kenya 1929-1939. Ph.D. Thesis, West Virginia University.

Neigus, D.L (1971). Conflict over Land; A study of Expansion and Inversion in Gusii Society. Thesis, Harvard College

Njiru, E. (1990). *Effects of Tea Production on Women's Work and Labour Allocation in Embu District*. M.A. Thesis, Nairobi University: Nairobi.

Njogu, E. (2002). *Household Food Security and Nutritional Status of Children in Tea and Non-Tea Producing Households in Ndia Division Kirinyaga District*. Unpublished Thesis: Kenyatta University.

Nyanchoka, J. (1984). *The Law of Succession Act and Gusii Customary Law of Inheritance* M.A. Thesis. Nairobi: University of Nairobi.

Omwoyo, S. M. (1997). The Colonial Transformation of Gusii Agriculture, MA Thesis, Kenyatta University: Nairobi.

Orvis, S.W (1989). *Political Economy of Agriculture in Kisii: Social Reproduction & Household Response to Development Policy*. PhD Thesis. University of Wisconsin, Madson

Tanui, P.(2002) Differential Gender Access to Agricultural Resources in Kenya: The Impact on Agricultural Production in Nandi District From 1954-2000.

Wafula, S. (1981) "Colonial land policy and the North Kavirondo African Reserve to 1940." M.A Dissertation, University of Nairobi.

G. **Internet Sources**

https://www.landesa.org/what-we-do/china/

https://www.landesa.org/what-we-do/china/

Kameri-Mboti, P. (2005). *Land tenure, land use and sustainability in Kenya: Towards innovative use of property rights in wildlife management.* International Environmental Law Research Centre. Geneva, Switzerland. Retrieved February 16, 2018, from www. capri.cgiar.org

Qvist, E. (1995). *Women's access, control and tenure of land, property and settlement.* Retrieved May 30, 2019, from www.sli.unimelb. edu.au

UN, (1980). UN Action for Women Press information. Women Aid International. Retrieved March 30, 2018, from **http//:www. highbeam.com UN+1980.html**. *Kenya.* Retrieved May 20, 2019, from www.jstore.org/stable/151481

Glossary of Gusii Terms Used in The Book

Gusii Terms	Meanings
Abakumi (Omokumi singular)	Highly respected or famous Gusii elder.
Abanyanchanchara	People associated with laziness/hunger/famine.
Aegwa	Being given something.
Amasaga	Communal working groups.
Boma	Cattle enclosure/kraal.
Borabu	Frontier or land which is vacant.
Boremo (Oboremo noun)	Land.
Chinsoni	Gusii informal code of conduct.
Ebiombe	Self-help groups.
Ebirachuoki (Ekerachuoki singular)	Indigenous plants that have stick-like leaves that produce white liquid (usually used in demarcating land).
Ebisarate	Enclosed huts were mainly used by young men and elders to look after and protect livestock.
Ebusa	Local brew.
Eero	Traditional sitting room.
Egesaku	Group of people who share the same ancestry or lineage.
Egetiro	Steep hill/landscape/an uphill task.
Egesiria	Traditional hoe made of iron.
Egiateko	Upheaval (e.g. widespread disease attack or floods, invasion by enemies).
Ekenyoro	Small village/geographical area occupied by a few homesteads.
Emetagara (Omotagora singular)	Indigenous plants whose leaves when warmed on fire are used for massaging aching/hurting muscles.

Emonga	A small piece of land set aside for elderly men or family patriarchs for their subsistence.
Enyomba	Family house in a given homestead. Also used for classifying Kisii sub-clans.
Kemogondo (Omogondo noun)	Farmland or working on the farm.
Kenyambi (Ekenyambi noun)	Type of grass whose roots run deep and is difficult to cultivate.
Mokungu (Omokungu noun)	Woman or a wife.
Moserengeti	A person who is verbose or talks a lot.
Obwata (bwata a verb)	To hold in your hands/arms.
Omobe	Bad/evil person.
Omochie	Homestead.
Omogaka	Male elder/family patriarch.
Omoroka	Short leafy shrub used for making hedges or boundaries.
Omotwe	Head.
Omwaka	Season or year.
Omwobo	Season of short rains.
Wimbi	Kiswahili word for finger millet.
Vijiji (Kijiji singular)	Kiswahili word for a village/a small geographical area.

Appendices

Appendix I: Informed Consent Letter

Dear Respondents,

I am a D. Phil. student at Moi University. It is a requirement for the course to carry out a research project. I am thus currently soliciting information on the topic "Gender relations in ownership and control of land in Gusii 1920-1970". This research is purely academic and any information provided shall be treated with confidentiality. Please kindly participate and respond appropriately to the questions given below. Your contributions are highly appreciated.

Thank you very much in advance.

Questionnaire Number..................... Date of interview ....

Let me take this opportunity to thank you for taking part in this study.

Yours sincerely,

MALLION K. ONYAMBU

Appendix II: Interview Schedule

I am a D. Phil. student at Moi University. It is a requirement for the course to carry out a research project. I am thus currently soliciting information on the topic "Gender relations in ownership and control of land in Gusii 1920 - 1970". This research is purely academic and any information provided shall be treated with confidentiality. Please kindly participate and respond appropriately to the questions given below. Your contributions are highly appreciated.

Thank you very much in advance.

Questionnaire Number ....Date of interview ....

INSTRUCTIONS

Please do not write your name anywhere on this questionnaire. Information provided will be treated with the utmost confidentiality. You are requested to read each question carefully and provide your honest response. Please tick (√) on your appropriate response.

SECTION A: Background Information

Age.............

Gender.........

Level of education .... occupation ....

Sub-location............

1. During the pre-colonial period did women own land in this community? [Yes], [No].

   If yes, did she have total control over the access and use of the land?

   If, No, why...

2. How is women's access and control of land guaranteed?..

3. During the pre-colonial period, who made the ultimate decision on how land was to be used?

   [a] The clan [b].The household head [c] husband (d) wife (e) Both husband and wife.

4. Do you own land? [Yes], [No].

   If yes, how did you acquire it?

   [a]. Bought [b].gift [c] inherited [d] late husband's land.

5. Did both Gusii men and women have a right to access land before 1895? [Yes], [No].

6. Did both have a right to use land without any hindrances during Pre-Colonial Period?

7. If both women and men had the right of access and use, how were those rights protected in Pre- Colonial Period?

8. Who was the custodian of the individual's land rights in the Pre-Colonial Period?

9. In case of violation of these rights, how was justice established in the Pre-Colonial Period?

10. Which was the main food crop among the Gusii in Pre-Colonial Period?

11. Were there reasons that would make an individual not have land on which to grow food crops in the Pre-Colonial Period?

12. If there was, which gender was most affected and why?

13. Did colonialism have any impact on women's ownership of land in this society?

    [Yes], [No]. Explain how and why.....................

14. Did the White man take any land from your parents/ close relatives or friends? [Yes], [No].

15. What effects did land alienation (taking away African land) have on the rights of access and use between men and women in Gusii?

16. Do you have the land registered in your name [Yes], [No]....... explain your answer

17. Do you have a title deed? [Yes], [No].

    Why...

18. If you had money, would you buy land and register in your name...............

    Explain your answer......................................

19. What factors hinder women from acquiring?

20. According to you, who is the legitimate owner of the land?

    Give a reason for your answer ....

21. 21. Who is entitled to inherit family land?

    [a] Sons [b].daughters [c] Both.

    Explain your answer ....

22. Do women have the power and authority to transfer or sell land? [Yes], [No]

    Explain your answer ....

23. Is a daughter allowed to inherit land in your clan/family? [Yes], [No]

24. If No, what do you think could be the barriers for women (daughters, divorcee, married) from inheriting land in their clan/family?

25. What are the threatening factors to women's access to land under customary tenure? Clan/family land?

26. How effective are women's strategies in increasing their access to land under the current land tenure systems?

27. What measures can be taken to improve women's access to land?

Appendix III: Interview Schedule For Chiefs/Assistant Chiefs

1. For how long have you served as a government official in the location?

2. Which crimes are prevalent in the area?

3. What mechanism do you use to deal with these crimes?

4. Is the land in your location surveyed?

5. When did land consolidation and registration begin in this location/sub-location?

6. How is land owned in this location?

7. Are there land-related cases brought to your office as the chief/ assistant for arbitration?

8. How was the land owned/controlled in this community during the pre-colonial period?

9. What was the place of women in regard to land ownership in the pre-colonial period?

10. How did the onset of colonialism impact women's ownership of land in Gusii?

11. In your own opinion did colonialism hinder or enhance women's rights to land?

12. Do you think the subsequent independent government in Kenya has addressed issues related to land ownership by women?

13. How did policies pass during the Kenyatta regime impact women?

14. How did the policies passed during the Moi regime affect women on land ownership?

15. Did the passage of a new constitution during the Kibaki regime enhance women's Acquisition of land?

16. Do you find the new constitution of 2010 in tandem with cultural practices as relates to land ownership among the Gusii of Kisii County?

17. When dealing with land ownership disputes between a husband and wife, what informs your decision? (a) the constitution (b) the cultural practice of the community (c) both............. Explain your answer.......................

18. What would you suggest to be done to strengthen and empower women to enable their own land in Gusii?..

Appendix IV: Focus Group Discussion Guide

1. Where did the Gusii migrate from?

2. How were the Gusii governed during the Pre-colonial period?

3. What was the economic activity of the Gusii during the pre-colonial period?

4. How was land administered during the pre-colonial period?

5. In your assessment, did women have the security of tenure then?

6. When was the colonial impact first felt in Gusii?

7. How did the coming of the British affect the administration of land among the Gusiis?

8. How did the colonial land policies impact women's right to land?

9. When did Kenya become independent?......................who was the president?

10. During the Kenyatta regime, how was the question of land handled in Gusii?

11. Did women participate in the Adjudication process?

12. In your opinion, to what extent did the Kenyatta regime enhance women's right to land?

13. What steps did the Kenyatta regime take to secure women's right to land?

14. In your assessment, to what extent did Kibaki enhance women's right to land?